Rhode Island
and the Union
1774–1795

Northwestern University Studies in History
Number Five

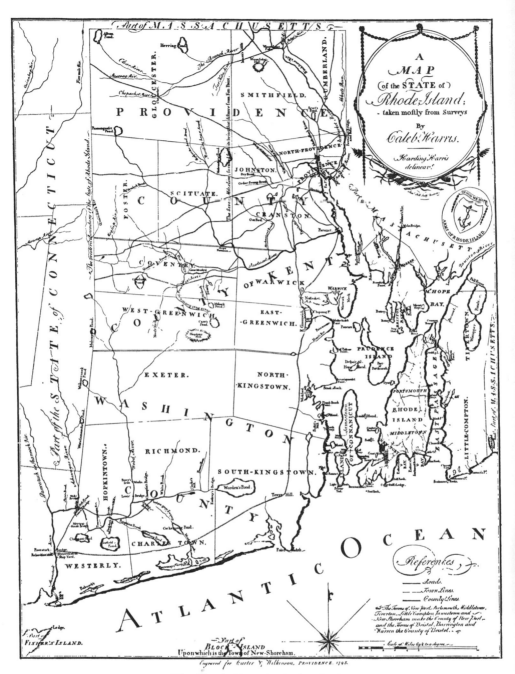

The Harris Map of Rhode Island.
Drawn in 1795, this was the first map ever made from extensive surveys of the state.
Courtesy of the John Carter Brown Library, Brown University.

1774-1795

Rhode Island
and
the Union

IRWIN H. POLISHOOK

NORTHWESTERN UNIVERSITY PRESS

EVANSTON   1969

The publication of this book has been aided
by contributions from friends of
JAMES ALTON JAMES.

Irwin H. Polishook is Associate Professor of History at
Herbert H. Lehman College of the City University of New York.

DEDICATED TO THE MEMORY
OF MY MOTHER AND FATHER

Contents

Preface

IT IS NOW seventy years since an extended study of Rhode Island during the Confederation era has been published. The intervening years have seen the collection of many new sources and changes in points of view, particularly regarding paper money and the Constitution of 1787, all of which seem to call for a fresh appraisal of the period. Although scholars have treated various parts of this subject in other works, this book offers a narrative and analysis based on the most important available sources and full consideration of the problem of Rhode Island and the Union.

Building a nation was not an easy process for the American people. We sometimes forget, because of the comparison with the new nations of the twentieth century, that the organization of the United States of America was an unexpected development of great complexity. More particularly, the precise form of national government that emerged from the Revolutionary era was the by-product of a functional interaction between the problems of the country, considered as a whole, and the formidable challenges facing the individual states. For each of the American states and their peoples, a judgment concerning the Union depended upon their estimate of the value received, real or imagined, from the central government established during the War for Independence. The fluctuations in every state, supporting or denying greater loyalty and power to the national government, seem to demonstrate that decisions regarding the federal system were rendered out of local experience.

It is just such a local experience that I have examined in this book. Despite the focus on an individual state, it seems to me that the local dimension provides an excellent opportunity to see revealed the vital forces that brought the United States into being. As will be apparent in this volume, I have found no single interpretation that can connect the different historical factors at work during the entire period from 1774 to 1795. Rhode Island reacted to the federal Union according to its own state-centered needs, which varied with time and circumstance, and often was influenced by bitter internal divisions. This approach serves to explain the contradictory policies of Rhode Island regarding the organization of a national government for the United States.

A historian, like his history, is not the product of a single influence or period of time. I have a number of debts to acknowledge for the years when this book was in progress. No one has contributed more to the completion of this volume than Professor Clarence L. Ver Steeg of Northwestern University. His continuing support as a teacher and scholar was crucial at every point in the development of the work. Professor David S. Lovejoy of the University of Wisconsin first introduced me to the study of Confederation Rhode Island and offered valuable criticism of the book. His help is gratefully acknowledged. Special encouragement to publish the book came from the late Professor James B. Hedges of Brown University. His evaluation of an early version of the work and suggestions were of great value. Professor Robert H. Wiebe of Northwestern University was also kind enough to offer a detailed commentary on the study that was most useful in revising it for publication. The many archives, historical societies, and libraries that were visited in the course of this research are noted in the bibliography. I am especially grateful to the very able and helpful people who work in the Rhode Island Historical Society, the Newport Historical Society, the John Carter Brown Library, the Rare Book Room and American History Division of the New York Public Library, the New York Historical Society, and the many depositories of the Rhode Island town records. I owe a special word of gratitude to the late Mary L. Quinn of the Rhode Island State Archives. Her years of dedicated service continue to be invaluable to succeeding generations of historians. Professor Gray C. Boyce of Northwestern University was most gracious and considerate in making arrangements for the publication of this book. I am also pleased to acknowledge the assistance of Mr. H. Russell Kay of Northwestern University Press in bringing a better book into print. Mrs. Bernice Linder typed the manuscript efficiently and with care. The Social Science Research Council and the American Association for State and Local History provided financial assistance at different points in the preparation of this project. Finally, my wife, a historian in her own right, has contributed substantially to whatever quality this volume may have. Needless to say, where the book fails to satisfy, I am fully responsible.

                                                                      I. H. P.

Note

The reader's attention is called to the following abbreviations of archival sources:

B.U.L.	Brown University Library
H.L.	Houghton Library, Harvard University
H.S.P.	Historical Society of Pennsylvania
J.C.B.L.	John Carter Brown Library, Brown University
M.H.S.	Massachusetts Historical Society
N.A.	National Archives, Washington, D.C.
N.H.S.	Newport Historical Society
N.Y.P.L.	New York Public Library
R.I.H.S.	Rhode Island Historical Society
R.I.S.A.	Rhode Island State Archives

Rhode Island
and the Union
1774–1795

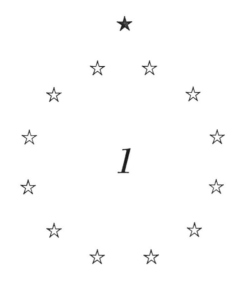

A Union of Necessity

THE AMERICAN REPUBLIC began informally in the autumn of 1774 with the gathering of delegates to the First Continental Congress. Eleven colonies sent representatives to this epochal meeting, a convention called to resolve the controversies that threatened civil war in the British Empire. The delegates came to Philadelphia with compromise and accommodation uppermost in their minds; all were instructed by their respective legislatures to agree upon measures that would prevent further strife between Great Britain and its North American colonies. Everyone hoped that concerted protests through an intercolonial congress, when given the unanimous support of the thirteen colonies, would bring reconciliation with the mother country. Independence was the desire of very few in 1774. Events in the Revolutionary conflict, however, overreached the desires of Americans at that time. And this first congress of delegates, which sought to end the crisis with Great Britain, was a forerunner of the political union of the colonies

3

that culminated in independence and a first national constitution under the Articles of Confederation.

Although the colony of Rhode Island spoke of its devotion to the British Empire it chose delegates to the Philadelphia Congress and strongly supported the protests of the American colonies. The leaders of the Rhode Island colony saw clearly the dangerous turn that Anglo-American relations had taken and assumed their place in the vanguard of the movement for unity. They advanced the American cause with a determination "to cooperate with other colonies in every respect for obtaining a redress of grievances, and establishing the rights and liberties of all the colonies upon an equitable foundation." [1] As if to underscore the gravity of the crisis and the resolution of Rhode Island in supporting the collective protest, the colony selected its two most eminent political statesmen, Stephen Hopkins and Samuel Ward, both former governors, as delegates to the First Continental Congress.

Rhode Island's participation in the intercolonial drive for unity during the early stages of the Revolutionary crisis stands in striking contrast to its traditional independence and distrust of the neighboring provinces. The main lines of Rhode Island's development up to the middle years of the eighteenth century were characterized by steadfast isolation from the other American colonies. One historian declared that the colony's traditional policy had been "To mind their own business and to insist none others should mind it for them." [2] This isolation was the product of circumstances surrounding the birth of the colony in the third decade of the seventeenth century, circumstances whose influence continued into the eventful years of the Revolutionary period.

Rhode Island began its corporate life under the influence of Roger Williams' unorthodoxy and with the support of several generations of dissenting immigrants. The colony was founded, Charles II announced in 1663, as a "lively experiment" in religious liberty. [3] Beyond the expe-

1. John R. Bartlett, ed., *Records of the Colony of Rhode Island and Providence Plantations in New England,* 10 vols. (Providence, 1856–65) , VII, 267.

2. James N. Arnold, "The Causes of the Popularity of the Revolutionary Movement in Rhode Island," *Narragansett Historical Register,* IV (1885) , 85. See also Frank G. Bates, *Rhode Island and the Formation of the Union,* Columbia University Studies in History, Economics, and Public Law, X, No. 2 (New York, 1898) , 11–44.

3. This was the famous expression used in the royal charter which was the colony's constitution. The charter is printed in Bartlett, *Records,* II, 1–21.

rience of any other American colony, the Rhode Island experiment was unique for its emphasis upon spiritual freedom and the separation of church and state to ensure that principle. For this reason the colony stood apart from its neighbors, unorthodox in an age when orthodoxy forbade toleration and demanded a firm union between minister and magistrate. When the province became a haven for the religious refugees of the entire world, particularly with the influx of the Quakers, Rhode Island became even more an object of hatred and distrust. Pertinent is the history of the New England Confederation, founded in the middle of the seventeenth century, which refused the entreaties of Rhode Island to enter into this first, rudimentary political union. In fact, the Confederation itself was directed as much against the supposed threat posed by Rhode Island as against the other dangers that alarmed the Puritans of New England.[4] Rhode Island's neighbors manifested their antagonism by combining against the unorthodox colony.

The Rhode Island tradition of isolation and distrust was fostered by two additional influences of importance, especially for the Confederation period: boundary controversies and the issuance of paper money. The boundaries of the Rhode Island colony were never firmly fixed during the early years of settlement. The original founders fled into the wilderness with little thought of patent and charter privileges, relying for their right to land and settlement upon direct purchases from the natives. The limits of these initial purchases were not well defined. This meant that the colony was always burdened by boundary disputes with its neighbors, in which the territorial integrity of the settlement was brought into question by assiduously pressed claims from Massachusetts and Connecticut. Success in these assertions of proprietary rights would have destroyed the colony;[5] as it was, the boundary con-

4. Samuel G. Arnold, *History of the State of Rhode Island and Providence Plantations: From the Settlement of the State, 1636, to the Adoption of the Federal Constitution, 1790*, 2 vols. (New York, 1859–60), I, 155–58 (hereafter cited as Arnold, *History of R.I.*); Charles M. Andrews, *The Colonial Period of American History*, 4 vols. (New Haven, 1934–38), III, 23–24; Harry M. Ward, *The United Colonies of New England 1643–1690* (New York, 1961), pp. 136–56.

5. Technical aspects of the boundary controversies and appropriate maps may be studied in John H. Cady, *Rhode Island Boundaries 1636–1936*, State of Rhode Island and Providence Plantations, State Planning Board, Special Report No. 7 (Providence, 1936). A perceptive look at these boundary squabbles, with attention to the political overtones of the rival claims and the desire of some New Englanders to rid America of the Rhode Island menace, is provided by Samuel H. Brockunier, *The Irrepressible Democrat: Roger Williams* (New York, 1940). The problem of con-

troversies between Rhode Island and its neighbors managed to embitter intercolonial relations throughout the colonial period. Although a boundary compromise in 1746 adjusted the frontiers in a manner favorable to Rhode Island's claims, the disputes continued into the nineteenth century and were ultimately settled by a decision of the United States Supreme Court.

The colonial paper-money problem—in which Rhode Island was a principal actor—was an aspect of the past that had a key influence in the Confederation era. This problem stemmed from an extremely unfavorable balance of trade and payments that persisted between the North American colonies and the mother country in the period before 1776. As a consequence, whatever specie came into these British possessions went out even more quickly in payment for foreign products. This hard fact of economic life left the northern colonies without sufficient gold and silver to serve as a medium of exchange. The result was a demand for substitutes, including paper currency, to relieve the pressures on commerce caused by the absence of a circulating medium. The New England region in particular, deficient in the production of an agricultural surplus and dependent upon the earnings of trade and commerce for a livelihood, was in dire need of a substitute for hard currency. An initial solution was the coinage of money in America, and in 1652 Massachusetts established the first mint in the colonies, which issued the famous pine-tree shilling. This specie emission was soon followed by other issues of paper currency whenever the need for revenue was great, such as in time of war, so that paper money served not only in place of specie but also as a device of governmental finance.[6] Eventually, the American provinces began to resort regularly to the printing press as a palliative for their financial ills.

Rhode Island also issued paper money whenever the need arose. The charter colony of Rhode Island, however, had much greater freedom in arranging its monetary policies than had most North American

flicting claims to the Narragansett country is most recently treated in Douglas E. Leach, *Flintlock and Tomahawk: New England in King Philip's War* (New York, 1958), pp. 16–18; Richard S. Dunn, "John Winthrop, Jr., and the Narragansett Country," *William and Mary Quarterly,* 3d ser., XIII (1956), 68–86; and Robert C. Black, III, *The Younger John Winthrop* (New York, 1966).

6. The best studies are E. James Ferguson, "Currency Finance: An Interpretation of Colonial Monetary Practices," *William and Mary Quarterly,* 3d ser., X (1953), 153–80; and Curtis P. Nettels, *Money Supply of the American Colonies before 1720* (New York, 1934). A succinct summary for Rhode Island is given in the "Report of Governor [Richard] Ward, to the Board of Trade, on paper money," Newport, January 9, 1740, Bartlett, *Records,* V, 8–14.

provinces, particularly Massachusetts. The Rhode Island colony operated under a royal charter that granted almost complete authority to
the American settlers. Except for the perfunctory reservation that colonial laws were to be as consistent as possible with those current in England, the province could enact whatever legislation it pleased. Rhode
Island was virtually independent; the colony elected all its public
officials, and its grant of self-government was so complete that Rhode
Island successfully denied that the king and his Privy Council could
disallow acts of the General Assembly. Hence while the royal governor
of Massachusetts Bay forbade all further emissions of paper money in
the early eighteenth century, Rhode Island labored under no similar
injunction until the parliamentary prohibitions of 1756 and 1764 put
an end to the colony's flirtation with paper currency.

The colony and its enterprising merchant class made the most of
their freedom. Eight issues of paper money were struck off the press in
the colonial years.[7] In the absence of competing New England emissions, Rhode Island currency circulated freely into the bordering colonies, where these bills were prized as the only available surrogate for
hard money. This made it possible for Rhode Island merchants to secure New England products for their carrying trade and to profit
greatly, if indirectly, from the remarkable advantages which their
royal charter offered. Paper money was helpful in other ways. In periods of economic decline, the inflationary impact of paper money
acted as a spur to trade and commerce. Likewise, the funds of paper
money authorized by the General Assembly were of considerable benefit to an underdeveloped colonial economy as a dynamic source of
capital and credit. Merchants and other entrepreneurs often favored
paper-money emissions which they found to their advantage and
beneficial to the economy of Rhode Island as well. In Massachusetts,
on the other hand, the privileges which Rhode Island enjoyed were
viewed with bitterness, a sentiment that changed to hatred whenever

7. The first Rhode Island emission came in 1710. It was followed by seven others,
not including the most famous emission of 1786. The standard work on these
emissions—but hardly an adequate one—is Elisha R. Potter and Sidney S. Rider,
"Some Account of the Credit or Paper Money of Rhode Island: From the First
Issue in 1710, to the Final Issue, 1786," *Rhode Island Historical Society Tracts*,
1st ser., No. 8 (1880). Two revealing accounts of colonial paper money and the
Rhode Island emission in particular are the works of John B. MacInnes, "Rhode
Island Bills of Public Credit 1710–1755" (Ph.D. diss., Brown University, 1952); and
Leslie Van Horn Brock, "The Currency of the American Colonies 1700–1764: A
Study in Colonial Finance and Imperial Relations" (Ph.D. diss., University of
Michigan, 1941), esp. pp. 195–202, 235–36, 313–17.

the Rhode Island bills were excessive and depreciated in value relative to specie.[8] The Rhode Island experience with paper money was thus a special source of strength for the colony, even while these emissions might on occasion prove objectionable in the New England region. In consequence hatred and mistrust of Rhode Island, inveterate from its settlement, increased.

At the conclusion of the colonial period, Rhode Island was a province whose relations with its neighbors were based on fear and suspicion. The innovation of religious freedom had been propounded in an age when that freedom was looked upon as arrant ungodliness, if not sedition. Further causes for bitterness were boundary controversies with the surrounding colonies, conflicts whose intensity derived from the fact that Rhode Island's territorial integrity was threatened. The final cause for disenchantment was paper money. Merchants in Massachusetts looked with displeasure upon succeeding paper-money issues in their Narragansett neighbor to the south. Moreover, with the economy of New England in a precarious balance and dependent on trade, the Rhode Island adventure with paper currency was a cause for conflict that rankled long after the last colonial emission in 1755. For these reasons the enthusiasm of the colony for a union with the American provinces in 1774 requires some investigation and explanation.

A Turn from Isolation

Rhode Island had long been vigorous in pressing its privilege of freedom from the encroachment of Great Britain. The colony claimed a virtual independence of the mother country and always resented interference with its treasured prerogatives. The province feared any innovation in its political and economic life that came from without, and it assailed the imperial reorganization after the French and Indian War. This resistance to change hardened into a fixed determination to

8. Bray Hammond, *Banks and Politics in America: From the Revolution to the Civil War* (Princeton, 1957), pp. 17–23. See also Richard A. Lester, *Monetary Experiments: Early American and Recent Scandinavian* (Princeton, 1939); and Joseph Dorfman, *The Economic Mind in American Civilization,* 3 vols. (New York, 1946–49), I.

defend the *status quo* at all costs, despite the dangers that such a policy entailed. As the prospect of war became more real, Rhode Island put itself on a war footing and prepared for the ensuing struggle.[9]

Actual fighting commenced late in the spring of 1775 after the momentous clash at Lexington, although the earlier period of peace was nothing more than a time of uneasy armed truce. By the end of 1775 enemy warships dominated Narragansett Bay and had entered Newport harbor, the colony's largest port, thereby endangering the seacoast communities of Rhode Island. Within days an evacuation of Newport had begun, and before another year was gone, under the threat of a British armada of more than 130 ships of war and transports, the island of Rhode Island itself was abandoned.[10] The security of the entire colony was put in extreme peril. With over 400 miles of shore line on Narragansett Bay and the ocean, Rhode Island faced the likely prospect of an immediate and overwhelming defeat as soon as the Revolutionary struggle began in earnest.

War is never a pleasant prospect, and no people engage in hostilities without taking steps to assure a strong military posture. This was true of Rhode Island. The major problem facing the colony was the certainty that British naval forces would attack from the sea and doubtless conquer the commodious harbor of Newport. Enemy occupation of the colony's largest town, dominating the northeastern seaboard, threatened Rhode Island—to say nothing of the fledgling United States—with military and commercial disaster. Because of this the General Assembly sent a special representative, Nathanael Greene, on a precedent-shattering mission to confer with the Connecticut colony in 1774 about the possibility of a common defense of the Narragansett region. The job, evidently, was beyond Rhode Island's ability, and we have in this bid an indication that age-old enmities and suspicions

---

9. Bartlett, *Records,* VII, 260, 264–66, 306. The definitive account of the coming of the Revolution in Rhode Island is David S. Lovejoy, *Rhode Island Politics and the American Revolution 1760–1776* (Providence, 1958) (hereafter cited as Lovejoy, *R.I. Politics*) ; a still useful supplement is Arnold, *History of R.I.,* II, 251–65.

10. Joseph Anthony to Aaron Lopez, Exeter Township [Pa.], January 27, 1779, Charles F. Adams *et al.,* eds., "Commerce of Rhode Island 1726–1800," *Collections of the Massachusetts Historical Society,* 7th ser., IX, X (1914–15) , 49–50; Governor Cooke to the R.I. Delegates at Philadelphia, Providence, July 18, 1775, Papers of Nicholas Cooke of Rhode Island, Mss., H.L., No. 10; Governor Cooke to John Hancock, Providence, December 8, 1776, Papers of the Continental Congress, 1774–1789, State Papers of New Hampshire and of Rhode Island and Providence Plantations, 1775–1788, Mss., N.A.

might be submerged in a common cause.[11] A second consideration that led Rhode Island to take a more receptive attitude toward cooperation with its neighbors was the material sacrifice which the Revolutionary struggle would obviously require. Rhode Islanders hoped that a cooperative war effort might lead to a better defense of their homes and distribute the economic burdens of the conflict more equally among the colonial partners. This thinking dominated Rhode Island policy on intercolonial and interstate matters thoughout the active phases of the American Revolution.

Rhode Island's novel desire for intercolonial cooperation was first manifested by a strong sympathy for the people of Boston after Parliament passed the Coercive Acts. The Rhode Island towns applauded the violence in Boston and elsewhere that had been directed against the importation of tea; they protested that attempts to tax the colonists and punishment of resistance to illegal impositions were part of a diabolical plot to usurp American freedom. When Parliament struck at the city following the Boston Tea Party, Rhode Island's freemen were resolute in Boston's defense. Everywhere in Rhode Island there was an identification with the suffering Bostonians—inconceivable in the past—and pledges of material support. Revealing also were forebodings openly expressed throughout the colony that the threat to Boston was a danger to all. A Newport town meeting told of its "deepest sense of the injuries done to the town of Boston, by the act of Parliament putting an end to their trade and destroying their port," adding that the "same power may at pleasure destroy the trade and shut up the ports of every other colony in its turn." The remedy suggested in Newport and elsewhere was union with the other embattled colonies.[12] In Providence, the colony's second most important center, the freemen were forceful in insisting that the town would "heartily join with the Province of Massachusetts Bay, and the other colonies" to defend

11. Bartlett, *Records*, VII, 311–12.
12. Newport Town Meeting, May 20, 1774, *Newport Mercury*, May 23, 1774. Important also are the resolutions of the Charlestown Town Meeting, July 4, 1774, an influential agricultural community in the southern part of the mainland, and a Portsmouth Town Meeting, May 19, 1774. See the *Newport Mercury*, June 6 and July 18, 1774. The Portsmouth freemen were told during the course of their debate that the Coercive Acts had a "most extraordinary nature, and fatal tendency"; they were warned that the British "are taking every measure to disunite the colonies, thereby to render the noble opposition to their arbitrary and destructive measures abortive; we hope a firm union of all the colonies will still subsist. . . ."

American freedom. The town's deputies in the General Assembly were specifically instructed to favor "the firmest union." [13]

Under this unanimous and emotional pressure from its towns, Rhode Island joined in the march toward intercolonial unity. The General Assembly declared that "a firm and inviolable union of all the colonies . . . is absolutely necessary for the preservation of their rights and liberties." To secure this unity, the legislature welcomed the suggestion that led to the First Continental Congress, binding its delegates "to procure a regular, annual convention of representatives for all the colonies." [14] This declaration was a bold step on the road to colonial union and nationhood.

Rhode Islanders were thus agreed that union of the American provinces was of fundamental importance to the cause of freedom. The people were repeatedly urged throughout the war to put away all past suspicion and fear of the neighboring states, "to lay aside every separate interest, all private views and considerations, and heartily unite and bravely exert your whole combined strength, and influence, in support of your whole combined dear native country. . . ." [15] The military necessity governing this policy was driven home time and time again by countless official and private estimates of the colonial situation in general and the Rhode Island dilemma in particular. The United States commander-in-chief, George Washington, on more than one occasion cautioned the state's leaders that no single state could defend itself against the might of Great Britain. He insisted that "if each state were to prepare for its own defence, independent of the others, they would all be conquered in a short time, one by one." [16] A reminder was hardly necessary, for Rhode Island quickly felt the sting of war after 1775. The Rhode Island governor, Nicholas Cooke, a retired merchant who reluctantly accepted the position when his loyalist predecessor was deposed, was fully apprised of the urgent military reasons for an American union. "From the Nature of the war and the circumstances of the colonies I think every idea of a partial and colonial

---

13. Providence Town Meeting, May 17, 1774, William R. Staples, ed., *Annals of the Town of Providence* (Providence, 1843) , p. 235; for the sentiments of Westerly and other towns consult the *Providence Gazette*, May 28, 1774.

14. Bartlett, *Records*, VII, 246.

15. Letter from "A Countryman," *Newport Mercury*, February 7, 1774; letter from "New England," *Providence Gazette*, May 4, 1774.

16. Washington to Governor Cooke, Morristown, January 20, 1777, Bartlett, *Records*, VIII, 114.

defence ought to be given up," wrote Cooke to General Washington during the first month of 1776. "There must be a supreme superintending power to exert and direct the force of the whole for the defence and safety of all." [17] Cooke surmised that in the absence of complete cooperation each colony's defense would be insufficient and its conquest by the British inevitable. He ventured the guess that unless the other colonies helped Rhode Island the province would have to be abandoned.

Of increasing concern also were the costs of the conflict, a burden which promised to be far greater than Rhode Island could shoulder alone, unaided by its sister states. The delegates in Congress were repeatedly instructed to gain the assent of the united colonies to the concept of a common defense, in which the costs of the war would be distributed equitably and each state would be reimbursed from a common treasury for any disproportionate contribution that it might make. When this policy was approved by the nation's representatives in the Continental Congress, Governor Cooke was jubilant. "By this strong Cement," he declared, "we hope the Colonies will be so intimately incorporated as to become (by the Blessing of God) impregnable." [18]

Rhode Island, therefore, took a leading part in the movement for an American political union—a union of necessity.[19] Every local and personal interest or fear, the leaven of the colonial past, had to be forgotten before the common danger. This consideration was the hallmark of Rhode Island policy. A former governor and political leader of the

17. Cooke to Washington, Providence, January 21, 1776, and Cooke to General Charles Lee, Providence, January 21, 1776, both in "Selections from Papers in the Public Offices of Rhode Island & Georgia," The Sparks Manuscripts, H.L.; Cooke to the Rhode Island Congressional Delegates, Ward and Hopkins, Providence, January 21, 1776, Bartlett, *Records,* VII, 451.

18. Matt B. Jones, "Revolutionary Correspondence of Governor Nicholas Cooke, 1775–1781," *Proceedings of the American Antiquarian Society,* n.s., XXXVI (1926), 237–38.

19. In this regard it is important to remember that military and security considerations were paramount throughout the colonial period among the forces looking toward intercolonial unity. Each of the ten intercolonial conferences between 1684 and 1751 were the result of these influences. The most famous conference, the Albany Congress of 1754, aimed at achieving military security in North America. Even more significantly, the conference acknowledged that to foster united action a political union was required, and the Albany Plan of Union was the result. For details consult Robert C. Newbold, *The Albany Congress and Plan of Union of 1754* (New York, 1955), pp. 28, 120. Another discussion and approach to the problem of the development of intercolonial unity is Richard L. Merritt, *Symbols of American Community 1735–1775* (New Haven, 1966).

southern section of the state, Samuel Ward, summarized this very succinctly:

> To be or not to be is now the Question. Every private View, Passion and Interest ought to be buried; We are embarked in one Common Bottom, if she sinks we all perish; if she survives the storm, Peace and Plenty (the offspring of Liberty) and every thing which will dignify and facilitate human Nature will be the Reward of our Virtue.[20]

But virtue, so often tied to practicality, dictated an entirely new course in Rhode Island's relations with the other American colonies.

The Wisdom of Change

Evidence was not long forthcoming that the decision to cooperate with the American states was a wise one. The overriding problem with which the state had to deal was that of military security; to protect the state from a disabling conquest was the key element in Rhode Island's military planning. Almost immediately after the Revolution began, the British occupied as much as one-third of the state's territory, including Newport and parts of the seacoast of Narragansett Bay. Only the mainland areas of Rhode Island were relatively free of hostile armies; this circle of freedom fortunately contained the productive farmlands of the state's Washington County, the famous Narragansett country.[21] Despite this bit of good luck, the need for men and material

20. Ward to Richard Ward, Philadelphia, November 11, 1775, *Correspondence of Governor Samuel Ward, May 1775–March 1776*, ed. Bernhard Knollenberg (Providence, 1952), pp. 121–22.

21. The southern region of the Narragansett country was famous for its verdant lands and agricultural produce. This area bore the brunt of paying for the war because the second richest region of the state, the island of Rhode Island, was under enemy occupation. The earnings usually supplied by commerce, particularly in Newport, were also drastically curtailed. This meant that the military necessity of protecting the Narragansett region, the only producing area of Rhode Island, was doubly urgent. Information on the Narragansett country may be garnered from Edward Channing, *The Narragansett Planters: A Study in Causes*, Johns Hopkins University Studies in Historical and Political Science, 4th ser., III (Baltimore, 1886); and William Davis Miller, "The Narragansett Planters," *Proceedings of the American Antiquarian Society*, n.s., XLIII (1933), 49–115.

—the sinews of war—was far in excess of what the beleaguered state could provide. Rhode Island was driven in its extremity to call upon the United States and the New England provinces for aid in defending itself. Soon after the initial battles of 1775, because of Rhode Island's desperate appeals for help, a convention of the New England states met to confer upon the joint defense of the whole section.[22] A better avenue through which to channel requests for a combined defense of Rhode Island was the Continental Congress, and to this body the General Assembly addressed numerous calls for troops and supplies. The state's delegates in Congress were bombarded with instructions telling them to seek increased continental battalions in Rhode Island. They were also asked to secure congressional pressure upon the neighboring provinces to assist the state with military forces.

An urgent problem was the scarcity of food and provisions in the state. Rhode Island never had an appreciable food surplus in the colonial period, and the war seemed to hold out the probability of extreme privation, even starvation. Nicholas Cooke's successor as governor, William Greene, explained that, owing to the disruption of the Revolution, "we have been under the cruel Necessity of taking the Inhabitants from their Farms, in the Seasons of plowing, planting, sowing and gathering in their Crops; by which means Husbandry hath been neglected, the State is impoverished, and we are now almost upon the Verge of a Famine." [23] Likewise, the Reverend James Manning, President of Rhode Island College, despaired that the shortage of food in Providence was so great that many people might starve to death.[24] An impending dearth of provisions led Governor Cooke to ask the neighboring states to supply quantities of grain and other foods for the relief of Rhode Island; the state's congressmen were asked to bring the problem to the attention of Congress, in hope of securing a congres-

22. Charles Hoadly and Leonard W. Labaree, eds., *The Public Records of the State of Connecticut, 1776–1796,* 8 vols. (Hartford, 1894–1951) , I, 120–21.
23. Greene to John Jay, President of Congress, Providence, April 26, 1779, State Papers of Rhode Island, Mss., N.A.
24. Manning to Moses Brown, Providence, March 25, 1779, Moses Brown Papers, Mss., R.I.H.S., III, 7A, No. 611; Ezekiel Cornell to unknown correspondent [Governor of Rhode Island?], Newport, November 6, 1779, Charles Francis Jenkins Collection, M.O.C., Mss., H.S.P., Box I; *Providence Gazette,* January 10, 1778. The want of provisions affected the British invaders of Rhode Island who were unable to find enough food for their needs in the Narragansett region. See Howard W. Peckham, *The War for Independence: A Military History* (Chicago, 1958) , p. 99.

sional call for enough food to prevent starvation and a collapse of the Revolution in the Narragansett state.[25] Responding to Rhode Island's critical situation, Congress appealed to New York and Connecticut to offer immediate succor to their "starving Sister." [26]

Another indication of Rhode Island's need for cooperative action after 1774 came when the inflation of the Revolutionary years was first felt. Precipitous increases in the price level that resulted from excessive emissions of paper money and the scarcity of articles for sale produced an unprecedented problem for the United States. The proposed solution was equally unprecedented. As inflated prices rose to inordinate heights, demands were voiced for government regulation of prices. Legislative action, it was assumed, would successfully combat the engrossers, extortionists, and speculators supposedly responsible for increasing prices. Massachusetts proposed that a New England convention be called to deal with the related problems of an expanding currency and inflated prices. The first of these price conventions met in Providence late in 1776, with four New England states in attendance. The proceedings of the delegates were sent to Congress, where the nation's representatives gave their formal approval to this futile effort to gain stability in prices through government regulation. Spurred on by its New England members, Congress recommended this course of action to the similarly plagued middle and southern states.[27] Intercolonial unity, sponsored by the New England states, reached out to embrace the entire nation.

The Rhode Island apprehension that its material contribution to the war effort would be disproportionately greater than that of many other states was verified at the end of the conflict. Though the figures will never be determined with certainty, several estimates were made

25. Hoadly and Labaree, *Records of Connecticut*, II, 187–88; John Fell, "Diary," in *Letters of the Members of the Continental Congress*, ed. Edmund C. Burnett, 8 vols. (Washington, D.C., 1921–36), I, 252.

26. John Jay to Governor Clinton of New York, Philadelphia, February 8, 1779, Burnett, *Letters*, IV, 60.

27. Edmund C. Burnett, *The Continental Congress* (New York, 1941), p. 423; William B. Weeden, *Economic and Social History of New England 1620–1789*, 2 vols. (Boston, 1894), II, 797; Albert S. Bolles, *The Financial History of the United States from 1774 to 1789: Embracing the Period of the American Revolution* (New York, 1879), pp. 158–73. The manuscript records of this and all other price conventions of the New England states are in the Rhode Island State Archives. A printed version appears in Hoadly and Labaree, *Records of Connecticut*, I, 585–620; II, 562–79.

which indicate the relative size of Rhode Island's expenditures.[28] The first claim which the state presented for repayment by the nation totaled more than $5,000,000; almost $600,000 was later added to the Rhode Island claim. Eventually the United States Treasury acknowledged that more than $1,800,000 was due to the state, though there was anguish in Rhode Island because the sum fell far short of expectations.[29] After deducting advances made by the federal government, Rhode Island was the fourth-largest creditor of the nation for common expenses incurred during the American Revolution; in proportion to its population, the state was second only to South Carolina among the federal creditors. This circumstance provides an important confirmation of the economic factors which impelled the state to embrace the cause of an inter-American political union, at least prior to 1781. Rhode Island saw that the war would be costly, probably beyond its ability to pay, and it sought to guarantee that each state would contribute toward independence according to its wealth. This idea was incorporated into the Articles of Confederation and served as the basis for repayments which were arranged in the years after the adoption of the Constitution of 1787.[30]

A National Constitution

The most dramatic event in this early enthusiasm of Rhode Island for a Union was represented by the state's speedy ratification of the Articles of Confederation.[31] The Continental Congress completed its

28. One reason why an exact accounting was impossible was that during the hurried events of the Revolution Rhode Island's books were poorly kept and many expenditures went unrecorded; another difficulty was the fact that many vouchers sent to Philadelphia were captured by the British or lost, and the Rhode Island copies were not honored. See "Report of the Commissioners to the General Assembly," October, 1791, Rhode Island Records, 1646–1851, 29 vols., Mss., R.I.S.A., Vol. XIV, pp. 76–78.

29. "Report of the Commissioners to the General Assembly," May, 1792, Reports to the General Assembly, 1728–1860, 15 vols., Mss., R.I.S.A., Vol. V, pp. 41, 52; Report on the Registered State Debt With Certificates, 1849, Ms., R.I.S.A., p. 53.

30. The clause in question was Article 8 of the Articles of Confederation.

31. The General Assembly debated the Articles on several occasions before ratifying them on February 8, 1778. For the dates and documents of ratification, see *Secret Journals of the Congress of the Confederation,* 4 vols. (Boston, 1824), I, 402–64.

work on the plan of union late in 1777, after an extended and trying period of labor. In November of that year the proposed constitution was sent out to the states with a penetrating explanation of the task involved in making a constitution for the new nation. "To form a perfect union," confessed Congress, "accommodated to the opinions and wishes of the delegates of so many states, differing in habits, produce, commerce and internal police, was found to be a work which nothing but time and reflection, conspiring with a disposition to conciliate, could mature and accomplish." The Confederation was offered as the best frame of government upon which the delegates could agree, an imperfect plan, perhaps, but the only one "which affords any tolerable prospect of general ratification." [32] Considering the extreme dangers that threatened the very existence of Rhode Island, its prompt and hearty approval is hardly surprising. As far back as 1775, Governor Cooke had boasted for the benefit of General Nathanael Greene of the state's undivided commitment to the Union. "There hath not been the least Division in the General Assembly from any Motive of a Departure from the common cause," exulted the elderly Governor. "On the contrary the Firmness of the General Assembly is perfectly to be depended upon." [33] Despite Rhode Island's intransigence in future years, fear and common danger cemented the affections of the American states during the Revolution.

The General Assembly voted its ratification of the Articles of Confederation unanimously.[34] Although the legislature proposed a series of desired amendments, these were suggested with a meaningful condition: "the completion of the union is so indispensably necessary," said the Assembly, that, if the amendments were rejected, the delegates in Congress were "not to decline acceding, on the part of this state, to the articles of confederation." [35] The Continental Congress was held in

32. Circular of Congress, York-Town, Pa., November 17, 1777, William R. Staples, ed., *Rhode Island in the Continental Congress: With the Journal of the Convention that Adopted the Constitution 1765–1790* (Providence, 1870), p. 131; Worthington C. Ford *et al.*, eds., *Journals of the Continental Congress, 1774–1789* (Washington, D.C., 1904–37), IX, 932–35.

33. Cooke to Greene, Providence, September 25, 1775, Cooke Papers, Mss., H.L., No. 9.

34. Rhode Island Records, Mss., R.I.S.A., Vol. 10, pp. 49–51; Bartlett, *Records*, VIII, 362; *Providence Gazette*, February 24, 1778; Ford, *Journals of the Continental Congress*, XI, 663.

35. Journals of the House of Deputies, 1774–1790, Mss., R.I.S.A., February 15 and 16, 1778. For the discussion of the amendments by Congress see Ford, *Journals of the Continental Congress*, XI, 638–39.

high esteem in Rhode Island, and the Confederation itself was proclaimed the "Grand Corner Stone" of independence.[36]

Despite the fact that Rhode Island's ratification of the Union was unanimous, there were some signs of reserve in the years before 1781. The delegation in Congress, for example, was authorized to adhere to all congressional measures in 1776, but "with the greatest care to secure this colony, in the strongest and most perfect manner, its established form, and all the powers of government, so far as relate to its internal police and conduct of our own affairs, civil and religious," [37] a reservation of monumental importance in later years. Other Rhode Islanders were uncertain of the wisdom of giving great power to any central government, even on a temporary basis, after the troubles with Parliament. One anonymous publicist asserted that the scope of congressional authority reached no further than to consult with and advise the states, rather than to direct national affairs with the compelling force of sovereignty; the individual states were supreme, and any change in this order of things could be accomplished only with the consent of the state assemblies. More particularly, this informant noted specifically: "The purse-strings ought to remain as a sacred deposit . . . in the hands of the yeomanry of each colony, respectively, or their representatives." [38] Nor did ratification of the Articles of Confederation submerge the state's individuality in the collective whole. There were still Rhode Islanders to be found who might exclaim: "The State of Rhode-Island and Providence Plantations is perhaps as free as any in the known world"—as free of Congress, one may presume, as any other authority.[39]

But as long as necessity dictated, there could be little doubt that Rhode Island's acceptance of the Union would be full. The state's hearty embrace of the nation was part and parcel of its willingness to fight a war for freedom and independence. In this, Rhode Island duplicated the motives of its sister states,[40] although its repudiation of

36. Rhode Island Delegates to Governor Greene, York, Pa., June 20, 1778, Burnett, *Letters*, III, 311.

37. Bartlett, *Records*, VII, 526–27. Burnett, *Continental Congress*, p. 168, observes that many of the states added this reservation to the credentials of their delegates; see also in this regard the important commentary of Merrill Jensen, *The Articles of Confederation: An Interpretation of the Social-Constitutional History of the American Revolution 1774–1781* (Madison, 1940; 4th ptg., 1962), pp. 161–76, 185–90.

38. Letter from "An Independent Whig," *Providence Gazette*, April 24, 1775.

39. Letter from "A Farmer," *Providence Gazette*, April 3, 1779.

40. Burnett, *Continental Congress*, pp. 213, 248, 340–41.

tradition was remarkable in degree. As long as the military danger continued, until the closing phases of the war in 1781, Rhode Island's relations with the Union were characterized by firm ties of friendship and trust.[41]

41. For the last military threat to Rhode Island, see Nathanael Greene to Governor Greene, September 22, 1780, Bartlett, *Records*, IX, 245; and Howard C. Rice, trans. and ed., *Travels in North America in the Years 1780, 1781 and 1782 by the Marquis De Chastellux*, 2 vols. (Chapel Hill, 1963), I, 63. An interesting appraisal of this danger at the end of the war is presented by William B. Willcox, "Rhode Island in British Strategy, 1780–1781," *Journal of Modern History*, XVII (1945), 304–31. Willcox suggests that the state was spared another full-scale onslaught only because of the friction that existed among the officers of the British land and naval forces in America.

Political and Economic Background

THE DELICACY AND URGENCY of Rhode Island's attachment to the United States did not become clear until after 1781. During the Revolution only an occasional voice warned that the fabric of Union was held together by threads of a most tenuous nature. The onset of peace saw the state begin the process of repudiating the nation. This backtracking followed a complex course throughout the Confederation years, and was intimately related to Rhode Island's own internal needs and pressures. How the state and its people responded to the economic and financial crisis of the postwar period is inseparable from Rhode Island's constitutional structure and the opportunity it offered for political change. Rhode Island's repudiation of the United States took place within the context of a political and economic background of the utmost relevance.

Government

After the American Revolution the constitution of Rhode Island remained the royal charter granted by Charles II in 1663. The colony became independent by the simple expedient of renouncing allegiance to the British monarch and striking the king's name from all political and judicial documents[1] Perhaps most noticeable were the legislative sessions that now closed with the invocation, "God save the United States," in place of the honored, "God save the King."[2] The ease with which Rhode Island became free merely confirmed the colonial traditions of the state, for it had always been virtually independent; a new course after 1776 was less difficult for Rhode Island than for most other states. The charter had ceded all powers—legislative, executive, and judicial—to the colony, without a reservation of substance other than the injunction that colonial laws "be not contrary and repugnant unto, but as near as may be agreeable to the laws of our realm of England, considering the nature and constitution of the place and people there."[3] This system had proved agreeable during more than one hundred years of colonial status, and Rhode Islanders boasted of its suitability for the state's experiment in independence.

The government of Rhode Island was divided into the characteristic three-part pattern, with a governor and bicameral legislature exercising complete authority under the charter. The state's legislature, the General Assembly, was composed of two distinct parts, each given equal authority. The upper house, or Assistants, was made up of twelve officers selected at large by the freemen at the annual elections in April; they included the two principal executive officers, the governor and deputy governor, and ten assistants who acted only in a legislative capacity. The upper house operated as a second chamber of the

1. In its Declaration of Independence the General Assembly wrote that George III, "forgetting his dignity," had attempted to establish a tyrannical government and force it upon Rhode Island (John R. Bartlett, ed., *Records of the Colony of Rhode Island and Providence Plantations in New England,* 10 vols. [Providence, 1856–65], VII, 522–26; *Providence Gazette,* May 18, 1776).

2. Bartlett, *Records,* VII, 501, 577, 595.

3. *Ibid.,* II, 9. A good summary of Rhode Island's constitutional history is offered by Patrick T. Conley, "Rhode Island Constitutional Development, 1636–1775: A Survey," *Rhode Island History,* XXVII (1968), 49–63, 74–94.

General Assembly, and its approval was necessary for the enactment of any piece of legislation.[4]

The lower house, or House of Deputies, was composed of representatives of the towns elected semiannually by the freemen in April and August. Because of its more frequent elections and larger membership, the House of Deputies was traditionally the more important of the two branches of the state legislature. The deputies took the most active role in lawmaking, and the bulk of the state's legislation originated with them; furthermore, the fullest consideration of any legislative business usually came in the more numerous lower house.

The representation of the towns in the House of Deputies was fixed by the charter of 1663. There was no proportional representation beyond the weighted delegations given to the four shire towns of the colony—Newport, Providence, Portsmouth, and Warwick. Newport elected six deputies to the lower house; Providence, Portsmouth, and Warwick four each; and every town incorporated after 1663, regardless of its size or wealth, chose two representatives to the General Assembly. By 1786 there were thirty towns in Rhode Island, making a total of seventy members in the House of Deputies. The static representation set down in the charter might have had some merit in the period before 1700, when the four original towns still were clearly pre-eminent, but it had lost all meaning in the Confederation era. In 1774, the largest town in the state, Newport, was entitled to elect the biggest delegation of six deputies. Providence, next in size with roughly half Newport's population, sent four members to the Assembly. But Portsmouth and Warwick, with one-third and one-half the population of Providence, respectively, could elect the same number of deputies as the larger town. The disparity did not end here: fifteen other towns had a greater population than Portsmouth in the year 1774, yet they were given only two members in the lower house, half the number which Portsmouth could claim under the ancient charter.[5] This disproportionate representation was especially severe among towns admitted in the period after 1663. For example, Jamestown, with 563

4. An excellent discussion of the upper house in Rhode Island during this period may be found in Jackson T. Main, *The Upper House in Revolutionary America 1763–1788* (Madison, 1967), pp. 86–92, 182–87.

5. This is based on the calculations in David S. Lovejoy, *Rhode Island Politics and the American Revolution 1760–1776* (Providence, 1958), p. 15. See also Arthur May Mowry, *The Dorr War: Or the Constitutional Struggle in Rhode Island* (Providence, 1901), p. 77.

inhabitants in 1774, elected two deputies, while Scituate and South Kingstown, with populations of 3,601 and 2,835, sent the same number of deputies to the lower house.[6]

The curious fact characterizing this situation of static representation in the pre-Revolutionary era was the satisfaction of the mass of freemen with the system. There were no complaints before 1776 that an unequal representation of the towns was in any way injurious to the interests of the citizens of the colony.[7] Probably the absence of discontent was symptomatic of the freemen's acceptance of the governments which this system produced and the conviction that any attack on specific articles of their treasured charter might be misconstrued as an attack on the charter itself. The charter was the rock upon which the colony's liberty and independence from the mother country rested; it had to be free from any suspicion. In addition, the inflexible representation set down in the charter gave an added weight in the General Assembly to the two major commercial towns, Newport and Providence, which increased the influence of the merchants in Rhode Island politics. The influence of the mercantile towns was of central importance in many of the political and economic controversies that marked Confederation Rhode Island.

In the Rhode Island system of government the executive branch was shorn of almost all authority; the chief functions of the governor were to preside at meetings of the upper house of the legislature and to act as the state's highest officer. He possessed no power over legislation whatever, other than as a member of the second chamber, having no veto over any laws passed by the General Assembly.[8] One colonial

6. *Providence Gazette*, July 2, 1774; Bartlett, *Records*, VII, 299.

7. Lovejoy, *R.I. Politics*, p. 15.

8. The issue of the Governor's veto was settled in 1731 when the Governor, John Jenckes, refused his assent to an act of the General Assembly emitting £60,000 in paper money. The question then arose: Did the governor possess a veto over legislative bills? Petitions and counterpetitions on the subject were sent to England, where the King's attorneys and the solicitor general declared: "That in this Charter, no negative voice is given to the Governor, nor any power reserved to the crown of approving or disapproving of the laws made in this colony." The significance of this decision cannot be overestimated. It clearly indicated that the constitution of Rhode Island was to be its charter, which provided the basic framework for the colony's structure of government; all institutions and officials derived their power from this charter. Under the terms of the colony's basic law, the governor had no role in legislation other than to proclaim acts of the Assembly. In addition, the king himself had no veto power over any Rhode Island statute, thereby freeing the colony from the meaningful royal disallowance which the crown exercised elsewhere. The General Assembly was thus free of both governor and king in one stroke! (Bartlett, *Records*, IV, 456–61.)

official described Rhode Island's chief executive as "a mere nominal one, and therefore a cipher, without power and authority; entirely controlled by the populace, elected annually, as [are] all other magistrates and officers whatsoever." [9] Agreeing with this estimate, another commentator, noting the contrast between the absence of strong executive authority and the enhanced power of the elected house of the General Assembly, denounced the colony's political system as a "Quaker mob Government"—heinous, no doubt, on account of its principal religious influence as well as its democratic tendency.[10] Besides serving as chairman of the meetings of the upper house, the governor was authorized to convoke the legislature into special sessions and acted as commander-in-chief of the armed forces of the state, though the latter role was very carefully circumscribed by the legislature.[11] The governor's influence in public life derived from his position as the state's leading official and his personal importance as a political leader. He had no appointive power.[12]

In effect, Rhode Island was governed by a single branch of government, the General Assembly, which held the full measure of authority granted to the colony and later the state under the charter of 1663. The Assembly exercised all legislative power and also had great power over the executive and judicial operations of the state.

To begin with, all laws and taxes were authorized by the legislature alone, usually originating with the House of Deputies. The General Assembly was the branch of government which could levy taxes, incorporate new towns, regulate the boundaries of all local jurisdictions, determine the time, place, and method of elections in the state, admit

9. Statement of Lord Chief Justice Daniel Horsmanden of New York, 1773, *ibid.*, VII, 182–83.

10. Francis Brinley to Francis Nicholson, Newport, November 4, 1709, Miscellaneous Bound Documents, Mss., M.H.S., Vol. VII.

11. During the American Revolution whatever initiative the governor might have been able to exercise in military affairs was restricted by the organization of an *ad hoc* council of war which was given control over state military policies when the Assembly was not in session. The governor and deputy governor both served as members of this council, but they had only one vote each and, except as officiating officers, were in no way more influential than other members of the group.

12. Prior to the Revolution the Rhode Island governor, instead of the crown, appointed all naval officers in the colony. When independence was achieved this minor appointive power, derived through English laws, was taken away by the legislature and exercised solely by the Assembly. During the Confederation period—in 1787—in order to augment the governor's revenues, he was authorized to appoint naval officers again and to share in their fees. See Rhode Island Records, Mss., R.I.S.A., Vol. 25, p. 109.

freemen, and decide all policies that concerned Rhode Island's relations with other states and foreign nations. The legislature was the agency through which the sovereignty of the people was expressed; and being but one remove from the source of all power, it held this power in point of fact.[13]

The real test of the power of the General Assembly may be observed in its appointive powers and the vast dimension of its influence in judicial affairs. Here the range of authority was great. The legislature, not the executive, chose all public officers, administrative and judicial, not directly elected by the freemen. Every appointment lasted for one year. This brief tenure increased an officeholder's dependence upon the General Assembly. The list of legislative appointees included sheriffs, customs officials, public notaries, tax collectors, and militia officers, as well as the five members of Rhode Island's highest court, the Superior Court of Judicature, and all the judges and clerks in the state's system of inferior courts. Furthermore, the Assembly's superintendence of judicial affairs went beyond its responsibility to appoint men to every judicial position in the state. The General Assembly also served as the highest appellate court in Rhode Island; it held the sole pardoning power, and monopolized complete authority in the impeachment and removal of public officials. The legislature capped its list of prerogatives by possessing direct and appellate jurisdiction in every matter relating to the probate of wills, and it might intercede at any stage in the administration of an estate.[14]

13. For a brief but incisive commentary, consult S. S. Rider, "Omnipotence of the General Assembly," *Book Notes*, I, No. 6 (1883), 3; and "Legislative History in Rhode Island," *ibid.*, IV, No. 27 (1887), 103–4. Thomas Wilson Dorr, taking stock of this situation in 1837 when the charter still served as Rhode Island's constitution, observed that "nearly all the powers . . . [of government] are accumulated without restraint or limitation in the Legislative Department." (See Reform Resolutions Presented by Thomas W. Dorr, January 13, 1837, Rejected January 21, 1837, General Assembly, Acts and Resolves, Miscellaneous, Folder XII, R.I.S.A.) The problem of the extent of the Rhode Island Assembly's power was argued in an interesting suit before the United States Supreme Court in 1829, the case of *Wilkinson* v. *Leland et al., U.S. Reports, Peters*, II, 627–62. One of the attorneys in the argument before the nation's highest court summarized the history of Rhode Island's structure of government by stating that the legislature "always has exercised supreme legislative, executive, and judicial power."

14. For the place of the judiciary in the Rhode Island political system see Edward S. Stinnes, "The Struggle for Judicial Supremacy," in *State of Rhode Island and Providence Plantations at the End of the Century: A History*, ed. Edward Field, 3 vols. (Boston, 1902), III; Harold D. Hazeltine, "Appeals from Colonial Courts to the King in Council, With Especial Reference to Rhode Island," in *Papers from the Historical Seminary of Brown University*, No. VII, ed. J. F. Jameson, (Providence,

The constitution of Rhode Island, therefore, placed in the state legislature almost complete authority—legislative, executive, and judicial. This grant of power was enormous, and the state was often dominated by an Assembly that chose to make full use of its authority. Events in the state's history during the Confederation period, particularly the paper-money interlude after 1786, must be understood against this background of an all-powerful legislature. There was no "minimized state" in Rhode Island, as one historian has suggested, for this implies a system in which the government is in some way bound by limitations in its structure or by the terms of a fundamental law. This was not the case in Rhode Island; the General Assembly, like the British Parliament, could do whatever it pleased. Nor was the philosophy of Rhode Islanders in any way an "extreme conception of Jeffersonian democracy," finding most virtuous that government which governed least.[15] The General Assembly was more than willing to make energetic use of its wide range of powers, especially when such use seemed to be the will of the majority.

Democratic Localism

The concentration of political power in the General Assembly was a striking aspect of the Rhode Island constitution. Just as striking, however, was the susceptibility of the state government to control by the people. If the Rhode Island constitutional system is to be characterized by any special term or phrase, it would be "democratic localism," a product of popular control of the General Assembly by the majority of voters and the vital role of the town as an institution of political life.

The democratic and local basis of the state's political structure was openly recognized by Rhode Island's political leaders throughout the Revolutionary period, as indeed it had to be if they were to remain in power. The Rhode Island deputy who served his town in the lower house of the legislature was controlled by a broad, active, and politically intelligent electorate. The freemen made effective use of their

---

1896) , 324–28; and Thomas Durfee, "Gleanings from the Judicial History of Rhode Island," *Rhode Island Historical Society Tracts,* 1st ser., No. 18 (1883) .

15. Both concepts are expounded in Hillman M. Bishop, "Why Rhode Island Opposed the Federal Constitution: Political Reasons," *Rhode Island History,* VIII (1949) , 115–26.

power by electing those candidates who promised to follow the popular will, and confirmed their strength by retiring from service those
officeholders who failed to gain favor. The instrument of election was
the town meeting, and the same institution served as the medium
through which deputies learned of the wishes of their constituents. A
Rhode Island official was, in a sense, the ambassador of the people
rather than their representative. He was considered the rubber stamp
of the townsmen. One delegate to the state's constitutional convention
in 1790 expressed this view when he quoted the motto: "The Voice of
the People is the Voice of God." [16] The democratic nature of the
Rhode Island constitution had long been apparent to the imperial bureaucracy, and it had tried on several occasions before 1760 to annul
the charter; by this means it was hoped that the supremacy of the government in London might be assured and one of the empire's most difficult provinces harnessed. Even some Rhode Islanders looked with
trepidation upon the state's political system, fearing the power of the
people. Theodore Foster, a Rhode Islander who served as one of the
first United States senators, confided to his diary in 1777 that "A Form
of Government so extremely democratical as ours is liable to commit
greater Error in the Administration of public Affairs than where the
Government is Monarchical or Aristocratical." [17] But the future senator further admitted that popular government produced less turmoil
in the long run than a system in fewer hands, because when the people
participate in governing themselves they are more likely to be content.

When the Revolutionary crisis came in the 1760's, the traditions and
institutions of political life in Rhode Island were so drawn as to permit democratic control of the government. The key to this control was
the frequency of elections in the state and the fact that virtually every
male inhabitant might qualify to vote. The governor, deputy governor, and all state-wide officers were chosen each year in an annual poll
of the freemen, who cast their ballots at town meetings late in April.
The members of the lower house were elected twice a year, during the
third week in April (simultaneously with the general officers) and
again during the third week in August. The frequency of these elec-

16. Robert C. Cotner, ed., *Theodore Foster's Minutes of the Convention held at
South Kingstown, Rhode Island, in March, 1790, Which Failed to Adopt the Constitution of the United States* (Providence, 1929), p. 37.

17. [Notation in the *North American Almanac*, June 3, 1777], Theodore Foster
Collection, Mss., R.I.H.S.

tions, particularly of the lower house, ensured that candidates would be responsive to popular demands. Whenever a public officer failed to mirror the grass-roots sentiments of the freemen, as in the paper-money overturn of 1786, he was voted out of office.

The elective process itself reflected the philosophy of the state's political structure. Each freeman cast his vote at town meetings regularly convened for this stated purpose. Every man's choice was registered by means of a list of candidates which he dropped into a hat; state law attempted to guarantee freedom of choice by requiring a secret vote upon the request of a single freeman and a second to his motion.[18] The ballots were counted on the spot by the moderator of the town meeting, who then entrusted the town's choices to the first deputy selected to represent the town in the legislature.[19] The tabulations were taken to the annual May session of the General Assembly, which met, as the charter required, in Newport. There all the votes were officially recorded by the two houses of government meeting together in grand committee. This instance of proxy voting, retaining the concept of a convocation of all the freemen, was symbolic of the democracy of the state's political system. Those individuals who were elected were sworn "to do equal justice unto all persons, poor and rich . . . without partiality, according to the laws established by the General Assembly." [20]

Popular control of the General Assembly was further advanced by the pattern of voting in Rhode Island. The charter itself did not specify any suffrage qualification, and presumably all men admitted as freemen of the colony were able to vote. Because of pressure from the home government, however, a property requirement was first established in the year 1723/24. During the Confederation period any freeman could cast a ballot if he held a freehold of £40 value or an estate which rented for 40 shillings, both calculated in lawful money.[21] Since lawful money was relatively cheap in Rhode Island throughout the period after 1776—as in former years—because of frequent emissions of paper currency, any male taxpayer could qualify. In 1788, with a pop-

18. Rhode Island Records, Mss., R.I.S.A., Vol. 13, pp. 425–26; Bartlett, *Records,* X, 263–64.
19. These records are often recorded in the town meeting books; sometimes they give the name of every voter and his choices for state offices. Where they exist these documents provide an important source of information in Rhode Island's history. A good example is the Exeter Annual April Town Meeting, 1766–1801, Mss., R.I.H.S.
20. *U.S. Chronicle* (Providence), April 1, 1784.
21. A succinct summary is given by Mowry, *Dorr War,* pp. 18–21.

ulation of nearly 60,000 persons, probably more than 7,000 Rhode Islanders were eligible to vote.[22]

Despite this pattern of democratic and local control of the state's political structure, the evidence from the remaining records indicates that in most elections, although the majority of adult males could exercise a franchise, few actually took the opportunity to vote. In Rhode Island's largest towns, Newport and Providence, extant manuscripts show a pattern of voter participation that varied from a relatively high proportion in some years to an extremely meager vote in others. In 1784 and 1785, for example, there were 80 and 77 ballots for general officers in Newport at a time when the total number of freemen eligible to vote was approximately 325; in 1789 and 1790, however, when the number of freemen exceeded 400, those voting numbered 305 and 365, respectively.[23] This would indicate that for Newport, at least, the proportion of participating voters varied from less than one-third in some years to almost 90 per cent in others. The story in Providence was much the same. There, in 1784, only 94 out of an electoral roll of more than 500 voted, while in 1787 and 1790, years when the town-meeting manuscripts reveal that there were exactly 521 and 527 freemen, the total number of voters was 333 and 348, respectively. The ratio of voters to those eligible in Providence varied from a low of less than 20 per cent in 1784 to almost two-thirds in 1790.[24]

The explanation for this phenomenon is to be found in the nature of the political issues of the period. In 1784 there were no issues of moment to divide and attract the freemen; consequently, voters chose to stay home on election day. So dormant were political controversies in 1784 that, for the first time in a decade, only a single party could be

22. Two analyses of the percentage of voters in Rhode Island are Lovejoy, *R.I. Politics*, pp. 16–18 and 197 n. 32; and the comprehensive work of Chilton Williamson, *American Suffrage from Property to Democracy 1760–1860* (Princeton, 1960), pp. 17, 26–27. Williamson suggests that probably between 50 and 75 per cent of all adult white males over twenty-one were freemen before the Revolution, although he also quotes with approval Cadwallader Colden's report that all Rhode Islanders who wanted could vote. The voting estimate above is taken from the *Newport Herald*, April 10, 1788; population information is gathered in Evarts B. Greene and Virginia Harrington, *American Population Before the Federal Census of 1790* (New York, 1932), pp. 61–70.

23. Newport Town Meetings, Mss., April 21, 1784, April 20, 1785, April 15, 1789, and April 21, 1790. (When citing the town meeting manuscripts no reference will be made to their location in the different town and city depositories throughout Rhode Island. For this information, see the bibliography.)

24. Providence Town Meetings, Mss., April 21, 1784, April 18, 1787, April 21, 1790.

found contesting the elections for the highest offices in the state.[25] By the years 1787 and 1790 the situation had changed radically. During the former year the paper-money struggle was at its high point, while 1790 coincided with the prolonged contest over ratification of the federal Constitution. In each case the freemen flocked to the polls in greater-than-usual numbers. The records for the rest of the state show a repetition of this pattern, except that the level of voter participation was generally below that of Newport and Providence. But when the issues of a campaign seemed to be decisive, as in 1786 and 1790, ordinary Rhode Islanders turned out in force to exercise their franchise.

Despite the low proportion of freemen who participated in most elections, the vital factors to be considered are whether those eligible to vote would do so when aroused by the issues in any single election and whether they would cast their ballots decisively to favor candidates committed to their interests. The evidence indicates that this was so. Rhode Island's freemen, though often somnolent, could accomplish their purposes by means of the ballot.

The most vigorously contested elections of the Confederation era occurred in 1786, 1787, and 1790. In 1786, after a long period of exhortation, those who advocated fiscal relief for the majority of Rhode Island farmers and an emission of paper money organized a political party and put their program before the voters. In opposition stood the merchants, firmly in support of the incumbent administration headed by William Greene of Warwick. In every one of the state's thirty towns the number of voters increased greatly over previous years, with the bumper crop of electors overwhelmingly in favor of the country party's new program of public relief and its candidate for governor, John Collins. Coventry, an inland agricultural town, saw its voting rolls double in size in 1786, with William Greene collecting only 44 votes to 148 for John Collins. Just one year earlier Greene received the almost unanimous ballot of 90 freemen out of the 91 who chose to vote.[26] Another agricultural town, West Greenwich, which had favored Greene with all its 61 ballots in 1785, gave the Governor only 13 votes in 1786; his opponent gained the approbation of 136 freemen.[27] Likewise, Coventry again favored the paper-money candidate, John Collins, with 187 votes

25. This is based on a manuscript notation in the town meeting records of Providence, cited above, which appears in Book No. 7, page 17. The notation is probably that of Theodore Foster, the Town Clerk.
26. Coventry Town Meeting, Mss., April 20, 1785; April 19, 1786.
27. West Greenwich Town Meeting, Mss., April 20, 1785; April 19, 1786.

in 1787, against 21 for his mercantile opponent, William Bradford, a Bristol attorney.[28] And in 1790, when the Constitution and re-entrance into the federal Union were policies before the voters, the people of West Greenwich gave all their 110 ballots to the candidates and party which seemed least inclined to favor ratification.[29]

Political suffrage in Rhode Island was thus of a contradictory nature. Property qualifications for voting, tied as they were to real estate and rental values expressed in inflated currency, did not act as a substantial bar to the franchise. The average Rhode Islander could easily qualify to vote in any election. This liberality was perhaps confirmed by the fact that in no known instance during the period covered by this study was there any public criticism of the laws regulating suffrage requirements nor even a suggestion that they be changed. The same was true of the pre-Revolutionary era.[30] Paradoxically, no more than three-fourths of the number of qualified males over twenty-one became freemen. Moreover, as we have seen, in any election a 60 per cent turnout of those eligible would have been a large ballot for the state; citizens of Confederation Rhode Island were apparently as delinquent in voting as their contemporary descendants. Yet if any particular election was a critical one, where issues were important and clearly defined, voting would increase substantially. When Rhode Island's freemen were aroused or a party in power had lost touch with the people's demands, the democracy inherent in a liberal suffrage enabled the majority of voters to secure their desired policies through the electoral process.

Popular control in Rhode Island political life was further enhanced by the role of the town in the state's constitutional system. Just as the General Assembly was sovereign in state-wide affairs, so the town was supreme where the locality was concerned. Added to this was the role of the town in the state's legislative process. Although the Assembly served as the institutional forum for determining the most important Rhode Island policies, by tradition and practice the opinions of the freemen expressed in their town meetings carried great weight. Few controversial decisions were made by the General Assembly between

28. Coventry Town Meeting, Mss., April 18, 1787.
29. West Greenwich Town Meeting, Mss., April 21, 1790. Though there were 110 freemen who voted in this election, only 74 took the trouble to cast their ballots six months later when Rhode Island chose a member of the United States House of Representatives.
30. Lovejoy, *R.I. Politics*, p. 17.

1774 and 1795 before the freemen had had their say in their town meetings, and any course of action agreed upon in the state's highest councils was referred back to the towns for confirmation. It is this combination of influence on local and state politics which gave Rhode Island's towns a major role in the state's history during the Confederation era.

Except for the original communities that combined to create Rhode Island and Providence Plantations in the seventeenth century, the towns were organized by the General Assembly. Normally they were constituted from outlying regions of existing towns and were given the power of self-government after they had petitioned the legislature. Most of the towns contained relatively small numbers of people, with only Providence and Newport able to make claim to an urban status. The population of Rhode Island was nearly 52,000 in 1783, when a census showed that Newport had the largest population in the state, slightly over 5,500 inhabitants, followed by Providence with about 4,300. No other town contained more than 3,000 people, and only nine (including Providence and Newport) exceeded 2,000. Rhode Island was still largely rural, with political power spread among thirty towns in the tiny state.

The government of the town was divided into a town council and town meeting, both institutions roughly analogous to executive and legislative departments. The council was the lesser body, operating as the administrative and executive arm of the town meeting, sometimes exercising judicial functions. It was elected yearly by the freemen. Among the most important responsibilities of the council were such diverse duties as tax collections, registration of titles and land conveyances, care for the poor, and superintendence of the construction and upkeep of local highways. Under special circumstances the council might also act as a court of probate for the town, administering the adjudication of wills and admitting to adjudication intestate estates.

The town meeting of all the freemen was a far more important institution. It was the supreme governing power in the locality. The town meeting appointed all public officers, set up the vast complex of rules which governed each community, and divided any taxes levied upon the towns by the General Assembly. Every local policy was decided by the vote of all the freemen at the many town meetings which gathered throughout the year. But even more important—at least for our purposes here—was the direct and vital influence which the town meeting exerted over state affairs.

The power of the town meeting in the formulation of state policies came first from its selection of the members of the General Assembly and executive officers. The town meeting was the local electoral unit for choosing all general officers and for the semiannual election of representatives to the House of Deputies. Frequency of elections gave the freemen, through the instrumentality of the town meeting, a powerful control over state affairs. Town representatives in the lower house were thought of as deputies of the locality—their official designation —if not as ambassadors of the people. Deputies were selected to mirror the will of each town, and they would not fail in that task if they hoped for re-election. The towns also influenced their deputies by paying their salaries as assemblymen—a factor that bent the will of more than one recalcitrant. Of greater force in binding the deputies was the towns' practice of instructing their representatives in almost every matter of public policy. The deputies were expected to follow these instructions, with little discretion left to the individual. In 1789, in the midst of the struggle over the federal Constitution, a town meeting in Cranston took special care to explain the solemn obligation of the deputies with regard to their formal instructions. The deputies were told that whenever a matter had been fully discussed by the freemen and in the Assembly, and when there were no specific instructions, they were free to use their own judgment. "But whenever there is any instructions or Particular Occasion from your Constituents," cautioned the townsmen, "you are strictly [to] adhere to the same and use your influence for Obtaining it." [31] Similar admonitions might have come from any town in Rhode Island. The instructions themselves were sometimes written directly by the assembled freemen at the town meeting; more usual was the practice of having a special committee appointed for the purpose of suggesting a declaration of policies, which would be reconsidered, amended, and adopted at a subsequent meeting of the freemen. These instructions covered a broad range of matters throughout the Confederation years, and the town meeting manuscripts show that the freemen were rarely silent on any important aspect of governmental policy.

A further avenue of local influence in the state's constitutional structure may be found in the part played by the town meeting in the writing of legislation. There evolved in Rhode Island during the seven-

31. Cranston Town Meeting, Mss., April 7, 1789.

teenth century the practice of referring legislation under consideration by the General Assembly to the freemen at their town meetings before final determination by the legislature.[32] This practice of referendum was used frequently during the Confederation period. All sorts of proposed laws were sent to the towns by the Assembly between 1774 and 1795, including matters of critical national importance. Referral to the people ensured that, in Rhode Island, decisions on national policies often depended upon the balance of town meetings for or against a particular issue. The two most significant questions relating to national affairs which the freemen considered at their town meetings were the Impost of 1781 and the Constitution of 1787. Both were debated and discussed in the towns before the General Assembly acted. The Impost of 1781 was the first proposed amendment of the Articles of Confederation; it was designed to give Congress a permanent revenue from taxes on international commerce. The plan gained the assent of eleven of the United States before Rhode Island blocked its seeming success with an implacable veto. Before the Assembly acted, it submitted the Impost directly to the towns. There the amendment was discussed, and the negative judgment of the majority of towns provided the grounds for Rhode Island's repudiation of the proposal. Similarly, the Constitution of 1787 was the object of a searching and prolonged appraisal by the towns before Rhode Island finally entered the new governing system in 1790. Only in Rhode Island did the people vote individually on the Constitution, and on several other occasions between 1787 and 1790 the freemen expressed their disapproval of the document through their town meetings. This popular appraisal and reappraisal of the federal Constitution provided the basis for Rhode Island's tardy re-entrance into the United States. The will of the people, repeatedly tested in the town meetings, was adamant in a matter of transcendent national importance.

The relationship of town government to the General Assembly cannot be drawn with precision, though by tradition the role of the town was very great. Suffice it to say that a loose federal structure marked Rhode Island's government, with state authorities in a superior position but with the localities exercising considerable influence. In cer-

---

32. Samuel H. Brockunier, *The Irrepressible Democrat: Roger Williams* (New York, 1940), pp. 168–71; Amasa M. Eaton, "The Right to Local Self Government," *Harvard Law Review*, XIII (1899), 441–54, 570–88, 638–58; XIV (1900), 20–38, 116–38.

tain respects the General Assembly was clearly absolute, as with regard to taxation, though the towns often protested loudly about their assessments. Any local tax collector who failed to fulfill the Assembly's call for funds was himself responsible for the entire sum and might be imprisoned for any shortage. On the other hand, the towns seem to have retained a shadowy superintendence over the whole range of local police powers, independent of the Assembly, even where state and local policies came into conflict. When in 1785 and afterwards the legislature ordered inoculation of the population against smallpox and the organization of hospitals for that purpose, several of the towns refused to go along. Neither Warwick nor New Shoreham accepted the Assembly's decree. In New Shoreham, the townsmen after prolonged discussion decided not to accept the legislative request and brazenly wrote in their records that "in open Town Meeting [they] do give Directions to the said [Town] Council not to Grant any Consideration to Admit of Inoculation being brought in said Town. . . ." [33] Likewise, the federal nature of the state-town relationship was very much in evidence in the summer of 1776, when the British navy threatened to destroy the town of Newport. To meet the danger, the freemen voted to defend the town, and all inhabitants were called upon to assist in building strengthened fortifications. This action caused discontent, particularly among those still loyal to the mother country, and protests were heard that independent action by the towns in so vital an area of public policy violated the constitutional balance that existed between state and local authorities. Many felt that the defense of Rhode Island should be undertaken only with the consent of the Assembly, especially in view of the delicate military crisis of 1776. The General Assembly received these complaints, according them extensive consideration. It declared that, by tradition, Newport and all the towns "were sufficiently authorized to make and ordain acts, orders and regulations, binding upon their respective inhabitants, in all cases whatever, for their advantage, safety and defense. . . ." [34] One can hardly imagine a broader grant of power to the locality. But this authorization was qualified by a vague reservation—much like the one imposed upon the colony in the royal charter—that township actions should be as consistent as possible with state law and never directly repugnant to any current statute.

33. Warwick Town Meeting, Mss., December 6, 1783; New Shoreham Town Meeting, Mss., July 12, 1785.
34. Bartlett, *Records,* VII, 555.

Politics

The structure of politics in Rhode Island was thus uniquely susceptible to popular control, and the institutions and traditions of the state
were designed to reflect the force of this democratic localism. Despite
this democratic bias the state's political life was not self-generating. It
required leadership in order to thrive. Superimposed upon the poten-
tiality of popular control was the influence of a governing elite made
up chiefly of families that had guided the colony since its earliest days
and had more recently found wealth and status along the shores of
Narragansett Bay. This elite was freely and frequently elected by the
people and was responsive to their will. There were also the outlines
of what might be called a modern party system in Rhode Island. The
state's leaders were traditionally divided into two groups of factions or
parties, a division which manifested itself in this period with some of
the apparatus of modern-day politics and much of its democratic nature.

The American Revolution and the following era found Rhode Island's political rulers drawn mostly from the professional class, the
merchants, and the large-scale farmers—men whose wealth and leisure
provided opportunities for public service. The commercial towns,
however, dominated the stage of public life. This was true primarily
because the trade marts which surrounded Narragansett Bay, particularly Newport and Providence, were more prosperous than those in the
interior, and the leaven of prosperity was political power. At almost
any time in Rhode Island's history before 1795, one might expect to
find the general officers of the state selected from among inhabitants of
the commercial towns. For instance, four of the five governors who
served the state between 1774 and 1795 came from either Newport or
Providence, all were merchants, and each had contacts throughout
New England.[35] Moreover, the mercantile families were influential and
important in Rhode Island since its earliest days, a fact which the continuing public service of the Wantons, Arnolds, Champlins, Ellerys,

35. For biographical details on the Rhode Island Governors one may consult the
Dictionary of American Biography, IV, 307; VI, 322–23; VII, 576–77; XIX, 412;
Biographical Cyclopedia of Representative Men of Rhode Island (Providence, 1881),
pp. 108–9; and Thomas Williams Bicknell, *The History of Rhode Island and Providence Plantations*, 3 vols. (New York, 1920), III, 1108–13.

and Browns would seem to confirm. Mercantile influence was further extended by the manufacturing, retail, and general commercial interests of these men, which gave them influential connections in the rural towns. The Providence merchants included among their enterprises not only foreign and domestic commerce and financial interests, but also distilleries, iron manufactories outside the main towns, candleworks, tanneries, slaughterhouses, paper mills, and retail stores which catered to customers from the entire state.[36] This network of commerce and manufacturing gave rise to an interest in politics and political power.

In the countryside we find an analogous role exercised by the wealthier farmers, men who qualified in the town manuscripts as "Gentlemen" and "Esquires," and the professional classes, particularly lawyers. Here, too, the importance of a family connection cannot be overlooked, for wealth and leisure added to a birthright in one of Rhode Island's founding families meant political power. The Greenes, Hazards, Durfees, and Stantons had long served as political leaders of the country towns. Joseph Stanton of Charlestown, one of the largest and wealthiest of Rhode Island's agricultural towns, is a good example of a country politician. He was reputed to have owned a tract of land four-and-a-half miles long and two miles wide during the Confederation period in the midst of the famous Narragansett country of Washington County, a considerable freehold in tiny Rhode Island. Stanton's holdings also included 40 slaves and 40 horses, and his large dairy produced milk and cheese products for which southern Rhode Island was long renowned. Because of his wealth, distinguished family, and education, Joseph Stanton was a man of power and influence in Rhode Island; he was, indeed, said to have "owned a lordship in Charlestown." [37] All of this was reflected in Stanton's lengthy career of public service. First elected to the General Assembly in 1768 at the age of twenty-nine, he served until the outbreak of the Revolution in 1775 and again between 1793 and 1801. During the Revolution Stanton

36. See the account in Franklin Stuart Coyle, "The Survival of Business Enterprise in the American Revolutionary Era (1770–1785)" (Master's thesis, Brown University, 1960), p. 10; and Arthur M. Schlesinger, *The Colonial Merchants and the American Revolution, 1763–1776* (New York, 1939), pp. 27–28.

37. *Biographical Cyclopedia*, p. 47. Stanton had the same given name as his father, grandfather, and great-grandfather, so that the Joseph Stantons dated back to the time when Indians dominated the southern part of Rhode Island; Stanton's mother, Mary Champlin Stanton, came from an equally prominent Newport commercial family.

commanded Rhode Island troops as a general in the state militia, and following the war he devoted himself to Rhode Island politics, acting as one of the leaders of the paper-money forces which captured control of the state government in 1786. After Rhode Island ratified the federal Constitution, Stanton became one of the state's two senators over the opposition of the Federalist party.

The Rhode Island constitutional system was also characterized by a tradition of party politics that was surprisingly modern in many respects. This party tradition had its origin in the colonial sectional conflict between rival political factions headed by Samuel Ward, of Newport and Westerly, and Stephen Hopkins of Providence. Though the activities of these factions bear a remarkable modernity, with nominations, campaigns, patronage, and even corruption, the absence of any dividing principles between them and a considerable emphasis upon personalities separated the pre-Revolutionary tradition from today's party politics.[38] The Ward-Hopkins controversy was a struggle for control of the colony's government and the profits that might ensue; it lasted from 1755 until 1770. Involved was a conflict between two strictly sectional factions, one centered in northern Rhode Island and including Providence, the other, including Newport, dominating the southern regions of the colony. Issues in the struggle were few and far between, with personal ambitions and sectional advantages the objects of combat. Governmental dominance brought with it power and prominence for the successful faction, profits from patronage and special favors for members of the winning party, and a welcome shift of the burden of taxation from the shoulders of a victorious section.[39]

Such things were worth fighting for, and the interminable wrangling of Rhode Island politicians gave the state a highly developed political tradition. At the root of Rhode Island's party system was the patronage which a victorious party might distribute. Victory for one party was often a signal for the proscription of the other, with a careful distribution of fishes and loaves to the party faithful. This happened in 1786, the year of the paper-money revolution in state politics. Paper-money men were rewarded with scores of jobs at the disposal of the General Assembly; wherever possible, holdovers were removed from

38. The best study is Lovejoy, *R.I. Politics,* particularly pp. 48–69. A confirmation of Lovejoy's conclusion was supplied by Mack E. Thompson, "The Ward-Hopkins Controversy and the American Revolution in Rhode Island: An Interpretation," *William and Mary Quarterly,* 3d ser., XVI (1959), 363–75.
39. Lovejoy, *R.I. Politics,* pp. 2–3.

office. Establishment of the paper-money system itself meant the creation of 66 new positions as administrators of this system of public relief; invariably, these posts went to leaders of the country party.[40] The profit involved in the paper-money system was sometimes quite handsome; for example, one justice of the Court of Common Pleas, Abraham Mathewson, received £1,780 16s. 8d. in confiscated debts, of which only £1,169 was turned over to the state.[41] The remainder went to Judge Mathewson, who collected a minimum fee of 5 per cent, plus added charges for attorneys, sheriffs, and printers. The public business could be good business for those lucky enough to serve in office, and this helps to explain the cohesiveness and fervor with which party politics was endowed in Rhode Island.

Even lesser lights among the supporters of a successful party expected some benefit for their labor, just as those in opposition waited in dread of dismissal. For this reason the amenable publisher of the Providence newspaper, the *United States Chronicle,* Bennett Wheeler, was given the patronage of printing Rhode Island's laws in 1787, as well as a lucrative post as collector of excise for Providence County. In contrast, the anti-paper-money and Federalist publisher of the *Newport Herald,* Peter Edes, was denied any emolument from the state's printing orders.[42] At the very same session of the General Assembly, in May, 1787, even before the legislators assembled to choose a new slate of officers for the next political year, the entire list had been selected in advance by a country party caucus.[43] The guiding principle for appointment and reappointment was the loyalty with which each candidate for patronage upheld the paper-money system during the trying year of 1786. A more pointed instance of patronage politics came at the May meeting of the 1789 Assembly, right in the midst of the pa-

40. The names and numbers of administrators of the paper-money system are found in the *Providence Gazette,* May 13, 1786.

41. General Treasurer's Papers, Lodged Money, Mss., R.I.S.A. This miscellaneous collection of manuscripts contains an incomplete number of accounts by judges throughout Rhode Island of money that had been lodged with them and then surrendered to the state in accordance with the requirements of the paper-money laws. Mathewson's accounts are to be found here, as well as those of other judges. In another instance, reported by Justice William Miller of Bristol County, the charges for a confiscated debt of £6 6s. were £3 15s.; likewise, Justice Robert Stanton of Washington County reported one case of a confiscated lodgment of debt in which the fees came to £8 2s. 6d. out of a total sum of £10 7s.!

42. Irwin H. Polishook, "Peter Edes's Report of the Proceedings of the Rhode Island General Assembly, 1787–1790," *Rhode Island History,* XXV (1966), 33–42, Pt. 1.

43. *Newport Herald,* May 10, 1787.

per-money and constitutional entanglements. So hard and fast had party divisions become in this critical year that the country leadership broke a long-standing Rhode Island custom when it appointed a full slate of justices of the peace for the respective counties without any regard for the nominations presented by the elected representatives of the towns. The legislators from Newport and Providence, unanimously opposed to the party in power, were denied the slightest consideration for the first time in anyone's memory.[44]

These perquisites of patronage had an especially important place in Rhode Island's political system when a party courted the good will of an influential town leader. In such cases, preferment and profit were offered in hope of securing the votes of a local politician's following. Benjamin Arnold of Warwick is a good example of such a politician. He came from a family that had seven votes in the Warwick town meeting and a following among the town's freemen. A large family and local connections made Arnold a politician to be courted in Warwick. In 1790, during the crucial campaign which was to determine whether or not Rhode Island would rejoin the United States, Arnold was careful to sound out the two major parties before committing himself to any candidate for office. He wrote to the country party nominee for governor, Arthur Fenner, Jr., of a desire to place his son Thomas in the profitable post of sheriff of Kent County. He complained of failure in this endeavor during the previous administration of Governor Collins, despite four years of loyal support, lamenting particularly the money he had spent and the bitter disappointment he had suffered. Arnold told Fenner plainly that if he did not secure an ironclad pledge of his son's appointment, he would accept the competing offers of John Brown, the Providence merchant, for his support.[45] The influence of these local leaders was not to be disdained, and competing parties were vigorous in their efforts to win them over. Another important merchant, Welcome Arnold of Providence, was ever solicitous of the pleasures of these local politicians. His son-in-law, Tristam Burges, told of the lavish table Arnold kept to entertain these men and the care he took to know of their business affairs and business needs.[46] The

---

44. *Ibid.*, May 14, 1789.
45. Arnold to Arthur Fenner, Jr. [April, 1790], Papers Relating to the Adoption of the Constitution of the United States, Mss., R.I.S.A., p. 102.
46. Tristam Burges, Memoir of Welcome Arnold, unpublished biography, R.I.H.S., 1850; G. H. Peckham to Welcome Arnold, Little Rest, April 1, 1783, and I. Perry to Welcome Arnold, South Kingstown, January 4, 1790, Welcome Arnold Papers, Mss., J.C.B.L.

influence of this great merchant and entrepreneur was always at the disposal of the politicians of the state, as, we may also presume, was his wealth.

Although the system of party politics in Rhode Island was thus surprisingly modern in many respects, it was perhaps most so in its nominating procedures and campaign practices. The choice of candidates for state office was generally initiated by a caucus of leading politicians in either of the two current parties or factions, with the formal determination of a party slate—or "prox," as it was termed in Rhode Island —made in an open meeting of interested voters. By 1790 this meeting of voters, which confirmed those selected by a party caucus, was labeled a nominating convention,[47] where every freeman might be given an opportunity to present his views. A nominating convention would be assembled by means of a notice in the newspapers, in which the party's leaders announced their intention to consult with the voters about the forthcoming list of candidates for public office. When a party already held office, the incumbent governor would be most prominent among those sponsoring nominations and a convention; an out-party's initiative would come from a group of its most distinguished citizens.[48] In either case, no matter how candidates were proposed for office, a general attendance of the freemen was always expected. Any deviation was vigorously condemned, for it was judged "no small Usurpation of Power," said a Rhode Islander in 1789, "that a few individuals of the State should thus engross to themselves a Right which belongs to the Freemen at large; it being an inherent Principle of our Constitution not only to Choose but to nominate our General Officers also." [49] When the issues in a prospective campaign were not of great interest, as in the years before 1786, the governor's slate would dominate the field, though competing lists of candidates might also appear, sponsored by interested factions throughout the state. Sometimes candidates were chosen without foreknowledge for a local ticket, and often a public disavowal in the newspapers was later required, usually accom-

47. Neil Andrews, "The Development of the Nominating Convention in Rhode Island," in *Papers from the Historical Seminary of Brown University*, No. I, ed. J. F. Jameson (Providence, 1894), set the date for the first formal convention at 1790. For an example of caucusing among Rhode Island politicians, see Samuel Ward to Welcome Arnold, Warwick, April 7, 1786, Frederick S. Peck Collection, 1761–1845, Mss., R.I.H.S., Box VIII.

48. An excellent example is the "Letter of the Coalition Committee," *Providence Gazette*, April 3, 1790.

49. Letter from "A Freeman," *ibid.*, April 11, 1789; and *ibid.*, September 5, 1789.

panied by an embarrassed pledge of support for the regular candidates.[50] Such nominations represented dissension within the party for local reasons or the desire to defeat a single unpopular candidate by offering a local favorite in his place.

Nominations for office were generally completed by the beginning of February. The campaign followed immediately afterward and lasted until the third week in April, when the election took place. An assiduous candidate took things into his own hands, arranging, upon designation for office, to print and distribute his party's slate throughout the state. Important also were consultations with local politicians and friends.[51] From this point on the campaign consisted, as in our own day, of an effort to weld together an effective and cohesive party machinery, of strenuous attempts to win and hold local and state-wide support through promises of patronage, and, finally, especially after 1785, of a debate on the issues and alignment of candidates in support of particular policies and principles.

It was this intrusion of principle into the Rhode Island political system that separated the politics of the Confederation era from the colonial factional struggle. As the Revolutionary crisis grew more grave in the late 1760's, the factional contest came to an end by mutual consent. The two chief political parties, those headed by Stephen Hopkins and Samuel Ward, compromised their differences, and a coalition of factions was the result.[52] By 1770 the Ward-Hopkins controversy was only a memory, and Rhode Island entered into the struggle for independence without its traditional party divisions.

The Revolutionary aftermath of the coalition was a period in which the party system was revived, this time with issues of principle at its base. Despite the unity which the British threat had brought to the state, the prolonged war sowed the seeds for the bitter campaigns of

50. See letter of John Brown, *ibid.,* April 11, 1783, and George Champlin to Welcome Arnold, Newport, March 30, 1790, Welcome Arnold Papers, Mss., J.C.B.L.

51. William Channing to Theodore Foster, Newport, April, 1779, Correspondence, Foster Collection, Mss., R.I.H.S., Vol. I. Foster was expected to serve as Channing's lieutenant in Providence County. For another characteristic bit of politics see Samuel Ward to Mr. Gorton, Warwick, April 14, 1783, Ward Papers, Mss., R.I.H.S., Box 2.

52. Samuel G. Arnold, *History of the State of Rhode Island and Providence Plantations: From the Settlement of the State, 1636, to the Adoption of the Federal Constitution, 1790,* 2 vols. (New York, 1859–60), II, 281–84. Lovejoy, *R.I. Politics,* pp. 151–52, suggests that the electoral preponderance of the Hopkins faction was also important in forcing the Ward supporters to accept a coalition, because after 1768 the latter group had little hope that they could win an election.

the Confederation. As noted earlier, Rhode Island was an active and important theater of combat throughout the Revolutionary War, with British forces in control of the Narragansett seacoast almost to the last. This made normal commercial activity impossible during the trying days of revolution. The richest of the Rhode Island towns had their economic life disrupted and were barred from contributing substantially to the general taxation and other material sacrifices which the American Revolution called forth. A valuation of the state undertaken as late as 1780 made no surveys in Newport, Portsmouth, Jamestown, Middletown, or New Shoreham—towns actually occupied, devastated by the enemy, or in constant danger of attack. These towns paid no taxes.[53] The onerous burden of supporting the war effort fell upon those towns free of the enemy, particularly the agricultural communities of southern Rhode Island. The inequity inflicted by the fortunes of war, which forced the country towns of Washington County to pay more than their pre-Revolutionary share of the state's costs, was borne without a murmur during the early days of the conflict, when everyone thought victory would be only a matter of time. But as the war dragged on, discontent became rife among the southern farmers.

Disaffection in the country towns took the form of a rising tide of complaint about the unequal distribution of representation in the General Assembly. The fact that Newport, Portsmouth, Warwick, and Providence enjoyed larger delegations in the lower house of the Assembly was condemned as indefensible, particularly because of the inability of the commercial towns to contribute their prewar proportion of the tax burden. The situation of Newport and Portsmouth, both dominated by the British and depopulated and disrupted by war, was especially provoking, because they continued to have their ante-bellum representation and influence in state affairs. It was also charged that the weighted representation enjoyed by the commercial towns produced the unequal assessments of the war period. Winning the Revolution had resulted in an issue of significance that would divide town and country throughout the years of the Confederation.

Soon the complaining towns of agricultural Rhode Island began to consult together about their common grievances. Leaders among the country farmers met to discuss the sad situation of the agricultural towns as paymasters of the Revolution and the overrepresentation of the seacoast communities in the legislature. Finally, in April, 1782, this

53. Bartlett, *Records,* IX, 273, 279.

discontent found expression in a convention that was held at Little Rest Hill, South Kingstown, now part of the modern city of Kingstown.[54] Delegates from Westerly, South Kingstown, Charlestown, Exeter, Richmond, and Hopkinton attended the meeting. The convention adopted a formal resolution of protest which it sent to the General Assembly, denouncing the disproportionate representation of the commercial towns in the legislature. The South Kingstown delegates declared that this ancient inequality was the result of a system of representation based upon neither population nor wealth but on a formula fixed forever in the seventeenth-century colonial charter.[55] As for the charter itself, formerly a sacrosanct document beyond reproach, the Charlestown Town Meeting said it was no longer to be revered, and the townsmen called for a new state constitution, "Suitable for a Free People." [56] To challenge the charter in this way before 1775 had been unthinkable. The delegates at the Little Rest Hill conclave suggested that a constitutional convention be called, made up of two delegates from each town, to draw up an entirely new frame of government for Rhode Island.

While the proposal to reform the charter was not raised again after 1782, the issue of representation in the General Assembly continued to agitate the towns throughout the Confederation period.[57] For many of Rhode Island's farmers the very existence of "freedom" and "constitutional liberty" depended upon every town's having an equal voice in the public councils. Doubtless, too, suspicion grew that the commercial towns, particularly Newport and Providence, had an ulterior purpose in perpetuating the old weighted representation they enjoyed in accordance with the colonial charter; possibly, they always hoped to "oppress" the agricultural communities through unfair taxation.[58] The American Revolution ended with Rhode Islanders once again divided over politics, only this time the division arose out of an issue of principle. The bitter rift over paper money and other related financial

54. South Kingstown Town Meeting, Mss., April 1, 1782; Richmond Town Meeting, Mss., March 6, 1782.

55. Charlestown Town Meeting, Mss., April 14, 1782 (No. 3, p. 28), preserves this most important protest to the Assembly.

56. *Ibid.*

57. Charlestown Town Meeting, Mss., March 13, 1784; Johnston Town Meeting, Mss., June 7, 1784; Hopkinton Town Meeting, Mss., March 16, 1784; Richmond Town Meeting, Mss., April 21, 1784; and Exeter Town Meeting, Mss., April 5, 1784. For a hostile reaction to the proposal to give each town the same number of deputies in the Assembly see Portsmouth Town Meeting, Mss., October 4, 1784.

58. Exeter Town Meeting, Mss., April 21, 1784.

questions that occurred in 1786 rested upon this bedrock of mutual recrimination and mistrust. The meetings and conventions of the early 1780's produced a common spirit of grievance among the agricultural towns that united them in the years to come and provided an opportunity for the most important country politicians to meet and know one another. A cohesive agricultural interest with an integrated leadership, hostile to the commercial towns, was a by-product of winning Rhode Island's independence. The politics of the American Revolution was thus a preparation for the party battles of the Confederation period.

Another Legacy

The economic and financial legacy of the American Revolution was also of primary importance in Rhode Island after 1783. The first problem that the state faced when peace arrived was reconstruction. The war brought great destruction, and merely to replace what had been lost was an assignment of considerable magnitude. The British threat in the Revolution was not limited to the seacoast, for the narrow confines of Rhode Island's boundaries placed the state under a virtual siege throughout the war.[59] Before hostilities ceased, the British occupied nearly one-third of the state's territory, including one-fourth of its farms; unoccupied areas were constantly pillaged by enemy foraging expeditions. The largest town, Newport, suffered the greatest losses of the Revolution. Its wharves, houses, and farms were despoiled, and its inhabitants were dispersed into every part of New England and the United States. Monetary damage in Newport alone was reported at $412,920.[60] The adjoining town of Middletown reported destruction in excess of $130,000.[61] Providence, though protected by its inland station, complained of the impact of the British naval blockade and a commercial crisis that precluded its meeting urgent assessments for the

59. For the war in Rhode Island see Arnold, *History of R.I.*, II, 377–430.

60. "Jonathan Easton's Ratable Estate," *Newport Historical Magazine,* II (1881), 60–61; J. P. Brissot DeWarville, *New Travels in the United States of America: Performed in 1788* (New York, 1792), pp. 201–2. The dollar figure for Newport has been converted from pounds sterling at a rate of $3.33 = £1; this conversion formula will be used throughout the book.

61. "The Destruction of Property in the Town of Middletown, R.I., During the Revolution," *Newport Historical Magazine,* II (1881), 241–43.

war effort.[62] The decline of population in Rhode Island between 1774 and 1783 was precipitous. The state lost about 7,000 of its 58,000 inhabitants, with the sharpest drop in population concentrated in Newport and Providence counties.[63] The ravages of war, in terms of both men and material, had to be repaired before peace would ever come to Rhode Island.

Next in order of peacetime priorities was the re-establishment of Rhode Island's commercial structure. The state's commercial life was a shambles at the end of the war. Commerce was especially crucial to Rhode Island because the state failed to produce enough staples for export; its productivity was limited by the lack of both natural resources and a spacious hinterland on which to depend for products to send abroad. Rhode Islanders depended on imports to supply their needs. The resulting unfavorable balance of trade could be met only through earnings from commerce, since there was no surplus of agricultural goods or manufactured products.

The merchants of Rhode Island were among the leaders in the American carrying trade. The special characteristic of their commerce, however, was the fact that the goods they carried were usually not of Rhode Island origin. Articles of trade came from other parts of the United States and the world, and the profits obtained from their reshipment made up the state's unfavorable balance of trade.[64]

This tenuous economic structure was obviously dependent upon numerous factors beyond the control of the Rhode Island merchants. In the pre-Revolutionary period the profits of this unique carrying trade were repeatedly threatened by restrictions placed on colonial commerce by the various measures of the old colonial system of Great Britain. For this reason Rhode Island may well have been the chief culprit in violating the mercantile system. The General Assembly's strong remonstrance protesting the Sugar Act of 1764 clearly delineated the peculiar dependence of Rhode Island upon trade for its livelihood. "The colony hath no staple commodity and does not raise provisions sufficient for its own consumption," explained the legislators. "Yet the

---

62. Bartlett, *Records*, VIII, 331.
63. Greene and Harrington, *American Population Before the Federal Census of 1790*, p. 7.
64. This point is convincingly elaborated by James B. Hedges, *The Browns of Providence Plantations: Colonial Years* (Cambridge, Mass., 1952), pp. 155–56, 324, 332.

goodness of its harbors and its convenient situation for trade, agreeing with the spirit and industry of the people, hath in some measure supplied the deficiency of its natural produce, and provided the means of subsistence for its inhabitants." [65]

When conditions of war during the Revolution interrupted the profitable course of Rhode Island's commerce, the state's means of subsistence were seriously deranged.[66] Just as serious, however, was the reciprocal impact of uncertain trade conditions upon financing the war. At the very moment when the Revolution produced a pressing need for greater wealth, Rhode Island was unable to enjoy unencumbered trade with the world. Financing the Revolution, therefore, was a problem of unequaled difficulty. One solution was to increase taxes. Previously, the costs of government in colonial Rhode Island were nominal, averaging in some years little more than $5,000 and requiring no general taxation.[67] The War for Independence brought this blissful state of affairs to an unhappy end, for the start of hostilities meant heavy taxation. The burden of taxes between 1779 and 1782 amounted to more than $8,570,000, with an annual assessment approaching $3,000,000.[68] The yearly rate of taxation amounted to one-third the tax ratables of the state for one period at the end of the war. Added to the ever increasing needs of the state were those of the national government, which by the terms of the Articles of Confederation was absolutely dependent upon the thirteen members of the Union for money. Rhode Island did its part in supplying the federal coffers. At the end of the war the state had contributed more than its proportion toward winning the Revolution. Even so, Rhode Island found itself falling short in meeting congressional appeals for funds and was forced to ask lamely for sharp abatements in the federal requisitions.[69]

The main reliance of Rhode Island in financing the war, as for the

65. Bartlett, *Records*, IX, 189–92; VII, 424–26.

66. Council of War of Rhode Island to the President of Congress, Providence, April 26, 1779, William R. Staples, ed., *Rhode Island in the Continental Congress: With the Journal of the Convention that Adopted the Constitution 1765–1790* (Providence, 1870), pp. 220–22.

67. Allan Nevins, *The American States During and After the Revolution 1775–1789* (New York, 1924), p. 493.

68. "A Table of Taxes . . . from February, 1779 to February, 1782, taken from the Treasurer's Book," Report on the Registered State Debt, Ms., R.I.S.A.

69. Bartlett, *Records*, IX, 501–2; Governor Greene to the Delegates in Congress, December 22, 1781, *ibid.*, p. 502.

nation, was not on taxation but on debt formation.[70] Paper money proved the easiest method of borrowing large sums from the public. The bills were made legal tender which had to be accepted by everyone at the risk of severe penalties. Paper currency was the largest single source of Revolutionary finance.[71] In Rhode Island paper-money issues exceeded £440,000 by the end of hostilities.[72] The redundancy of the paper bills in the states and the nation led to a spiraling inflation and the extinction of the purchasing value of the currency. Before the conclusion of the war, Congress and the state legislatures were forced to scale down the value of the paper money, thereby repudiating the bulk of the Revolutionary debt.[73] By doing this, the United States carried a smaller burden of indebtedness during the Confederation period.

The second important source of deficit finance for the Rhode Island government was an extensive program of loans, in which securities were exchanged for goods and services provided in the war, and also certificates given to soldiers in lieu of salaries and bonuses. This program of borrowing resulted in an internal debt for Rhode Island estimated at £150,000 (about $500,000) in 1783, and it continued to grow with additions of interest and principal after the Revolution. The internal debt was not repudiated—as in the case of paper money—or ever adequately scaled down in value in proportion to the inflation that occurred after 1776. This huge internal debt, therefore, remained to burden Rhode Island throughout the Confederation years; and when peace gave way to depression and economic decline, the burden of debt became intolerable.

Finally, financing the Revolution had another effect upon the subsequent history of the state, in particular on Rhode Island's relations

70. Clarence L. Ver Steeg, *Robert Morris: Revolutionary Financier* (Philadelphia, 1954), pp. 43–44; Curtis P. Nettels, *The Emergence of a National Economy 1775–1815* (New York, 1962), pp. 23–29.

71. See especially on this subject the comprehensive study by E. James Ferguson, *The Power of the Purse: A History of American Public Finance, 1776–1790* (Chapel Hill, 1961), pp. 44, 333.

72. Ralph W. Harlow, "Aspects of Revolutionary Finance," *American Historical Review*, XXXV (1929), table inserted between pages 68 and 69.

73. Congressional action on paper money came on March 18, 1780, when it was ordered that approximately $200,000,000 of the current bills be exchanged for $5,000,000 in new money, thereby repudiating almost seven-eighths of the federal debt in paper currency. See *ibid.*, p. 61; Ferguson, *Power of the Purse*, pp. 57–69 (the best account); Edmund C. Burnett, *The Continental Congress* (New York, 1941), pp. 406–27; or Lynn Montross, *The Reluctant Rebels: The Story of the Continental Congress 1774–1789* (New York, 1950), pp. 296–97.

with the Union. The state contributed heavily and disproportionately to the national war effort, and peace found Rhode Island a national creditor. As bankruptcy became an ever present possibility during the lean years of 1785–87, the state looked more and more to this expected credit as a source of solvency. There were insistent demands that the nation settle its accounts with the state and reimburse Rhode Island for its excessive expenditures,[74] but the task was easier contemplated than essayed. A settlement of accounts did not come during the Confederation; it was accomplished only several years after the establishment of the new federal government in 1789. In the interval, the strain in state and federal relations persisted.

The influence of the American Revolution was central to the controversies of the Confederation period. The war left great destruction in Rhode Island, and victory was won through tremendous expenditures. An important result was the conviction of Rhode Islanders that the best postwar policy was one which permitted the state and its people to rebuild before anything else. The problems of peace, most thought, should be approached with the self-interest of the state and its citizens the sole standard for judgment; competing national values would have to be sacrificed after a long and costly war. Given these attitudes, Rhode Island's unwillingness to strengthen the Union after 1781 is not surprising, especially since the state turned its back on the nation when it looked only for its own advantage.

The war affected Rhode Island history in other salient ways that would in time lead it out of the Union. The costs of the conflict could not be met from current resources, and the state was compelled to finance the Revolution by borrowing. A troublesome internal debt resulted that played a fundamental role in Rhode Island's subsequent development. Similarly, the existence of a large state debt made congressional monetary demands very awkward, considering the constant danger of bankruptcy for the state itself. Indeed, the domestic politics of Rhode Island's internal debt was the dynamic factor in the state's relations with the Union after 1786. Furthermore, the task of paying for the war fell unevenly upon the different parts of the state. The agricultural mainland towns were relatively free from enemy attacks and were obliged by fate to pay the price of independence. As years went by, however, they protested that some commercial towns, which paid little or no taxes because of the war, continued to enjoy an unequal rep-

74. See, for example, Bartlett, *Records,* IX, 561.

resentation in the General Assembly. The country paymasters of the Revolution demanded equality. These complaints produced meetings, petitions, and conventions among the southern agricultural towns at the end of the war, a precursor of the political alignments of the Confederation period. The question of equal representation injected an issue of principle into Rhode Island politics that would ultimately influence the development of postwar parties and the state's relations with the nation.

3

Rhode Island Defeats the Impost

ONE OF THE FIRST great struggles over the federal system came almost simultaneously with the achievement of peace. By 1783, Great Britain's hope that the colonies could be subjugated had been dispelled, and reluctantly it recognized the independence of the United States. But this triumph did not bring a secure peace to the new nation. For many Americans the preservation of independence called for a radical reform of the structure of the central government and its relationship to the several states.

Even before the masterful success at Yorktown in the fall of 1781, many believed that the Articles of Confederation was inadequate as a frame of government for the United States. The bonds of union seemed too loosely drawn during the Revolution; instead of pulling together throughout the war, the states appeared at the end to be drifting apart. In composing his last "Crisis" paper, Thomas Paine found a need to warn his fellow Americans of the danger of disunity. He boldly asserted that a stronger national government was required for the future greatness of the country, leaving his readers to understand that the Confederation would soon have to be repaired.[1]

Thomas Paine was not alone nor most vociferous in his contention. Attacks on the Articles of Confederation were commonplace from the beginning, centering on the fact that the federal system granted too much power to the states. Now, as peace approached, a chorus of discord was heard, to the effect that the federal structure would not meet the demands of peace. "I think there must be a total reform of the system," Congressman Jesse Root confided to Governor John Trumbull of Connecticut. "Congress must exercise the proper powers and establish all necessary executive boards and offices."[2] A majority of congressmen were coming to believe that the national government had to be strengthened. Their interest was perhaps less in enhancing the power of Congress than in reducing the power of the states,[3] for it was the laggardness of the states in their exercise of the nation's power—"shamefull deficiencies," decried James Madison—that was responsible for the inability of the country to meet the needs of the time.[4]

Two developments brought the problem of the national government to a crisis between 1780 and 1783. One was the military campaign at Yorktown; the other was the impending collapse of American finance.

In 1780–81, for the first time during the long-drawn-out contest with Great Britain, American forces were presented with a unique opportunity to bring the Revolution to an end with a successful military campaign. The possibility of large-scale French assistance on land and sea presented itself during this period. Of special importance was the presence of two powerful French naval squadrons in American waters, at Newport and in the French Indies. This made mastery of the seas, in combination with a land attack in the south, a matchless opportunity

1. "The Last Crisis," No. XIII, *Providence Gazette*, May 24, 1783.

2. Root to Trumbull, Philadelphia, January 8, 1781, and Connecticut Delegates to Trumbull, Philadelphia, January 16, 1781, both in Edmund C. Burnett, ed., *Letters of the Members of the Continental Congress*, 8 vols. (Washington, D.C., 1921–36), V, 520, 537.

3. Ezekiel Cornell to Nathanael Greene, Philadelphia, July 21, 1780; Cornell to Governor Greene, Philadelphia, June 18, 1780; and Jesse Root to William Williams, Philadelphia, January 29, 1781; all in *ibid.*, V, 281, 225, 546.

4. Madison to Thomas Jefferson, Philadelphia, April 16, 1781, *ibid.*, VI, 59; James M. Varnum to Governor Greene, Philadelphia, April 2, 1781, in William R. Staples, ed., *Rhode Island in the Continental Congress: With the Journal of the Convention that Adopted the Constitution 1765–1790* (Providence, 1870), p. 335; Washington to Joseph Jones, Morristown, May 31, 1780, Worthington C. Ford, ed., *Letters of Joseph Jones* (Washington, D.C., 1889), p. 11.

for the Revolutionary allies. In addition, the military situation was unusually favorable. With Clinton in New York and Cornwallis in Virginia, the major British armies were dangerously split, north and south. If American forces, aided by the French, were able to strike an overwhelming military blow against either of the two British armies, particularly that of Cornwallis, a substantial and possibly conclusive military victory might be achieved. With good fortune, United States commanders speculated, a smashing defeat might be inflicted upon the enemy and the independence of the nation assured.[5] Good fortune, however, was not to be left to chance, and, with a great victory in sight, a revamping of the chaotic situation under the Articles of Confederation was deemed necessary.

Finance was the most difficult problem facing the United States. Until 1780 the revolution against Great Britain had been sustained largely by emissions of paper money. Eventually these proved excessive, and Congress was obliged to end all future issues. Existing paper bills, calculated by E. James Ferguson at about $226,000,000, were consolidated at a rate of forty to one, with over $5,000,000 in new currency replacing the old money.[6] The nation now had a smaller debt to pay off than before, but there was still an urgent need for revenue, particularly to supply the army, even after Yorktown.[7] Indeed, so bleak did financial prospects for the United States appear that some spoke of investing power in a committee of public safety or a dictator.[8] The

5. John R. Alden, *The American Revolution 1775–1783* (New York, 1954), pp. 240–47; Howard W. Peckham, *The War for Independence: A Military History* (Chicago, 1958), pp. 164–83; Edmund C. Burnett, *The Continental Congress* (New York, 1941), pp. 459–60, 522–50; Lynn Montross, *The Reluctant Rebels: The Story of the Continental Congress 1774–1789* (New York, 1950), pp. 319–23. For specific details on how the Yorktown campaign was financed consult Clarence L. Ver Steeg, *Robert Morris: Revolutionary Financier* (Philadelphia, 1954), pp. 72–77; and Ellis P. Oberholtzer, *Robert Morris: Patriot and Financier* (New York, 1903), pp. 79–90, 110–13.

6. "Financial Committee Report," November 9, 1780, *Secret Journals of the Confederation,* 4 vols. (Boston, 1824), I, 177; Charles J. Bullock, *The Finances of the United States from 1775 to 1789, With Especial Reference to the Budget,* Bulletin of the University of Wisconsin, Economics, Political Science, and History Series, Vol. I, No. 2 (Madison, 1895), pp. 171–72; and E. James Ferguson, *The Power of the Purse: A History of American Public Finance, 1776–1790* (Chapel Hill, 1961), p. 67.

7. Ezekiel Cornell to Governor Greene, Philadelphia, June 27, 30, August 29, and September 10, 1780, all in Staples, *R.I. in the Continental Congress,* pp. 300, 309, 311–12.

8. Ezekiel Cornell to Governor Greene, Philadelphia, August 1, 1780, *ibid.,* p. 303; Cornell to Governor Greene, Philadelphia, May 30, June 24, 1780, John Russell Bartlett, ed., *Records of the Colony of Rhode Island and Providence Plantations in*

Revolution, in this respect, had reached a turning-point, and the future of the United States was at stake.

Another critical side of the financial problem was that of the public debt. Although much of what the United States owed its creditors had been repudiated in the paper-money exchange of 1780, the federal government still carried a debt of approximately $35,000,000. The nation had to provide for the interest on this past debt and make provision to repay the principal. Compounding the difficulties of the federal government was the failure of the states to meet their congressional requisitions. As a result, Congress was obliged to meet its continuing military and financial obligations by entering into new foreign loans. Unfortunately, members of Congress had little expectation that they could obtain further foreign credits, for no government abroad would lend money to a nation that gave every promise of defaulting on its debts. Unless new monies were obtained through foreign loans, the only alternative was bankruptcy.[9] Equally unsettling was the possibility that some of the states might themselves provide for that portion of the national debt held by their own citizens. What this might mean in terms of an orderly establishment of the nation's future credit and frank acknowledgment that the central government was unable to satisfy its own creditors was not obscure to most congressmen. The political implications of a state assumption of the federal debt seemed perilous. If the states took over the federal debt, as Pennsylvania recommended, the national credit and possibly the national government might be threatened.[10]

New England, 10 vols. (Providence, 1856–65), IX, 113, 229; Pennsylvania Gazette (Philadelphia), June 9, 1784.

9. Morris to Governor Greene, Office of Finance [Philadelphia], January 14, 1782, Letters to the Governor, 1731–1800, Mss., R.I.S.A., Vol. 17, p. 73.

10. The best discussions of this point may be found in Ferguson, Power of the Purse, pp. 143–45; E. James Ferguson, "State Assumption of the Federal Debt During the Confederation," Mississippi Valley Historical Review, XXXVIII (1951), 413; and Merrill Jensen, The New Nation: A History of the United States During the Confederation 1781–1789 (New York, 1950), pp. 388–98. For congressional concern over a possible state assumption of the federal debt, consult Jonathan Elliot, ed., Debates on the Adoption of the Federal Constitution in the Convention Held at Philadelphia in 1787; With a Diary of the Debates of the Congress of the Confederation; As Reported by James Madison, a Member, and Deputy from Virginia, Supplementary to Elliot's Debates, 5 vols. (Washington, D.C., 1845), V, 5 (hereafter cited as Elliot, Debates); Madison to Edmund Randolph, Philadelphia, December 10, 1782, and Virginia Delegates to Governor of Virginia [Benjamin Harrison], December 10, 1782, both in Burnett, Letters, VI, 559.

The Impost of 1781

Everyone thought it was impossible to secure further loans at home or abroad without positive assurance that Congress would repay its debts. The ingenuity of the nation's representatives was taxed to the utmost by a quest for money. Several committees of Congress considered these problems at the end of 1780 in the hope of coming up with workable solutions. Congress devoted much of its own precious time to active discussion of the financial alternatives open to it; the greatest evil of Revolutionary finance seemed to be the absence of a steady supply of money to the federal government. Without a fixed income, the nation's obligations could not be discharged nor provision made for future needs. The first glimmer of a plan came in November, 1780, when the congressional committee on finance recommended that Congress seek authority from the states for a national system of taxes on foreign trade, the revenues of which would be used to defray the costs of the war. The committee explained that the United States had lost its credit, and there was no prospect of foreign aid unless Congress gained a permanent revenue.[11]

During the next two months the delegates in Philadelphia continued to discuss the desperate condition of United States finance, considering in the process numerous proposals. A revenue from foreign trade was universally applauded as the most likely remedy. James Duane, an influential congressman from New York, wrote optimistically to General Washington that a solution for the country's financial chaos was at hand, as "a duty on imports and exports and prizes will be recommended," and if approved by the states, he added, "it must produce a considerable revenue."[12] Also contemplated by Congress was another measure of great importance, not directly related to the revenue problem but designed to overhaul the federal government. Congressmen talked much of changing the executive structure of the central government, eliminating the congressional boards that admin-

11. J. M. Varnum to Governor Greene, Philadelphia, January 8, 1780, Bartlett, *Records,* IX, 42; "Proceedings and Observations of the Committee on Finance," November 9, 1780, Burnett, *Letters,* V, 465.

12. Duane to Washington, Philadelphia, December, 9, 1780; Sullivan to the President of New Hampshire, Philadelphia, December 11, 1780; John Witherspoon to William Livingston, Philadelphia, December 16, 1780; all in Burnett, *Letters,* V, 478, 481, 488.

istered the nation's policies, and replacing them with single executive heads for each department of government.[13]

When Congress met on the morning of February 3, 1781, therefore, the issue of a revenue from trade was already agreed upon. All that remained was to decide on the exact form of the plan. Shortly after roll call, the renowned Dr. John Witherspoon, minister and president of the College of New Jersey, formally resolved that Congress be invested with the superintendence of international commerce and exclusive authority to lay duties upon imports into the United States.[14] This extensive request for congressional power was not approved. Later in the day a more limited grant of authority was voted by the members. Congress resolved, "as indispensably necessary," that the states give the federal government power to levy a 5 per cent duty on foreign imports and all naval prizes and prize goods. Revenues arising from this Impost were to be used to discharge the national debt. The resolution provided that the Impost would be for an indefinite term, expiring only when the entire debt had been paid off.[15]

Because of the urgency of the financial picture, Congress ordered its president to print the resolution and dispatch it immediately to the state legislatures for ratification.[16] Those congressmen who were present when the Impost was approved also reported quickly to their states. Everyone declared with unusual optimism that the affairs of the Union were now set on a proper track. The Impost was acclaimed as a reform which would certainly "retrieve the character of and give new confidence and importance [to] the United States." [17]

This was the background of the Impost of 1781. The plan, it should be noted, attempted to amend the nation's constitution, because Congress did not have any power under the Articles of Confederation to lay a tariff on trade or, for that matter, to levy any taxes at all. Had the Impost been ratified by all the states—as required for an amendment —this would have given the federal government a limited taxing power, a steady and growing revenue, and limited control over com-

13. Ezekiel Cornell to Governor Greene, Philadelphia, January 29, 1781, Staples, *R.I. in the Continental Congress*, p. 326.

14. Worthington C. Ford *et al.*, eds., *Journals of the Continental Congress, 1774–1789*, 34 vols. (Washington, D.C., 1904–37) , XIX, 102–3.

15. *Ibid.*, p. 112.

16. "Circular from the President of Congress to the Several States," Philadelphia, February 8, 1781, Burnett, *Letters*, V, 565.

17. Thomas McKean to the Speaker of the Delaware Council [Thomas Collins], Philadelphia, February 3, 1781, *ibid.*, 557.

merce through its administration of the tariff system—an impressive advance for a government without power or prestige, wholly at the mercy of its member states. It is revealing that this amendment was sent to the states before the Articles of Confederation had gone into effect as the first United States constitution. Maryland, the last state to accept the Articles, gave its approval early in March, 1781, almost a month after Congress had asked the states to change the then unofficial constitution. The very fact that Congress sought to reform a frame of government as yet inoperative merely underscored the urgency with which the Impost of 1781 was proposed.

The general context in which the Impost was created is also worth recalling. The Impost plan was only one of a series of measures looking toward a radical change in the structure of the national government between 1780 and 1783. The most dramatic step was the reorganization of the executive departments of the federal government, so that single executive heads ran the national administration in place of multi-member committees under the direct control of Congress. Congress hoped that this change would give decisiveness to the federal government. The appointment of Robert Morris to a position of superior authority in financial affairs was the most important and successful of the new appointments. As superintendent of finance Morris worked to improve the financial situation of Congress. He proposed a far-reaching program of national reform which antedated the achievements of Alexander Hamilton by nearly a decade, including organization of a national bank and an abortive suggestion that Congress fund and assume all the debts of the United States.[18] Morris' personal financial standing and energy guided the nation through the financial crisis of 1781–83 and supplied the funds necessary for the epochal victory at Yorktown. The significance of this many-sided attempt to reorganize the national government—through the Impost, new executive departments, and the financial activities of Robert Morris—is readily evident. It represented the force of United States nationalism on the march, a movement designed to strengthen the federal government by making Congress a focal point for the nation's sovereignty. Only such a solution, the nationalists believed, would save the Revolution and secure the peace.

The Impost was an integral part of the nationalist movement. It proposed to strengthen a weak central government and thereby set a

18. For Morris and his career at this time see the penetrating analysis in Ver Steeg, *Robert Morris*, pp. 65–131, 166–78.

crucial precedent for changing a constitution not yet in force. This first amendment, thought its adherents, might serve as an entering wedge for future expansion of congressional power. Once the states acceded to the congressional request for a limited taxing power and control over trade, the further growth of the national sovereignty would transform the nation. This explains why the Financier Robert Morris was so ecstatic, declaring that "the political existence of America depends upon the accomplishment of this plan." [19] He believed that the Impost was of fundamental importance as a precedent. Paradoxically, this was true despite the admitted fact that the Impost could not provide enough revenue to meet all demands for interest on the nation's debt, to say nothing of the principal. It would supply hardly more, confessed Morris, than "a Tub for the Whale." [20] The Financier placed the total debt at approximately $35,000,000; he estimated that returns from the proposed duty would not exceed $500,000, excluding the costs of collection, an unlikely sum for solving the country's financial woes.[21] Yet despite the inadequacy of the sum, as a first halting step the Impost was deemed a necessity. Without it the nationalist vision of enhancing the power of the federal government could not succeed.

Rhode Island Delays

The Impost went out to the states soon after its passage by Congress. Several states considered the plan quickly, and, although there were reservations and much dispute, the amendment was approved by eleven legislatures before the end of the summer of 1782.[22] Only Rhode Island and Georgia still had not ratified the plan; since the latter state was occupied by Great Britain, the adherence of Rhode Island would have brought the Impost into force.

19. Ferguson, "State Assumption of the Federal Debt During the Confederation," p. 413.

20. John C. Miller, *Alexander Hamilton: Portrait in Paradox* (New York, 1959), p. 87.

21. Ferguson, *Power of the Purse*, p. 146; Oberholtzer, *Robert Morris*, p. 108.

22. The best general account of the Impost struggle is Jackson Turner Main, *The Antifederalists: Critics of the Constitution, 1781–1788* (Chapel Hill, 1961), pp. 72–102.

For more than twenty months the Rhode Island General Assembly refused to act, confirming the fears of some nationalist spokesmen that success would not come easily.[23] Rhode Island's delay in ratifying the Impost occasioned several pleading letters from the state's congressional delegation, chiefly General James Mitchell Varnum and Daniel Mowry, both strong nationalists, urging the Assembly to consent to the amendment. Neither man, it seems, knew of the powerful opposition that fostered Rhode Island's inaction. On August 14, 1781, the delegates wrote home inquiring into the state's torpor with respect to the Impost. "We are at a loss," they said, "to conjecture the rumors which have induced the state of Rhode Island to delay complying with the requisition of Congress, respecting the five per cent duty." They expounded on the floundering state of the country's finances and the crippling weakness of the federal constitution in regard to matters of taxation and trade. An expansion of congressional power must come, they observed, and because of this "we are very desirous of knowing the Resolution of the state relative to the Duty upon imports and prizes." [24]

The new superintendent of finance, Robert Morris, was also concerned about Rhode Island's silence, fearing rightly that silence in this case did not mean consent. He wrote to Governor William Greene asking why Rhode Island hesitated to accept the Impost amendment. The governor responded with an explanation that the legislature was unable to decide, saying further that Rhode Island "shall wait until our sister states have adopted the same. . . ." Greene complained that Rhode Island had already given more than its fair share of the costs of the war and implied that the state would act cautiously before it contributed anything more, even indirectly through a tax on trade.[25] The Financier answered in a series of letters. He tacitly acknowledged that many states—including Rhode Island—had contributed heavily to winning the Revolution, but warned that the only alternative to sustained payment was bankruptcy. Morris declared that if every state waited until the others first fulfilled the needs of the Union and all accounts were equitably settled and distributed, "the Congress may spare

23. James Madison to Edmund Pendleton, Philadelphia, May 29, 1781, Burnett, *Letters*, VI, 103–4.

24. Varnum and Mowry to Governor Greene, Philadelphia, August 14, 1781, Staples, *R.I. in the Continental Congress*, p. 349; Varnum and Mowry to Governor Greene, Philadelphia, September 4, 1781, Burnett, *Letters*, VII, 207.

25. Greene to Morris, Providence, October, 1781, Bartlett, *Records*, IX, 485–87.

themselves the trouble of doing any further business, and their Constituents may spare themselves the expense of keeping them together." [26]

The Financier's suspicion that Rhode Island might be hostile toward a strengthened Union heightened during the summer of 1782. At that time the two new congressional delegates from Rhode Island, David Howell and Jonathan Arnold, seemed to bear out everyone's fears by their bitter opposition to a minor item in Morris' fiscal reorganization. Though the issue was small, it manifested Rhode Island's changing attitude in national affairs.

In his reform of the Treasury Department, Morris had proposed that federal requisitions be laid by the states as a separate tax and be collected independently of local levies. Federal taxes would thus be distinct from state impositions. In order to facilitate this program, federal commissioners were appointed by Congress to serve in the states and receive all federal funds. No commissioner was nominated to serve in his native state.[27] Howell and Arnold were vigorous critics of the plan on the floor of Congress. They explained that, according to the laws and traditions of Rhode Island, collecting taxes was a matter of internal concern and could not be arrogated to an out-of-state authority. A federal collector, they said, would illegally supersede in office the general treasurer of Rhode Island, who alone under the laws of the state could collect taxes. A federal official such as Morris proposed was unknown to the state's constitution.[28] The two delegates closed with an impassioned admonition to their fellow congressmen not to allow the Financier's proposal to pass, because its operation and tendency were "repugnant to the letter and spirit of the Confederation." The new members from Rhode Island who had replaced the nationalists,

26. Morris to Greene, Office of Finance [Philadelphia], December 29, 1781, January 3 and October 17, 1782, Letters to the Governor, Mss., R.I.S.A., Vol. 17, pp. 65, 70, 75. For other items, see Circular Letter to the States, Philadelphia, July 27, 1781, and Morris to the President of Congress, Philadelphia, February 11 and May 17, 1782, both in Papers of the Continental Congress, Letters and Reports from Robert Morris, Mss., N.A., I, pp. 113, 332, 463.

27. Morris to Governor Greene, Office of Finance [Philadelphia], October 21, 1782, Letters to the Governor, Mss., R.I.S.A., Vol. 18, p. 30.

28. Ford, Journals of the Continental Congress, XXIII, 666, 669; Arnold and Howell to Governor Greene, Philadelphia, October 19, 1782, Letters to the Governor, Mss., R.I.S.A., Vol. 18, p. 30. The state accepted a federal collector, Edward Chinn, in the spring of 1783; see Morris to Governor Greene, Office of Finance [Philadelphia], April 1, 1783, Letters to the Governor, Mss., R.I.S.A., Vol. 18, p. 66.

Varnum and Mowry, clearly signaled the state's unwillingness to support any longer the idea of a strong national unity. The future course for Rhode Island in relations with its sister states—as before with its sister colonies—was going to be one of intransigence.

The Impost came before the Rhode Island legislature on several occasions prior to the decisive vote late in 1782. Each time the issue was postponed. Rhode Island was one of the lesser states of the Union, and it wanted to act in concert with another state before defeating the plan. Unfortunately, no other state refused the proposal outright before 1782. It was also expected that by a continued postponement, instead of an immediate vote in early 1781, time would be gained to campaign against the Impost, to attack those who might support the plan, and to allow the towns enough leisure to instruct their deputies in the General Assembly to vote against this grant of power to Congress. Though advocates of the amendment boasted that delay would aid their cause, the opponents knew well that their own strength was growing. They wanted to be sure of a nearly unanimous rejection by the General Assembly, because in the summer of 1782 it was certain that Rhode Island would stand alone.[29]

Opposition to the Impost in Rhode Island was led by the merchants, men who were vitally interested in its defeat.[30] Their motives, sometimes openly expressed, were primarily economic, though usually couched in political terms. They showed no interest whatever in strengthening the Union; their political stance against changing the federal system was that of extreme states' rights. The war had interrupted the profitable course of Rhode Island's commerce, and the merchants wanted to see all lines of communication with the outside world swiftly restored. In order to achieve this, an unburdened commerce was necessary. The Browns, Arnolds, and other mercantile families, however, were realists. They knew very well that the federal government needed money. Rhode Island, after all, had its own expenses. They felt that when a tax was laid on trade it should benefit Rhode Island first—and only. Revenues that came from Rhode Island's

---

29. Joseph Brown to David Howell, Providence, September 8, 1782, and Joseph Nightingale to David Howell, Providence, August 25, 1782, Archives, Mss., B.U.L.

30. The connection between the merchants and the defeat of the Impost, as well as the states' rights position of this class of men, was first expounded in Hillman M. Bishop, "Why Rhode Island Opposed the Federal Constitution: The Continental Impost," *Rhode Island History*, VIII (1949), 3–4.

hard-won commercial success should not accrue to the credit of all states through the national treasury.[31] There was also considerable feeling against permitting the federal government to lay tariffs while simultaneously permitting states that might profit from sale of the western backlands won from Great Britain to retain their exclusive claims against those of the United States. All the states had to share equally in revenues from the West.[32] The merchants believed further that imposts on their trade ought to be used to ease the burden of internal taxation and pay off the elephantine state debt, of which they were the chief owners.[33]

Another economic factor bearing upon mercantile unwillingness to accept the Impost was the special character of Rhode Island's commerce. The state depended on trade to live, and in seeking articles for sale Rhode Islanders were compelled to look beyond their own frontiers. In other words, as James B. Hedges has explained, since Rhode Island had a dearth of products for sale, its merchants were obliged to "import in order to export." [34] The continental Impost posed a danger in this regard. It did not provide for drawbacks on duties paid when foreign goods were re-exported from Rhode Island. If these duties could not be passed on to the consumer in the form of higher prices, they would, of necessity, be absorbed by the merchants. Merchants feared that, if the duties fell upon the importer, their profit margins,

31. See, particularly, the letter from Nicholas Brown, the prominent Providence merchant, to David Howell, Providence, August 26, 1782, Brown Papers, Mss., J.C.B.L.

32. The question of the western lands had troubled Rhode Island since the beginning of the Revolution. Throughout the period between 1778 and 1782, Rhode Island's delegates in Congress were under explicit instructions to secure the surrender of the backlands to the nation for the equal profit of all the states. The Assembly's formal instructions may be read in Bartlett, *Records*, VIII, 365; IX, 562, 612, for February, 1778, June, 1782, and October, 1782. Important evidence on this issue may also be found in "Letter from a Gentleman at the Southward," *Providence Gazette*, October 26, 1782; Rhode Island Delegates [Howell and Arnold] to Governor Greene, Philadelphia, October 13, 1782 and "Madison's Observations on . . . Territorial Claims," May 1, 1782, both in Burnett, *Letters*, VI, 502, 341; *The Papers of James Madison*, ed. William T. Hutchinson *et. al.* (in progress; Chicago, 1962—) , II, 72–78.

33. For the mercantile interest in the relationship between an Impost and the state debts, see John Brown to David Howell, Providence, October 23, 1783, Mss., R.I.H.S., Vol. 14, p. 27, and Nicholas Brown to Nathaniel Appleton, Providence, December 13, 1784, Brown Papers, Mss., J.C.B.L.

34. James B. Hedges, *The Browns of Providence Plantations: Colonial Years* (Cambridge, Mass., 1952) , p. 324.

already threateningly low, would disappear.[35] The same merchants who denied Great Britain's attempts to tax their trade were not going to give this power to Congress without a struggle.

The Impost Debate

A campaign against the Impost first gained momentum in the winter of 1781–82, although the recalcitrance of Rhode Island's leaders was already well advanced by then. The occasioning factor in the state's open change of policy and new hesitation in advocating a stronger Union was the smashing success at Yorktown. This victory fostered a universal conviction that the war was coming to a close; the cause of American nationalism faltered as a result. Robert Morris, for one, found all further progress toward financial reform blocked by the indifference and studied negligence of the states.[36] The year 1781 was the high-water mark of nationalism before 1787. News of Yorktown ar-

---

35. [David Howell] "Thoughts on the Five Per Cent.," *Providence Gazette*, Supplement, October 19, 1782; Ford, *Journals of the Continental Congress*, XXIII, 799.

Forrest McDonald suggests that another primary reason for the Impost's defeat stemmed from a "sinister" plan of a group of Providence merchants, especially the Browns, to speculate in government securities. According to McDonald, the merchants pretended they would favor the Impost and convinced "mercantile correspondents in other cities that Rhode Island would soon also ratify." The result was an increase in the price of continental securities which these correspondents bought and a decline in the value of state issues which they sold. Afterwards, the defeat of the Impost depressed the price of United States debts while the value of state securities, which the Rhode Island merchants had acquired at low prices, rose sharply.

The difficulties with this explanation are formidable. To begin with, the sources McDonald utilized, including the Brown Papers in the John Carter Brown Library and the Rhode Island Historical Society, do not provide consistent evidence to sustain this conclusion. McDonald cites few particular items from the manuscripts he used so it is impossible to reconstruct his interpretation. Secondly, there is no evidence that the Providence merchants wrote to their "correspondents" saying Rhode Island was prepared to ratify the Impost. Again, no specific items from the merchants are cited which support McDonald's statements. The narrative given above as well as the sources used show the consistent opposition of the merchants to the Impost of 1781. For McDonald's views see *We the People: The Economic Origins of the Constitution* (Chicago, 1958), pp. 324–26, and *E Pluribus Unum: The Formation of the American Republic 1776–1790* (Boston, 1965), pp. 20–23.

36. Burnett, *Continental Congress*, pp. 523–24, 526.

rived in Rhode Island late in the fall of 1781, and, with victory, the military necessity to support the cause of national unity disappeared. With independence in sight, the defeat of the Impost was sealed.

Probably few readers took much notice of an innocuous letter from "Philo-Patrie" that appeared in the *Providence Gazette* on Saturday morning, January 19, 1782. This was the initial attack on the Impost amendment printed in the newspapers, but it was a relatively soft blow, considering the storm that was to come. Later in the month another writer blasted the Impost because it upset the comfortable balance that existed between the power of the states and the dependence of the central government. "Congress may call on us for money," he wrote, "but cannot prescribe to us methods of raising it; that is within our sovereignty, and lies solely in the power of our legislatures." [37] This same critic predicted that the Impost would introduce swarms of foreigners into the states, federal bureaucrats who would become as venal and corrupt as British customs racketeers before the Revolution. The problem of the Impost became, in this way, a matter of public debate, and the emotion of these first words foretold the vigor of the subsequent controversy.

The struggle began in earnest when James Mitchell Varnum, one of the state's representatives in Congress, returned to Rhode Island and took charge of the pro-Impost and nationalist minority. Varnum was born in Massachusetts but decided to stay permanently in Rhode Island upon graduation from Rhode Island College in Providence. He studied law and, shortly before the Revolution, had become one of the state's leading advocates. War found Varnum favoring the cause of his native land, and he served as brigadier general of the Rhode Island armies during the Revolution.[38] Varnum achieved a reputation as a lawyer of great ability and learning and as a public speaker of exceptional power. He mixed these talents with a fervent nationalism. In his letters from Congress, Varnum intoned a theme of expansive nationalism, with special emphasis on the faults of the Articles of Confedera-

37. Letter from a "Plain Dealer," *Providence Gazette,* January 26, 1782. In a succeeding letter on the Impost problem, the "Plain Dealer" asked Rhode Island's voters to "make it your business (and a serious business it ought to be) to examine into the conduct and characters of candidates at the approaching election" (*Providence Gazette,* February 2, 1782).

38. For biographical details on Varnum, consult the *Dictionary of American Biography,* XIX, 227–28; James M. Varnum, *A Sketch of the Life and Public Services of James Mitchell Varnum of Rhode Island* (Boston, 1906); and the best study, Wilkins Updike, *Memoirs of the Rhode Island Bar* (Boston, 1842), pp. 145–233.

tion. He was known to be "very desirous of inlarging" the powers of Congress.[39] In his view, the real trouble with the newly independent nation was an "absolute want of Government." [40] The only remedy was to entrust Congress with every power necessary to guarantee the peace and security of the United States. With such thoughts as these James Mitchell Varnum returned to his adopted state to fight for ratification of the Impost.

On March 2, 1782, Varnum began the publication of a series of essays in the *Providence Gazette* under the pseudonym of "A Citizen." His articles proved an able summary of the circumstances that led Congress to ask for the Impost amendment and the reasons why the national government wanted to exercise a greater scope of authority than it did under the Articles. Significant, too, was Varnum's elaborate discussion of political philosophy, out of which developed his concept of Congress as a central government capable of acting upon both individuals and the states, the very antithesis of the Confederation. The philosophy of the "Citizen" was symptomatic of the nationalism that propounded the Impost of 1781 and secured an entirely new federal system in 1787.

The fundamental principle in Varnum's articles was his belief that the federal Congress should be the focus of the national independence that had been won in the American Revolution. Independence in 1776 meant the sovereignty of the United States collectively, not of the thirteen states individually. As such, the Impost proposal was perfectly logical, even a fulfillment, because it enhanced the sovereignty of the new nation by giving Congress a permanent revenue. The Impost, Varnum insisted, was to be viewed in these terms, as an implicit and inherent right of the national government which the states were obliged to acknowledge. He admitted that a strict construction of the

39. Thomas Rodney, "Diary," Burnett, *Letters*, VI, 19.

40. Varnum to Wilkins Updike, Philadelphia, February 3, 1781, Updike Papers, 1673–1898, Mss., R.I.H.S., Vol. 1673–1804. Varnum took notice in this letter (written the day the Impost was passed by Congress) of Maryland's impending ratification of the Articles of Confederation and of other proposals to strengthen congressional power. But he doubted that halfway measures would suffice. "It is probable, I confess, that the Confederation will soon be concluded," he wrote. "But then, we shall be just where we are now, in a perfect state of Imbecility." It was just this spirit and attitude which lay at the heart of the nationalist movement in Congress. The nationalists were convinced that unless there was a basic structural change in the balance of federal and state relations, a change in the direction of the nation, the Union and the country would not survive. For this reason they were induced to recommend amending the Articles of Confederation even before it came into force.

Articles of Confederation might give a different impression, but such an impression was false and unintended. Congressional powers were not fully outlined in the Articles of Confederation because they were not always "capable of conventional description." He asserted even more strongly that the rights of government "cannot be reduced to certain rules, and are [occasionally] exercised only upon extreme necessity." [41]

Nor were these Varnum's conclusions alone. Congress itself more than once considered the deficiencies in its grant of authority, suggesting that its vast responsibilities for the nation must imply the right to use every means of fulfillment. A congressional committee reported in 1780 that at times extraordinary crises might arise which would render it necessary for the government to deviate from the apparent limitations of its grant of power. The committee asked Congress to consider "whether such times and exigencies do not now exist." [42] James Madison, in 1781 a congressman from Virginia and a vocal advocate of a strong federal government, suggested that, whenever the states refused to accede to the requisitions of Congress, the nation had an implied right to coerce the delinquent. These seemingly extralegal powers should be invoked, he remarked, only when to do so was palpably necessary, but they were implicit among the many powers already given to Congress and they derived from the sovereignty of the United States.[43] Similarly, another Virginian, Joseph Jones, spoke of the implied power of Congress to enforce its decisions in every phase of activity where a grant of responsibility existed, whether this power of enforcement was specified or not.[44] Thus Varnum's expansive assertion of national sovereignty and his desire to broaden federal power by means of theoretical implied rights were not unique. In the same way the Impost amendment itself was just one part of a larger framework of United States nationalism.

Varnum and his philosophy did not hold forth in the Rhode Island press without rebuttal. Letters and articles poured in so quickly that

41. *Providence Gazette,* March 9, 16, 1782.
42. Burnett, *Continental Congress,* p. 452.
43. Madison to Jefferson, Philadelphia, April 3, 1781, *The Writings of James Madison: Comprising his Public Papers and his Private Correspondence, including Numerous Letters and Documents Now for the First Time Printed,* ed. Gaillard Hunt, 9 vols. (New York, 1900–1910), VI, 57; Irving Brant, *James Madison and American Nationalism* (Princeton, 1968), pp. 136–41.
44. Jones to Thomas Jefferson, Philadelphia, April 6, 1781, Burnett, *Letters,* VI, 57.

John Carter, publisher of the *Providence Gazette,* Rhode Island's most influential journal, explained that he could not print every commentary on the Impost. The harassed printer said that when he omitted any letter it was not because he disagreed with the writer's point of view and was trying to shape the news; the cause was simply a lack of space, for which he was sorry. Despite the sordid motives attributed to Carter's failure to print everything, he stoutly maintained that the pages of his newspaper had always been and would "remain perfectly free and open to all parties." [45]

The most sustained reply to Varnum came from an unexpected source, Rhode Island College's former professor of natural philosophy, David Howell. On March 23, 1782, a series of articles began to appear intermittently in the *Providence Gazette* under the signature of "A Farmer." The anonymous author was David Howell, at that time an active and prosperous attorney in Providence closely associated with the Browns and other mercantile families, both professionally and by marriage.[46] His dispute with Varnum over the Impost showed him to be a keen and effective polemicist, one who could combine argument with a biting wit.

Prior to 1782 Howell had been a useful and ambitious citizen, a man successful first as a teacher and later as a self-educated lawyer. He served as a local justice of the peace, spent one term on the Superior Court of Rhode Island, was a member of numerous important public committees (such as one that revised the militia laws in 1776), and he even volunteered to act as "Captain" of the Providence fire department in 1779. Howell was, in short, a popular and active Rhode Islander, whose performance as the "Farmer" thrust him into prominence as a state-wide political figure. He added to all this a genuine devotion to the cause of freedom and liberty—which later on made him a leader in the movement to abolish Negro slavery—and an ambition to win important public office.[47]

45. *Providence Gazette,* April 20, 1782.
46. Biographical details on Howell are available in the *Dictionary of American Biography,* IX, 301; *Biographical Cyclopedia of Representative Men of Rhode Island* (Providence, 1881), p. 140; and [David Howell] "Tombstone Inscription," *Narragansett Historical Register,* V (1886), 70. Estimates of Howell's character are given in Henry Marchant to Alexander Hamilton, Newport, December 9, 1793, in Gaillard Hunt, "Office Seeking in Washington's Administration," *American Historical Review,* I (1896), 281–82, and William Ellery to Alexander Hamilton, Newport, December 16, 1793, Emmet Collection, Mss., N.Y.P.L., Em. 4168.
47. Joseph J. Smith, *Civil and Military List of Rhode Island* (Providence, 1900), *passim;* "Communication by James Manning and David Howell to the Senior Class,

The "Farmer" began his condemnation of the "Citizen" on a political note, denouncing the Impost as a tax that would subvert the liberties of all Americans. This he swore to prevent. David Howell conceived of British taxation and the Impost amendment as sharing the same stamp of despotism. Since he had risked everything against Great Britain, so he would again fight against the schemes of Congress. "From that fatal day when the stamp act was hatched by an infernal junto of British Ministers down to the no less fatal day, if heaven prevent not, when the five per cent. duties were recommended," avowed Howell, "I declare before God and the world, my principles and measures have been the same." Consequently, the pledge of Revolutionary times, "never to spare a tyrant, though shrouded under the name of parent, friend, or brother," which was once invoked against the mother country, was now applied against the national government of the United States.[48]

Sovereignty in the United States rested with the states. From this basis Howell bitterly attacked Varnum and the Impost plan. Varnum's contention that the act of independence created a collective sovereignty was decried as a barefaced grab for power. What especially aroused Howell's ire was the "Citizen's" insinuation that certain unspecified inherent rights and implied powers were accorded the federal Congress as its birthright, though, admittedly, they were to be exercised only in cases of grave emergency. Howell asserted that Congress had no latent or undefined power; it could claim no "magic charm" of prerogative, as had Great Britain. Even the most extreme necessity would not make such power visible, because it did not exist. "And I will add," the "Farmer" gibed, that "this extreme necessity is sometimes to be judged of by the most extreme villains and often pleaded to justify the most extreme villainies." The powers of Congress under the Articles of Confederation were explicit and established, being the result of compact and clear stipulation. Why, then, asked Howell, should there be talk of congressional authority as latent or implied, "or to lie hid, and as it were in ambush to the subject, and ready to pop out upon every occasion for his destruction?"[49] According to

---

June 8, 1775," in R. A. Guild, *Life, Times, and Correspondence of James Manning* (Boston, 1864), p. 241; Letter of David Howell, *Providence Gazette,* March 21, 1778; and David Howell, "Charge Delivered to the Graduates of Providence College on Commencement Day (September 17, 1791)," *Baptist Annual Register* (1791), 216–19.

48. *Providence Gazette,* March 23, 1782.

49. *Ibid.*

David Howell, those who talked of undefined, implied powers were a danger to the United States.

The "Farmer" took great pains to build on the strong tradition of self-government in Rhode Island. His words rang with the conviction that the states' rights principle was best for his fellow citizens. Howell emphasized that under the Articles of Confederation the division of state and federal power guaranteed the sovereignty of each state and that all power not expressly surrendered to the nation was reserved to the individual states.[50] Appealing to the traditions of Rhode Island's freemen and their experience of having ascendancy in local affairs, the "Farmer" apotheosized state control over taxation as vital to a free people.[51] The "Farmer" also attacked the Impost because the duties were to be collected by federal officers operating within the borders of Rhode Island. Howell subtly labeled the federal collectors "foreign officers," not answerable to the General Assembly, and, therefore, presumably irresponsible. It was better for the cause of liberty to keep the power of taxation as close to the people as possible, in the hands of the state, and not delegate this "jewel" to a foreign government such as Congress.[52] A Rhode Island brand of xenophobia was thus invoked to combat the Impost.

The contrast between Howell and Varnum with regard to political philosophy was striking. The one, nationalistic, looked toward a broad interpretation of the constitution to foster the nation's welfare; the other, a states' rights advocate, fearful of the arbitrary use of power, desired a limited grant of responsibility to the nation and a federal-state balance weighted in favor of the states. In 1782 Varnum adumbrated the philosophy of nationalism usually associated with Alexander Hamilton and a later period of our history. David Howell anticipated the philosophy of Antifederalism and the states' rights republican opposition to the Federalist party.

In some of his articles the "Farmer" digressed from states' rights to offer a more mundane explanation of why the state should reject the Impost. Howell began by attacking Varnum's picture of American finance as unduly pessimistic—a "high coloured painting," he wrote. He noted that if the nation's finances were as desperate as the nationalists claimed, no one would lend the United States money under any

50. *Ibid.,* March 30, 1782.
51. *Ibid.,* April 13, 1782.
52. [David Howell] "Thoughts on the Five Per Cent.," *ibid.,* Supplement, October 19, 1782.

circumstances.[53] Howell protested that the Impost would work against the commercial interests of the state by encumbering its trade with duties and blocking its markets. After the great devastation of the war, he reasoned, free trade would best encourage Rhode Island's prosperity. Moreover, the monies raised by the proposed tax on trade would not be credited to the state's accounts with the Union but would be received into the general revenues; this meant that the state would be deprived of a considerable source of taxes.[54] As a consuming state Rhode Island would also suffer. In the event the duties were passed on to consumers, those states, such as Rhode Island, that depended upon imports to satisfy their needs would again contribute unequally to the national treasury. Howell calculated that the just proportion of Rhode Island's obligations to the nation, relative to its population, would be increased by more than eight times if the General Assembly accepted the Impost amendment; for the trading towns of Newport and Providence it would be increased almost sixteen-fold. "Surely this is alarming!" the "Farmer" exclaimed.[55] He wrote that those with large families—farmers, tradesmen, and the poor—would be hardest hit by any increase in prices caused by duties on imported commodities.

The "Farmer" called attention to the irrevocable nature of the Impost. He asserted that, once granted, it would never be rescinded. Howell recommended, as a good principle, that the operation of any tax should have a specific purpose and terminal date. The Impost was supposed to liquidate the debts of the United States, but there was no limitation in time, amount, or character as to what these debts might contain. Without specific safeguards, warned the "Farmer," the amendment, if ratified, "will be like Adam's fall, unalterable, and affect . . . all our posterity." [56] Responding to Varnum's charge that opponents of the Impost offered no alternative sources of revenues, Howell suggested

53. *Ibid.*, March 30, 1782.

54. *Ibid.*, April 13, 1782; letter from "A Countryman" [probably Howell], *ibid.*, September 21, 1782; Howell to Welcome Arnold, Philadelphia, August 23, 1782, Simon Gratz Collection, Mss., H.S.P., Case 1, Box 7. Varnum, in a resumption of his articles on July 20, 1782, denounced Howell by arguing that trade was, in its very nature, interstate; therefore, any revenue from commerce belonged to the United States.

55. [David Howell] "Thoughts on the Five Per Cent.," *Providence Gazette*, Supplement, October 19, 1782. "The less commercial States," said Howell simply, "do not consume, compared with the more commercial States, so great a quantity of foreign goods as is proportionate to their wealth."

56. *Ibid.*, April 13, 1782.

a reorganized system of national requisitions, with every state bearing its just proportion of the debts of the United States.[57]

The "Farmer" articles of David Howell set the stage for Rhode Island's refusal to accept the Impost. His arguments served as ammunition for a succession of critics. When election time neared in the spring of 1782, the anti-Impost forces, led by the merchants and dominant throughout the state, offered Howell as an aspirant for the United States Congress, opposing James Mitchell Varnum. Twice before Howell had sought election to Congress, and on both occasions, in 1778 and 1781, he was soundly defeated. The earlier contest, in 1778, must have been particularly humiliating for the Providence lawyer. He was accused of having supported the Tories and of justifying their cause, charges very difficult to contradict because they were fed by rumors and undercover gossip. Howell was probably a victim of misunderstanding. He defended the Quakers and their neutrality in the war against Great Britain, upholding their right of conscience with respect to bearing arms and paying taxes. This brought on the allegation of Toryism.[58] In contrast, the campaign of 1782 was a resounding success, and Howell's smashing victory tasted that much sweeter for having succeeded defeat. Details of the electoral struggle are today unknown. In a letter to General Nathanael Greene, Howell reported that he had not the "most distant thoughts" of running for Congress until he was prevailed upon shortly before the election by some "respectable gentlemen" to permit his name to be printed against that of Varnum.[59] Since each man had a stated and well-known position on the issue of the Impost, Howell's triumph reflected Rhode Island's determination to veto the congressional amendment.[60]

As Howell prepared to take up his duties as congressman after the election, his articles as the "Farmer" came to an end. But the controversy over the Impost did not abate. In Howell's place, Theodore Foster, an attorney and town clerk of Providence, entered the fray as an

57. Letter from "A Citizen," *ibid.*, August 3, 1782; [David Howell] "Thoughts on the Five Per Cent.," *ibid.*, Supplement, October 19, 1782.

58. David Howell to John Pemberton, Providence, October 12, 1778, Pemberton Papers, Mss., H.S.P., Vol. 32, p. 109.

59. Howell to Greene, Philadelphia, October 18, 1782, Miscellaneous Manuscripts, N.H.S., Box 36, Folder 2.

60. *Providence Gazette*, May 4, 1782; Benjamin Cowell, *Spirit of Rhode Island, Sketches of the efforts of the Government and the People in the War of the Revolution* (Boston, 1850) , pp. 257–58.

antagonist in the *Providence Gazette*. Foster masqueraded as "A Free-holder," and in the fall began a series of letters that closely duplicated Howell's earlier castigation of the proposed amendment. The importance of Foster's efforts lay not in what he was able to add to the stock of complaints already advanced against the Impost. Rather, the "Free-holder" letters are of interest because they show the extent to which David Howell had crystallized the states' rights cause in Rhode Island. Foster's letters merit examination also because they attracted attention in national circles and brought rebuttals from Varnum and Thomas Paine.

Theodore Foster echoed Howell's states' rights preference when he congratulated the freemen for their delay in giving greater power to Congress. In grandiloquent fashion, he denounced the Impost as a grave violation of the Confederation, "at once destroying all the liberties of the several states, separately considered, reducing them to so many provinces of Congress, and tending to the establishment of an aristocratical or monarchical government." [61] With shotgun attacks, Foster fired all the arguments he could conceive against the proposal. He condemned the amendment as the "ground-work for the introduction of a perpetual standing army . . . subservient to the purpose of tyranny," noting that it would promote corruption and thereby further place an unequal tax burden on the people of Rhode Island.[62] The "Freeholder" boldly took up Varnum's taunt that there was no substitute for the Impost. He contended that the country's finances would never be put on a sound basis until all accounts between the states and the nation were adjusted and every member of the Union received its proper recompense. Without a settlement of accounts, every state, like Rhode Island, would find it impossible to aid the cause of fiscal stability. After all accounts were settled, Foster argued, the states

61. *Providence Gazette*, October 26, 1782; January 11, 1783.
62. Other critics of the Impost offered an even wider range of complaints against the amendment. One writer charged that the revenues were to be used to support a half-pay plan for revolutionary officers (letter from "The Plain Dealer," *ibid.*, September 7, 1782). Another publication, by one "S.A.," opined that the Impost would burden the poor with taxes and permit the merchants to escape taxation entirely. "S.A." suggested that mercantile opposition was a sham; they secretly favored the Impost. He remarked that Rhode Island's merchants operated with satanic guile, because they knew that if they openly supported the new taxes, everyone in Rhode Island would automatically be against them; by saying no to the Impost, the merchants knew that the freemen would say yes in return. "It is true the merchants appear against the duty, to deceive the country," wrote "S.A.," in the *Providence Gazette*, on April 20, 1782. "They know if they should appear in favor of the duty, the country would be against it."

should then assume their fair proportions of the national debt and supply federal requisitions as they saw fit. Foster also blasted the amendment as part of a larger scheme to consolidate the national debt with a new funded debt, secured in part by the Impost revenues. He criticized the funding concept as nothing more than an attempt to encourage speculation and corruption by establishing a permanent debt that would never be retired.[63]

Even before the "Freeholder" held forth in the Rhode Island press, the nationalists in Congress grew restless at the slow pace of their hoped-for reinvigoration of the federal government. Not only was Rhode Island blocking the Impost, but other states were withholding support for congressional efforts to meet the financial crisis. Accordingly, a resolution was passed by Congress authorizing four commissioners to visit the state assemblies during the summer of 1782. They were instructed to emphasize the deepening financial crisis of the nation and to advance the cause of fiscal reform.[64] The northern commissioners, Jesse Root of Connecticut and Joseph Montgomery of Pennsylvania, arrived in Rhode Island early in the summer. By that time Rhode Island was the only state besides Georgia which had not yet ratified the Impost amendment.

Root and Montgomery were very firm when they appeared before the Rhode Island legislature. They urged upon the General Assembly the necessity of complying with the wishes of Congress, especially the desperate federal requests for funds, and they reminded the legislators of the continuing needs of the army. The commissioners exerted their greatest effort on behalf of the Impost plan. Root and Montgomery warned the Assembly that responsibility for the inauguration of the Impost rested on its shoulders, and predicted that "the blame of present and future generations would be on us if the Impost were not accepted." [65] The legislators, however, were generally unmoved by these entreaties, satisfied as they were that Rhode Island had done as much as the most generous state in contributing to the war against Great Britain. Melancholy as the commissioners' story was, scoffed the Provi-

63. *Ibid.*, November 9, 1782. Foster called the settlement of accounts the "great herculean work in American politics." See also the letter from "Casca," *ibid.*, October 11, 1783.

64. James Madison to Edmund Randolph, Philadelphia, May 28, 1782, *Writings of Madison*, ed. Hunt, I, 198; Burnett, *Continental Congress*, pp. 528–29.

65. Joseph Brown to David Howell, Providence, July 13, 1782, Archives, Mss., B.U.L.; Jonathan Arnold to David Howell, Providence, June 29, 1782, Peck Collection, Mss., R.I.H.S., Box VI.

dence merchant Joseph Brown, it changed no one's mind, and the "ingenious and importunate" addresses of the national representatives were simply brushed aside.

Not as easy to ignore was Thomas Paine, who was persuaded to travel to Rhode Island and prepare a series of public letters in favor of the Impost and a strengthened Union.[66] Paine's intervention in the Rhode Island debate clearly demonstrates the national implications of the local conflict. Moreover, Paine's position—like that of Foster—continued the nationalist–states' rights division that already marked the war of words between David Howell and James Mitchell Varnum. Thomas Paine, the democrat and revolutionary, stood among those nationalists who wanted a greatly strengthened Union. Paine went on to Rhode Island in face of the General Assembly's initial rejection of the proposed Impost amendment. After this setback his efforts were deemed that much more essential, because Paine now had to convince Rhode Islanders to reverse their stand against constitutional reform. If this could be accomplished, the Impost plan might yet be salvaged.

Paine met the states' rights evocations of Howell and Foster with the claim that Congress was as truly representative of the people as the state assemblies. Congressmen, he declared, were elected by and of the people, and the frequency of their elections made certain an identification of interest between them and their constituents. Congress was directly responsible to the popular will. The members of Congress were fully subject to the same laws as any ordinary citizen.[67] The most important problems for the American people to consider, in Paine's

66. The six letters which Paine wrote under the pseudonym of "A Friend to Rhode Island and the Union" were published in the *Providence Gazette,* December 21 and 28, 1782, January 4, 11, 18, and February 1, 1783. The letters were written and published in the Philadelphia press before they appeared in Rhode Island. This would indicate that Paine's project was started before, or at the same time as, news of Rhode Island's veto of the Impost arrived in Philadelphia, during the second week of November. Publication of the letters in Philadelphia and elsewhere also suggests that in recruiting Paine the nationalists had more in mind than simply propagandizing in Rhode Island. They obviously wanted to see Paine's refutation of Howell and Foster republished throughout the United States. Paine's letters were rediscovered by Harry H. Clark and published in *Six New Letters of Thomas Paine: Being Pieces on the Five Per Cent Duty Addressed to the Citizens of Rhode Island,* ed. Harry H. Clark (Madison, 1939); they are conveniently reprinted in *The Complete Writings of Thomas Paine,* ed. Philip Foner, 2 vols. (New York, 1945), II, 333–66. See also Howard W. Preston, "The Varnum House," *Rhode Island Historical Society Collections,* XX (1927), 120, and Staughton Lynd, "Abraham Yates's History of the Movement for the United States Constitution," *William and Mary Quarterly,* 3d ser., XX (1963), 239 n. 34.

67. *Providence Gazette,* December 21, 1782.

mind, were the national debt and how it was going to be paid. Pointing to the inadequacy of the revenues derived from requisitions and to the inability of the federal government to raise new loans, he singled out a tax on international trade as the best solution for the nation's financial crisis.

The American democrat also exhibited a fervently nationalistic approach to the nation's future. Of what value was state sovereignty, he asked, in face of the overwhelming problems with which the United States had to deal in domestic and foreign affairs? "It is on our united sovereignty that our greatness and safety, and the security of our foreign commerce, rest. The united sovereignty must be something more than a name, and requires to be as completely organized for the line it is to act in as that of any individual State, and, if anything, more so because more depends on it." [68] The nationalist Paine pleaded for a Union in which the strength of all the United States might be brought to bear upon the problems that plagued the nation.[69] Thomas Paine did indeed stand "first on the lists of Federalists" in 1782–83, as he told an incredulous audience in the early years of the nineteenth century.[70]

In his letters Paine tried unsuccessfully to assure Rhode Islanders that their economic interests would not be adversely affected by the Impost. He asserted that a tax on trade fell on each state in proportion to its consumption of foreign goods, and on individuals in the same way. Because of this a small state like Rhode Island, which consumed fewer imported articles than more populous states, would pay less than others into the national treasury. Paine said that it would be improper to credit any one state with the amount of revenues drawn from a federal tax on its international trade, for the patterns of commerce in the United States were interstate in character and the money which came from a tax on imports was the "confederated patronage" of the United States.[71]

Of particular interest was Paine's attempt to break the unity of anti-Impost forces in Rhode Island by appealing to the country farmers to throw off the leadership of the mercantile community on the

68. *Ibid.*, December 28, 1782.
69. Paine argued that it was more valid to speak of the unity of the nation than of the independence of the states. "For if the nation be fully supported, our independence is made secure," he wrote. "The former is the mother, the latter the infant at her breast. The nourishment of one is drawn through the other." *Ibid.*, January 4, 1783.
70. *Writings of Thomas Paine*, ed. Foner, II, 913.
71. *Providence Gazette*, December 28, 1782, and January 4, 1783.

question of the Impost. One major purpose of the Impost, said Paine, was to take a revenue from trade and thereby lessen the burden of further land taxation and poll taxes. The merchants knew this very well and opposed the amendment only to "draw the neck of commerce compleately out from every share and portion of the public difficulty." Was it just, he implied, for the merchants to enjoy a profitable trade with the world scot-free of taxation while the farmer in the field contributed indirectly to the federal government through special levies laid on his land? The merchant drank his wine free of all duties because the Revolution did away with every burden on trade; but the farmer paid a sum on his cider because state excises were a substitute source of revenue.[72] This allusion to the role of the merchants in the anti-Impost fight brought a vicious attack on Paine's integrity in supporting the nationalist movement, one of many that he faced in his eventful life. Some suggested, among other things, that "Common Sense," Paine's sobriquet, had become a mercenary writer whose principles and talents were for sale to the highest bidder; he had sold out to the nationalist pack led by Robert Morris in Philadelphia. Paine answered his critics by warning the merchants that their repudiation of the Union might one day precipitate them into unexpected problems; the time might come when they had outgrown their states' rights principles, and then how difficult it would be to favor a powerful Union.[73] Later, when the Antifederalists in Rhode Island returned to the arguments of 1781–82 to keep the state from ratifying the federal Constitution, many merchants may well have groaned that they had not heeded Paine's prophecy.

Defeat

The efforts of Thomas Paine were of no use in stemming the tide of states' rights in Rhode Island. In fact, as mentioned before, Paine came to Rhode Island too late to avert the General Assembly's initial rejection of the Impost. Town and country were in firm alliance on the issue, and they simply waited for the best moment to veto the proposal. That time came in November, 1782.

72. *Ibid.,* January 11, 18, 1783.
73. *Ibid.,* February 1, 1783.

One suspects that Rhode Island's leaders would have preferred to put off a decision by never voting on the Impost at all, since its veto would invite a storm of criticism. But a decision could not be postponed forever. In Congress the patience of the nationalists was exhausted, and they waited with eager anticipation to learn of Rhode Island's stand. Only Rhode Island blocked the success of their program for constitutional reform; when Rhode Island gave its consent, the Impost would go into effect. Early in October the delegates in Congress cautioned the state's leaders that Rhode Island could no longer delay. David Howell wrote to Welcome Arnold and Theodore Foster that Congress sought a "Categorical answer" at the very next session of the legislature. He advised that the "fatal measure" must now be defeated.[74]

An indication that a decision was near came at the October session of the General Assembly. A vote on the Impost was once more postponed and the delegates in Congress were instructed to adhere closely in their actions to the Articles of Confederation and to fight against any infringement of the sovereignty of the state.[75] Since David Howell was the principal representative in Philadelphia, the resolution was superfluous. Much more important were the town meetings convened in all parts of the state to consider the Impost amendment. The freemen gathered to discuss the issue throughout 1782, and their deliberations were decidedly in opposition to giving more power to the Continental Congress. The decision of the town meeting in Barrington was probably typical. There the freemen "voted that the Deputies from this Town oppose the Act from Congress commonly called the Impost or 5 prct Act . . . and use their utmost Endeavor that said Act be not Adopted by this State." Similar decisions against the Impost may be examined in the town meeting manuscripts of East Greenwich, Bristol, Scituate, Westerly, Middletown, Cranston, and Newport.[76]

The Rhode Island General Assembly, under increasing pressure

74. Howell to Welcome Arnold, Philadelphia, October 9, 1782, Charles Francis Jenkins Collection, M.O.C., Mss., H.S.P., Box 3; Howell to Foster, Philadelphia, October 12, 1782, Correspondence, Foster Collection, Mss., R.I.H.S.

75. Welcome Arnold to David Howell, Providence, September 17, 1782, Welcome Arnold Papers, Mss., J.C.B.L.; Bartlett, *Records*, IX, 612.

76. Three towns—Jamestown, Gloucester, and West Greenwich, all agricultural communities—initially favored the Impost. Every one of them changed its opinion by the time the Assembly voted in November. The fact that other town meetings have left no record of their deliberations is not surprising. Some of the records are no longer in existence, having been lost to the ravages of time, carelessness, and fire. In many cases, also, the towns made no record of their deliberations.

from outside the state, finally put the Impost amendment to a vote on November 1, 1782. After an extended reading of the anti-Impost letters of the delegates in Congress, a one-sided debate ensued, with critics of the amendment dominating the floor. When the speaker of the lower house finally put the question, there was not a single favorable vote. Before a crowded assemblage, the fifty-three deputies present voted to reject the Impost.[77] Within five months of this action, as a conclusive defiance of the Union, the General Assembly adopted a state Impost plan in which all revenues taken from Rhode Island's trade would benefit the state alone.[78] The first and most nearly successful attempt to amend the Articles of Confederation was thus defeated by the veto of Rhode Island; the nationalists in Congress, however, were not to accept this frustration of their carefully worked-out plans without a vigorous counterattack.

77. Arthur Fenner, Jr. to David Howell, Providence, November 5, 1782; Solomon Drowne to David Howell, November 4, 1782, Peck Collection, Mss., R.I.H.S., Box VII; Nicholas Brown to David Howell, Providence, November 5, 1782, Brown Papers, Mss., J.C.B.L.; *Newport Mercury*, November 9, 1782; *Providence Gazette*, November 2, 1782.

78. Bartlett, *Records*, IX, 630, 669; *Providence Gazette*, March 8, 15, 1783; John Brown to David Howell, Providence, November 5, 1783, [typescript copy], Manuscripts, R.I.H.S., Vol. 14, p. 27.

4

Congress Attacks
the Delegates

IT WAS DAVID HOWELL who was destined to face the wrath of the
nationalists after Rhode Island rejected the Impost. This was evident
even before the General Assembly's negative vote of November 1, 1782.

Early in the summer of 1782 Howell proceeded to Philadelphia to
represent Rhode Island in the United States Congress. His arrival was
unwelcomed, and he was treated with cool formality by his fellow
delegates. The new congressman was an acknowledged leader of the
anti-Impost majority in Rhode Island and as such was held to be the
"successful opposer of a ruinous & exploded system." Writing home to
his Quaker friend, the philanthropist Moses Brown, Howell complained of low spirits and moods of depression during his first weeks in
Congress, exacerbated, no doubt, by his unfriendly reception in Philadelphia. Never before had he been more dispirited, said Howell, and

never more "deeply oppressed with the weight of public affairs . . . than since I have been in this city."[1]

At the time of Howell's arrival in Philadelphia a special committee of Congress had been organized to look into the reasons for Rhode Island's and Georgia's delay in ratifying the Impost. The real target was Rhode Island. Upon learning of Howell's coming to the city, the committee immediately asked him to appear and testify. Howell accepted the invitation with caution but also "with pleasure," he noted, because he felt that it would give him a good opportunity to lay his views before Congress. Despite the hostile climate in which Howell found himself, with congressmen investigating Rhode Island's thinly veiled intransigence, he was forceful in his testimony. His appearance reaffirmed the views he had earlier expressed as the "Farmer" in the Rhode Island press, but now there was perhaps more emphasis on economic issues. The new congressman probably surmised that the polemics which favorably impressed Rhode Islanders would be of no avail in Philadelphia.[2]

Howell admitted that a large revenue would eventually arise from a duty on international trade. He felt this fund should be given over entirely to the states. Rhode Island, Howell observed, had suffered greatly in the war, and a tax on imported goods ought in justice to be used for the rehabilitation of the battered state. Important also was the possibility that tariffs might unnecessarily burden commerce, raise the price of foreign goods, and, by increasing the demand for domestic substitutes, raise the cost of American produce as well. He again reiterated the merchants' fear that the tax might fall upon the importer if uncertain commercial conditions made it impossible to pass the amount of the duty on to the consumer in the form of higher prices. Finally, Howell pleaded that the Impost was an unfair form of taxation, because Rhode Island bought more foreign products than its sis-

1. Howell to Brown, Philadelphia, August 6, November 6, 1782, Moses Brown Papers, Mss., R.I.H.S.; Howell to Nicholas Brown, Princeton, July 30, 1783, Brown Papers, Mss., J.C.B.L.; Howell to Welcome Arnold, Philadelphia, November 17, 1782, Edmund C. Burnett, ed., *Letters of the Members of the Continental Congress*, 8 vols. (Washington, D.C., 1921–36), VI, 543; Howell to Deputy Governor Bowen, Annapolis, April 19, 1784, William R. Staples, ed., *Rhode Island in the Continental Congress: With the Journal of the Convention that Adopted the Constitution 1765–1790* (Providence, 1870), p. 489.

2. Howell to Governor Greene, Philadelphia, July 30, 1782, Staples, *R.I. in the Continental Congress*, pp. 381–85. (The discussion above of Howell's presentation before the committee is taken from this long letter.)

ter states and would inevitably pay a disproportionate share of the nation's taxes.

The Rhode Islander returned to his political objections in a more restrained manner than in his performance as the "Farmer." Howell still maintained his basic conviction that a federal Impost impaired the sovereignty and independence of his state; he asserted that the administration of the system by federal officials—Howell had to forbear calling them "foreign" officials before Congress—operating within the borders of Rhode Island but uncontrolled by the General Assembly or the people, would infringe on the state's freedom. He reminded his listeners of the American predilection for evading duties on trade and of the political danger of the numerous agents and the "vast expenses" needed to prevent smuggling. Howell estimated that when all costs were counted it might well be that the Impost would not afford enough money to make the plan worth-while. Furthermore, the unaccountability of the federal government to the states for the use of these revenues and the perpetual nature of the grant made the proposed amendment even more inadvisable.

In a concluding argument, Howell called attention to the pending question of the western lands. Rhode Island long maintained that the vacant territory west of the mountains had become the property of all the states by virtue of the combined effort in winning the war. No single state could justly lay exclusive claim to any territory formerly held by the British monarch. Rhode Islanders had the dream that an enormous revenue might arise from the sale of western lands, perhaps enough to liquidate the costs of the war, and the General Assembly was under pressure from its Revolutionary soldiers to secure portions of the new domain as a bonus for their military service.[3] Howell asked whether it was expected that Rhode Island "would part with all the benefits of its maritime situation until some assurance could be obtained of a participation in common with other states in the back lands. . . ." He made very clear the state's continuing belief that, as long as other members of the Union persisted in their exclusive claims, Rhode Island should keep the advantages of its commerce for itself.[4]

3. William Ellery to Benjamin Huntington, Annapolis, April 3, 1784, William Ellery Letters, 1783–1790, Mss., R.I.S.A.; Captain William Allen *et al.* to Colonel Jeremiah Olney, Saratoga, November 10, 1783, Olney Papers, 1775–1820, Mss., R.I.H.S., I.

4. John Russell Bartlett, ed., *Records of the Colony of Rhode Island and Providence Plantations in New England*, 10 vols. (Providence, 1856–65), VIII. 365:

Before withdrawing, Howell suggested two changes in the terms of the Impost amendment which, by implication, although he never made this certain, would make the plan acceptable to his state.

> 1st. That each state retain the power of choosing the officers of the revenue to be collected within its jurisdiction;
>
> 2nd. That the revenue arising from this duty be carried to the credit of each state wherein it be collected respectively, and deducted from their annual quota of continental requisition.[5]

Both proposals were unacceptable to Congress. To Howell's mortification, even his fellow delegate from Rhode Island, Ezekiel Cornell, was unwilling to favor these changes. After Howell had completed his presentation, Robert Morris, who had listened intently and patiently during Howell's deposition, requested that his objections be put in writing and that a copy be sent to the Treasury Department. Howell complied with Morris' request, giving nine reasons, all economic in nature, for refusing to embrace the Impost. The political implications of the amendment were subdued even more, and the material disadvantages of the plan were highlighted.

In a long letter to Governor William Greene, Morris minced no words in assailing David Howell. He declared that a duty on trade was a sumptuary tax which fell on individuals in direct proportion to the amount of goods they bought. Consequently, there need be no unequal burden on Rhode Islanders because they could readily avoid the tax by reducing their purchases of imported articles. An Impost, therefore, was voluntary and not disproportionate. The Financier asked the governor to consider that the southern states were probably greater consumers of foreign goods than Rhode Island, and they had consented to ratify the Impost. Dealing with some of Howell's other strictures, Morris questioned whether Americans would evade a duty laid by their own representatives in Congress: "nothing can be more infamous than to defraud our government," he wrote, supposing infamy a bar to

---

letter from "A Plain Dealer," *Providence Gazette,* November 8, 1782; Charles Thompson, "Notes of Debates," [August 27, 28, 1782, in Congress], and "Observations" of James Madison, both in Burnett, *Letters,* VI, 341, 458.

5. Howell to Governor Greene, Philadelphia, July 30, 1782, Staples, *R.I. in the Continental Congress.*, pp. 381–85. See also Nicholas Brown to David Howell, Providence, August 26, 1782, Brown Papers, Mss., J.C.B.L., for a source and reaffirmation of Howell's views.

smuggling. He asserted emphatically that large revenues would arise from a tax on international commerce, and they should be credited to all the states because the funds would come from consumer purchases throughout the nation.[6]

Congress waited patiently for several months after hearing Howell's testimony, hoping against hope that Rhode Island would accede to the plan. Finally, their patience exhausted, the nationalists secured the passage of a congressional resolution, on October 10, 1782, calling upon Rhode Island for a definitive reply on the Impost.[7] The Rhode Island delegates, Howell and Jonathan Arnold, reported the congressional demand in their correspondence back home, but they remained adamant in opposition to the amendment.[8] They recounted again, for the benefit of Governor William Greene, the now time-worn arguments against the Impost, reverting as before to the alleged political dangers that would accompany ratification, freely telling of their dread of a loss of freedom and the tyranny of Congress. Although rumors cropped up early in November that the state had rejected the plan, there was no official word. Under the prodding of Alexander Hamilton and James Madison, Congress voted on December 6 to send a delegation to Rhode Island to urge ratification of the Impost.[9] In an official letter to Governor Greene, Congress declared that the very safety and

6. Morris to Greene, Office of Finance [Philadelphia], August 2, 1782, Staples, *R.I. in the Continental Congress*, pp. 388–91. Morris wrote several letters to Rhode Island in a vain attempt to get the state to change its stand. He reminded Governor Greene that Rhode Island alone held up the Impost, because Georgia, which had also failed to ratify the amendment, was occupied by Great Britain and not expected to participate in congressional and national politics until the war was over. He said, in addition, that while some states had ratified with reservations (and he knew that Howell had sent these reservations on to Rhode Island), the Impost would take effect as soon as Rhode Island signaled its acceptance. See Morris to Greene, Office of Finance [Philadelphia], January 14, September 3, October 17, 1782, Letters to the Governor. Mss., R.I.S.A., Vol. 17, pp. 73, 75; Vol. 18, p. 9.

7. Worthington C. Ford *et al.*, eds., *Journals of the Continental Congress, 1774–1789*, 34 vols. (Washington, D.C., 1904–37), XXIII, 643–44.

8. Howell and Arnold to Governor Greene, Philadelphia, October 13, 15, 1782, Staples, *R.I. in the Continental Congress*, pp. 393, 394–98.

9. Ford, *Journals of the Continental Congress*, XXIII, 769–72; Arnold and Howell to Governor Greene, Philadelphia, December 7, 1782, Staples, *R.I. in the Continental Congress*, p. 402; Alexander Hamilton and Ezra L'Hommendieu to Governor Clinton, Philadelphia, December 9, 1782, *Public Papers of George Clinton, First Governor of New York, 1775–1795, 1801–1804*, ed. Hugh Hastings *et al.*, 10 vols. (New York, 1899–1914), VIII, 57; *The Papers of Alexander Hamilton*, ed. Harold C. Syrett and Jacob E. Cooke, 11 vols. (in progress; New York, 1961—), III, 206–9.

security of the United States would be gravely affected by the defeat of the Impost.[10]

The Rhode Island delegates bitterly denounced the congressional deputation. "Unless the present measure is calculated for downright *coercion* or to *overawe & terrify* the little state of Rhode Island to adopt the impost against their *interest & judgment*," Howell said on the floor of Congress, "I am at a loss for its object." He affirmed that Rhode Island, "tho the *least* in the Union & the *last* to decide upon this Question will do so with *the Same deliberation & independence of* Spirit, *uninfluenced* by *the determination* of the others. . . ." [11] The members of Congress were advised to support constitutional measures rather than castigate Rhode Island for its reluctance to adhere to an amendment it considered nefarious.

While Congress was wrangling over the proposal, news arrived in Philadelphia of Rhode Island's rejection of the Impost.[12] Defeat brought no abatement in the ardor with which the nationalists fought for the Impost. If anything, the fact that minuscule Rhode Island blocked the plan resulted in a more intense effort to induce the state to change its mind.

Congress resolved, over the heated objections of Howell and Arnold, to send the delegation to Rhode Island as a "precaution," despite the state's unanimous veto. It also established a special committee, composed of Alexander Hamilton, James Madison, and Thomas Fitzsim-

10. Congress to Governor Greene, Philadelphia, December 11, 1782, Staples, *R.I. in the Continental Congress*, pp. 402–3; *Papers of Hamilton*, ed. Syrett and Cooke, III, 209–10.

11. Howell to Nicholas Brown, Philadelphia, October 30, 1782, Brown Papers, Mss., J.C.B.L.

12. Official news of Rhode Island's failure to ratify the Impost was contained in William Bradford, Speaker of the Assembly of Rhode Island, to the President of Congress, East Greenwich, November 30, 1782, Papers of the Continental Congress, State Papers of Rhode Island, Mss., N.A., pp. 526–29. The note was endorsed: "Read Dec. 12, 1782 and referred to Hamilton, Madison and Fitzsimmons." (See also Bartlett, *Records*, IX, 683–84; and Ford, *Journals of the Continental Congress*, XXIII, 783–84, 788–94.) The Bradford letter gave three basic and several minor reasons for the Rhode Island negative: (1) the tax would be unequal, bearing harder on the commercial and consuming states; (2) the duty would introduce into Rhode Island federal officers who were not recognized by its charter, and the duty was, therefore, unconstitutional; (3) Congress would not be accountable to the states for this fund, and "would become independent of their constituents, and so the proposed impost is repugnant to the liberty of the United States." Among the arguments in a minor key were: (4) Rhode Island had already contributed a disproportionate share into the national treasury; (5) each state must contribute its federal quotas as it saw fit and thereby keep its influence in national politics.

mons, to investigate the reasons given by the General Assembly for its repudiation of the Impost plan. A factor which contributed to these decisions was Pennsylvania's renewed interest in solving the vexing problem of the nation's finances by an assumption of the federal debt by the states, a course of action now more likely to succeed because of the Rhode Island veto.[13]

The report prepared by Hamilton, Madison, and Fitzsimmons rebuked Rhode Island for its states' rights intransigence, making very evident the nationalist spirit in which the Impost had been born. "The truth is," the committee contended, "that no Federal Constitution can exist without powers that, in the exercise, affect the internal police of the component members." There could be no Union, no satisfactory federal government, without substantial encroachment on the power of the states. This lesson, learned so hard, was incorporated as a cardinal principle in the Constitution of 1787. The report contradicted the idea that an Impost would destroy the federal balance between the nation and the states. "The measure in question, if not within the letter, is within the Spirit of the Confederation," it declared with firm conviction. "Congress, by that, are empowered to borrow money for the use of the United States, and by implication, to concert the means necessary to accomplish the end." [14] A broad interpretation of the United States Constitution, as noted earlier, saw the light of day long before the Federal period.

On December 22, 1782, the deputation for Rhode Island set out northward, hopeful of success. After no more than a half-day's journey, it returned posthaste to Philadelphia with the startling rumor that Virginia, after hearing of Rhode Island's veto, had rescinded its ratification. The following day, a chagrined Virginian, James Madison, dolefully told a thunderstruck Congress that his state had repealed its ratification. "The most intelligent members were deeply affected," Madison remembered, "and prognosticated a failure of the impost

---

13. Virginia Delegates to the Governor of Virginia [Benjamin Harrison], Philadelphia, December 10, 1782; and Samuel Wharton to the Delaware Council, Philadelphia, January 6, 1783, both in Burnett, *Letters*, VI, 559; VII, 2–3; Jonathan Elliot, ed., *Debates on the Adoption of the Federal Constitution in the Convention Held at Philadelphia in 1787; With a Diary of the Debates of the Congress of the Confederation; As Reported by James Madison, A Member, and Deputy from Virginia, Supplementary to Elliot's Debates,* 5 vols. (Washington, D.C., 1845), V, 13.
14. Ford, *Journals of the Continental Congress*, XXIII, 406–9; *Papers of Hamilton*, ed. Syrett and Cooke, III, 213–23; Staples, *R.I. in the Continental Congress*, pp. 404–11.

scheme, and the most pernicious effects to the character, the duration, and the interests, of the Confederacy." [15]

The Affair of the "Extracts"

Despite the antifederal action of Virginia, the episode of Rhode Island and the Impost did not die easily. Rhode Island was still accorded full credit for the amendment's defeat, and the animus of the nationalists was hard to contain. They needed only a pretext to vent their rage, and this was provided by David Howell, whose indiscretion with regard to the secrets of Congress prompted a concerted campaign to destroy his influence and thereby secure a change of policy in Rhode Island. As the secretary of Congress, Charles Thompson, revealed, "so long as Howellian politics prevail in that state, I have no hope of their doing any thing that will strengthen or support the Confederacy." [16] An attack on Howell, then, was a blow against states' rights.

The delegates who sat in the Continental Congress were under a general injunction not to make public the proceedings of the members. Since Congress combined executive and legislative responsibilities in its function as the national government, secrecy was essential, especially when diplomatic or military affairs were discussed. During the first years of the Revolution the bar of congressional secrecy worked well, but even then there were few delegates who did not violate the ban in one way or another. At the end of the war, with peace in sight, congressional discretion was thrown to the wind.[17] Moreover, many congressmen considered themselves ambassadors of sovereign

15. Elliot, *Debates*, V, 17–18. Jackson Turner Main, *The Antifederalists: Critics of the Constitution 1781–1788* (Chapel Hill, 1961), pp. 92–94, analyzes the motives for Virginia's repeal and suggests that even if Rhode Island had not vetoed the Impost request, Virginia would still have withdrawn its ratification.

16. Jonathan Arnold to Governor Greene, Philadelphia, March 28, 1783, Bartlett, *Records*, IX, 686; Jonathan Arnold to Welcome Arnold, Philadelphia, February 25, 1783, Emmet Collection, Mss., N.Y.P.L., Em. 557; Thompson to Jacob Read, Philadelphia, September 27, 1784, Burnett, *Letters*, VII, 573.

17. The astute Gouverneur Morris charged after Yorktown that "our pretended private business" was not private at all, and that it was "known and talked of in every one of the states." In this instance, nothing less than the nation's peace policies were a matter of public knowledge. See Edmund C. Burnett, *The Continental Congress* (New York, 1941), pp. 435–36; and Burnett, *Letters*, I, "Preface," viii.

states rather than independent representatives, and they believed it was improper to withhold any important information from high state officials back home. An occasional lapse from the pledge of secrecy, therefore, was quite common and often embarrassing.

At the same time the Impost struggle was taking place, the United States initiated a series of difficult negotiations in Europe in an effort to secure foreign aid in the form of loans and financial assistance. American diplomatic agents abroad sought to capitalize on the enthusiasm in several European nations for the American cause, an endeavor made more likely of success after the victory at Yorktown.[18] David Howell, in common with most congressmen, tried to keep his state informed of all important national affairs, including the diplomatic negotiations abroad.

In a private letter to John Carter, publisher of the *Providence Gazette,* Howell took the liberty of disclosing the details of a loan John Adams was negotiating in Holland, and he declared that American diplomats reported the nation's prestige was at the highest point in its short career of independence:

> Our foreign affairs are in a good Train. The national importance of the United States is constantly rising in the Estimation of European Powers, and the civilized World. Such is their Credit, that they have of late failed in no Application for foreign Loans—and the only Danger on that Score is that of contracting too large a Debt. Instead of regretting that our Credit was no better established by an Impost, rejoice it went no further.[19]

Carter proceeded to publish extracts from Howell's letter in his newspaper, and, following the practice of the time, this choice bit of news was reprinted in one form or another in many journals throughout the United States.[20] The allegations made in Howell's correspond-

---

18. R. R. Palmer, *The Age of Democratic Revolutions: A Political History of Europe and America, 1760–1800; The Challenge* (Princeton, 1959), pp. 327–28; William Graham Sumner, *The Financier and the Finances of the American Revolution,* 2 vols. (New York, 1891), II, 58.

19. Howell to Carter, Philadelphia, October 16, 1782, Burnett, *Letters,* VI, 509.

20. *Providence Gazette,* November 2, 1782—the day after the General Assembly failed to ratify the Impost—and February 1, 1783. Howell's extracts were anonymously published under the headline: "A Letter from a Gentleman in Philadelphia to his Friend in this Town, dated Oct. 16 [1782]." These extracts were reprinted in the *Boston Gazette,* November 10, 1782; the *Freeman's Journal* (Philadelphia), March 12, 1783; *Pennsylvania Packet* (Philadelphia), February 18, 1783; *Thomas's The Massachusetts Spy* (Worcester), October 16, 1783; and *The Connecticut*

ence greatly embarrassed the nationalist movement because they indicated that the financial problems of Congress were on their way to a satisfactory solution. For this reason Howell's indiscretion became a *cause célèbre*.[21] Howell's extracts challenged a fundamental premise of the nationalists in Congress—that the nation had reached a critical period in its development—and, if Howell was not refuted, these disclosures threatened to impede the congressional quest for greater power.

The affair of the extracts first came to the attention of Congress on December 6, 1782.[22] A member told of reading in a Boston newspaper, under a Providence dateline, parts of a letter purporting to have been written by someone in Philadelphia giving full details of American loans and diplomatic activities abroad. Suspicions as to the author were immediately fixed on David Howell. "It was imagined," Madison wrote in his diary of the debates in Congress, "that a detection of the person suspected would destroy in his state that influence which he exerted in misleading its councils with respect to the impost." [23] A nationalist from North Carolina, the physician Hugh Williamson, suggested that a committee be appointed to investigate the matter and report to Congress; his motion implied that there was reason to suspect that the honor and character of the nation, as well as the financial health of the country, had been adversely affected by the information contained in the extracts. Congress agreed to write to the governors of Massachusetts (where the publication first came to the attention of Congress) and Rhode Island, asking them to inquire into the possible source of these revelations. Samuel Osgood, a Massachusetts congressman, objected to the implication that a member from the Massachusetts delegation might have committed this offense, and he demanded that only the governor of Rhode Island be asked to proceed with an investigation.[24] The committee reported on December 12. It condemned the now notorious extracts as dangerous and erroneous, because they gave a false picture of the supposed health of American finance; the committee recommended that, since the information had obviously

Journal (New Haven), November 7, 1782. For other disclosures by Howell of confidential affairs in Congress see Howell to Nicholas Brown, Philadelphia, August 3, 1783, Brown Papers, Mss., J.C.B.L., and Howell to Welcome Arnold, Philadelphia, August 10, 1782, Welcome Arnold Papers, Mss., J.C.B.L.

21. Burnett, *Continental Congress,* p. 533.

22. Ford, *Journals of the Continental Congress,* XXIII, 769–72.

23. Elliot, *Debates,* V, 12. Important also is Jonathan Arnold to Governor Greene, Philadelphia, December 6, 1782, Bartlett, *Records,* IX, 676.

24. Ford, *Journals of the Continental Congress,* XXIII, 791–93.

come from a member of Congress, the erring member should be apprehended and his misrepresentations corrected. Everyone was already certain that the delinquent was David Howell.

The next day, on December 13, facing detection by an aroused Congress, Howell admitted that he had supplied the information which John Carter initially published.[25] When Congress again took up the subject of the extracts, it agreed that an investigation in Rhode Island was now superfluous. But Alexander Hamilton, still smarting over the Impost debacle, was anxious to make Howell's behavior a matter of public record. He insisted that the resolution rescinding the letter to Rhode Island indicate that an inquiry was redundant because Howell had confessed his indiscretion.[26] Howell and his colleagues, Jonathan Arnold and the newly arrived John Collins, protested that Congress had no right to call any member to account for information sent to his constituents. Such a step, they declared, would endanger freedom of debate in Congress, hamper liberty of the press, and make the sessions of the national legislature independent of the people.[27] Howell was particularly stubborn in declaring that he "had written nothing but what he believed and could prove from authentic documents in possession of Congress." Jonathan Arnold added insult to injury by taunting the nationalists with the statement that he had written similar letters, "and was then about to write to the state and should write the same again." [28] The Rhode Island delegates denounced the "inquisition" of David Howell and complained that his persecution was the result of opposition to the continental Impost, a stand which his constituents fully approved. "He considers himself their servant," Howell explained, "and to them alone is he accountable for his doing."

Although David Ramsay, delegate from South Carolina and historian of the Revolution, urged that the Rhode Islander not be made a martyr, Hamilton and other Impost men insisted that Howell's name be entered on the congressional journals as having written the alleg-

---

25. Elliot, *Debates*, V, 15.

26. *Ibid.*; Ford, *Journals of the Continental Congress*, XXIII, 812.

27. Bartlett, *Records*, IX, 682.

28. Letter from "A Countryman," *Continental Journal* (Boston), January 30, 1783. This long letter is the best source of information about the actual debates in Congress. The fact that it presented accurate information on what was said should indicate that congressional secrecy was honored as much in the breach as in the observance. This anonymous writer was glowing in his estimation of Howell and Arnold and their defiance of Congress. He saw the entire attack on the Rhode Island delegates as the result of "ministerial vengence," and a desire to destroy Howell's public career.

edly fallacious extracts. The nationalists recommended that the secretary for foreign affairs, Robert Livingston, transmit to the governor of Rhode Island a representative selection from the diplomatic mail so that the critical state of American affairs might be known to the people of the state.[29]

The impact of these proceedings, as David Ramsay predicted, strengthened Rhode Island's determination to uphold its position and continue an independent course without wavering. Jonathan Arnold told Governor Greene and other state leaders that the nationalists in Congress held out the Impost as the only way to save the United States from disunion and collapse. Given their convictions, Howell's unpopularity was not surprising. The Impost of 1781 "was extolled as the infallible, grand political catholicon, by which every evil was to be avoided and every advantage derived," Arnold remarked. "Of consequence, everything done in opposition to that darling measure placed the doer in the most obnoxious point of view." [30]

The extract controversy came to an inconclusive end. Congress sent selections from the nation's diplomatic correspondence to Rhode Island, but the General Assembly fully supported Howell's actions.[31] On both sides, the evidence was read in different ways. The Rhode Island Assembly was reassured that Howell's information accurately pictured the state of American finance, and it congratulated the delegates for their "meritorious service" to the state and the "cause of freedom in general." The nationalists in Congress found no joy in such adulation. Although the United States had been able to enter into new and substantial loans between 1782 and 1783,[32] they were convinced that noth-

29. Elliot, *Debates*, V, 15–16; Ford, *Journals of the Continental Congress*, XXIII, 822; Staples, *R.I. in the Continental Congress*, pp. 416–17. All the documents in this controversy, including the actions of Congress and letters of the delegates, may be consulted in Letters to the Governor, Mss., R.I.S.A., Vol. 19.

30. Arnold to Greene, Philadelphia, January 8, 1783, Bartlett, *Records*, IX, 677–79. See also the letters of Elias Boudinot and James Madison in Burnett, *Letters*, VI, 545, 549; VII, 92.

31. Elias Boudinot to the Governor of Rhode Island, Philadelphia, January 16, 1783, Papers of the Continental Congress, Letters of the President of Congress, Mss., N.A.; William Greene to the President of Congress, March 18, 1783, Papers of the Continental Congress, State Papers of Rhode Island, Mss., N.A., pp. 530–35. A printed version may be found in Bartlett, *Records*, IX, 654, 666–67.

32. See Davis R. Dewey, *Financial History of the United States*, 11th ed. (New York, 1931), pp. 47–48; Charles J. Bullock, *The Finances of the United States from 1775 to 1789, With Especial Reference to the Budget*, Bulletin of the University of Wisconsin, Economics, Political Science, and History Series, Vol. I, no. 2 (Madison, 1895), p. 147; *Secret Journals of the Congress of the Confederation*, 4 vols. (Boston, 1824), IV, 253.

ing less than a permanent revenue would save the country from disaster. The critical situation of the nation was the result of an ineffectual Congress and financial instability. The Impost, had it been ratified by all the states, would have given at least some satisfaction on these two counts. David Howell was deemed responsible for the amendment's defeat; hence the rancor of Congress when his indiscretion came to light.

Another Pretext

Bitterness over the Impost did not subside as the war came to an end in 1783. There would be no forgiveness on the part of the nationalists in Congress. A second opportunity to attack Rhode Island and its delegates soon materialized. In this instance, the proceedings were irresponsible and reflected the growing malaise in congressional affairs.

During the early summer of 1784 the qualifications of the congressmen from Rhode Island were called into question, and an energetic effort was made to expel them from the federal government. "Some young men pursue the object of taking away our seats in Congress," wrote Howell to Deputy Governor Jabez Bowen, "as if it were of the first magnitude." [33] The case in question arose from the fact that Rhode Island elected its delegates in May of each year, at the same time the freemen chose all the general officers, and they were authorized by a statute passed in 1777 to sit in Congress longer than a year if the General Assembly sent no new members to relieve them. These practices and the provisions of the act of 1777 antedated the Articles of Confederation and were followed after that constitution became operative in 1781. However, the Articles of Confederation required that delegates to Congress were to be elected annually, and their term of service had to commence in November, not May. Rhode Island's electoral procedure seemed to violate the nation's constitution. The congressional committee on qualifications reported that the laws under which the Rhode Island congressmen were elected were unconstitutional, being superseded by the Articles of Confederation, and their mandate to sit in the national legislature for more than one year was illegal.[34]

33. Howell to Bowen, Annapolis, May 22, 1784, Staples, *R.I. in the Continental Congress*, p. 513; Burnett, *Continental Congress*, pp. 605–6.
34. Bartlett, *Records*, VIII, 290–91; Ford, *Journals of the Continental Congress*, XXVII, 377–79; Staples, *R.I. in the Continental Congress*, pp. 500–509.

While Congress bemused itself with the happy possibility that the federal councils might soon be wiped clean for a time of Rhode Island and David Howell, the distressing fact became known that if the Rhode Islanders were expelled there would be no quorum and congressional business would cease. So the attack was dropped and the issue was compromised. In deference to the purists, Congress resolved that no state might authorize its delegates to serve for more than a year without re-election, nor could a term in Congress begin except in November. Having said this, Congress declared that the Rhode Island elections, nevertheless, were constitutional. The members reasoned that the May elections were legal because, though coming in the spring, they "presumed that the said election was intended to be conformable to the Confederation," and that the year of service was supposed to begin in November.[35]

This formula did not bring an end to complaints about the qualifications of the Rhode Island delegates. John Francis Mercer, a congressman from Virginia, continued to challenge the right of any Rhode Islander to speak in Congress on the ground that they were no longer members. For days on end the nation's representatives spent many precious hours discussing this issue.[36] In time the dispute between Mercer and the Rhode Island delegation took on the color of a personal vendetta, with Mercer and others trying to vindicate what they considered the aggrieved honor of Congress by having Howell and his colleagues expelled. So heated did the wrangling become that Mercer challenged the Rhode Islanders to a duel in an effort to resolve the controversy. The entire business of the qualifications of the Rhode Island congressmen, observed James Monroe, was carried on with more "indecent conduct" than he had ever before seen in the national legislature.[37]

Just what Mercer's motives were in pursuing this issue with such fanaticism are today obscured, but he was ambitious and, as Jefferson related, "afflicted with the morbid rage of debate, of an ardent mind,

35. Ford, *Journals of the Continental Congress*, XXVII, 385–86, 389–90. Details are given in Burnett, *Letters*, VII, "Preface," xliv–xlv.

36. Ford, *Journals of the Continental Congress*, XXVII, 411–18, 420–25, and 484–87; and Virginia Delegates to Governor Benjamin Harrison, Annapolis, June 4, 1784, Burnett, *Letters*, VII, 543–44.

37. David Howell to Deputy Governor Bowen, Annapolis, May 22, 1784, Staples, *R.I. in the Continental Congress*, p. 514; Monroe to Jefferson, Annapolis, May 25, 1784; for a sample of Mercer's distaste for Rhode Island, see Mercer to Jacob Read, Philadelphia, September 23, 1784; both letters appear in Burnett, *Letters*, VII, 536, 591–92.

prompt imagination, and copious flow of words. . . ." [38] He apparently wanted to obtain a high federal appointment, and his obsessive ambition led him to court popularity and renown by humbling stubborn Rhode Island—the Confederation's dragon. In the upshot of the conflict, Congress wasted weeks of its time debating an obviously sterile question. It seemed throughout this unprofitable battle that the federal system was coming apart. One member of Congress confided to Thomas Jefferson that the qualifications struggle

> has Produced great diversity of sentiment, and more altercation than I have ever seen either in Congress or any other place, so that I begin to seriously apprehend we shall be forced to adjourn and confess to the World that the division of our councils has prevented the adoption of those measures which the interest of the Union so loudly call'd for at our hands.[39]

Reaction in the States

In contrast to the prevailing sentiment in Congress, public opinion in the states was divided over Rhode Island's veto of the Impost. Where certain states had ratified the amendment with suspicion and reservation, Rhode Island's recalcitrance was accepted without criticism and, in some instances, applauded. In other places, however, particularly the army, Rhode Island was roundly condemned. The range of opinion revealed quite clearly that reform of the federal system and a new frame of government would come about only when the dire forecasts of the nationalists in Congress were everywhere accepted without doubt. Not everyone in 1782 was convinced that the Union was about to collapse; this was the most formidable barrier to unanimity on the proposal to strengthen the federal system. When the day arrived that found the majority of Americans certain that the Union was in desperate need of change, a new federal constitution would be inevitable.[40]

38. Burnett, *Letters*, VII, 501 n. 6; Jefferson to James Madison, Annapolis, April 25, 1784, *The Papers of Thomas Jefferson*, ed. Julian P. Boyd *et al.*, 17 vols. (in progress; Princeton 1950—), VII, 119.
39. Samuel Hard to Thomas Jefferson, Annapolis, May 21, 1784, Burnett, *Letters*, VII, 533.
40. In fact, the Rhode Island delegates told Thomas Jefferson that Rhode Island would never approve the Impost until all the states were fully in favor of a

News of the Impost's defeat was carried throughout the United States by the press and by private correspondence of the members of Congress. For the nationalists, Rhode Island had struck a crippling blow to the country's future; their enmity could hardly be restrained. Rhode Island was execrated as an "evil genius of America," whose opposition to the continental Impost "injured the United States more than the worth of that whole state." [41] Connecticut citizens were told that Congress should have "purchased" Rhode Island or even "annihilated" the state, because in either case the United States would have suffered far less than it did in consequence of the amendment's defeat.[42] John Montgomery summed up the anger of many congressmen by declaring that the "Cursed State ought to be erased out of the Confederation, and I was going to say out of the earth, if any worse place could be found for them." [43] While nationalists attacked Rhode Island as a "perverse sister," public creditors sadly contemplated the "denial of justice" which the state's veto represented. Without new sources of revenue, they believed their debts would never be paid. In the army, Rhode Island's intransigence was a matter for concern and condemnation. With insufficient supplies and inadequate provision made for the payment of salaries, bonuses, and pensions, the men of the Revolutionary battalions, especially the officers, looked forebodingly upon the rejection of a plan to give greater revenues to Congress.[44]

Not everywhere in the United States was the Rhode Island action denounced. For some the state was a savior. "Her name will go down

---

strengthened Union, without reservations. When that day arrived, they declared, "Rhode Island would not solely oppose the will of the whole union, but in that case would yield." Jefferson to Governor Benjamin Harrison, Annapolis, May 7, 1784, *ibid.*, pp. 518–19; Jefferson to James Madison, Annapolis, May 8, 1784, *Papers of Jefferson*, ed. Boyd, VII, 232.

41. *State Gazette of South-Carolina* (Charleston), June 1, 1786; "A Fable," *Exchange Advertiser* (Boston), February 11, 1786.

42. "Policy of Connecticut," No. II, *The Connecticut Gazette and the Universal Intelligencer* (New London), April 9, 1784.

43. Montgomery to Edward Hand, Carlisle, July 26, 1784, Burnett, *Letters*, VII, 575. For further commentary in Rhode Island see reprints in the *Newport Mercury*, March 13, 1784; a valuable sidelight also appears in Dr. William Gordon to Nicholas Brown, Jamaica Plains [Boston], December 22, 1783, Brown Papers, Mss., J.C.B.L.

44. Madison to Edmund Randolph, Philadelphia, November 19, 1782, *The Writings of James Madison: Comprising his Public Papers and His Private Correspondence, including Numerous Letters and Documents Now for the First Time Printed*, ed. Gaillard Hunt, 9 vols. (New York, 1900–1910), I, 262; Captain William Allen to Theodore Foster, Camp Highland, August 14, 1782, Correspondence, Foster Collection, Mss., R.I.H.S.

to posterity with the highest renown and honor," said a writer in the Massachusetts press, instructing the General Court on the benefit of Rhode Island's veto: "she hath saved America." [45] In Philadelphia, readers of the city's competitive newspapers witnessed a vigorous debate over the merits of Rhode Island's action and the Impost amendment in general. One observer, "Democritus," stated in the spring of 1783 that he fully accepted Rhode Island's stand and was convinced that the Impost would have irretrievably shifted the balance of federal-state relations in favor of the nation. "Before long and ere we are aware of the change, we should become one great republic, instead of a combination of small states," he opined. "Absolute monarchy would be the consequence." [46] For this reason Rhode Island and its doctrine of states' rights were praised.

A different response to the Impost controversy appeared in the New England states, where the vehement nationalist campaign against Rhode Island was itself censured. One publicist in Boston, who avowed neutrality on the Impost question, expressed his troubled surprise that Congress pursued the Rhode Island delegates with such determination.[47] The Connecticut Assembly, otherwise a warm advocate of the Impost proposal, attacked the proceedings in Congress against its eastern neighbor on Narragansett Bay. The Connecticut Assembly also questioned assertions by the nationalists that Congress had unspecified "implied" powers which it might exercise in order to accomplish its purposes; this concept of congressional authority was said to be subversive of the federal system and an infringement on the powers reserved to the states alone. A Connecticut congressman, Jeremiah Wadsworth, personally congratulated David Howell for his role in blocking the federal Impost. "Rhode Island had saved the liberties of America once," he said, "and perhaps she might again." [48]

David Howell was not timid in fostering sympathy for Rhode Island and understanding of its states' rights fears. He actively sponsored a national anti-Impost movement by calling on influential newspapers to publish his articles and other manuscripts critical of the proposed amendment. Though Howell met with some reluctance, he did manage to persuade the generally nationalistic printers to publish the

45. Letter of "Cato," reprinted in the *Providence Gazette,* February 15, 1783; see also the letter of "Agricola," *Connecticut Courant* (Hartford), December 10, 1782.
46. *Freeman's Journal* (Philadelphia), March 26, January 1, 1783.
47. Letter from "Probus," *Independent Chronicle* (Boston), February 20, 1783.
48. David Howell to Deputy Governor Bowen, Annapolis, February 5, 10, 1784, Staples, *R.I. in the Continental Congress,* pp. 447, 473–76.

materials which he supplied them in excess.[49] He was also anxious to secure the support of his colleagues in Congress, dispensing anti-Impost tracts among the members—sometimes by leaving them on their desks at the beginning of the day—and wrote of the articles being widely read. "Some Gentlemen in this City highly approve of them," Howell informed Theodore Foster. The Rhode Island congressman carried on an extensive correspondence with influential people in all the states, and his principles became a standard behind which the states' rights factions rallied.[50]

In the face of Rhode Island's opposition Congress was stymied in its first attempt to strengthen the federal government. The only course left to the nationalists was to accept the state's veto as incontrovertible and attempt to gain Rhode Island's assent to another amendment. The result was the Impost of 1783, which attempted to conciliate Rhode Island and other adversaries of a national tax on international trade by making several fundamental concessions to the states' rights outcry of 1781 and 1782. Congress sent the states an Impost plan that was specifically limited to a period of twenty-five years, thus making certain that federal taxes on trade would not be perpetual; the states were also empowered to nominate the collectors, who would be chosen by Congress from among the nominees.[51] "In renewing this proposition to the states," Congress observed, "we have not been unmindful of the objections which have hitherto frustrated the unanimous adoption of it." [52]

The new revenue amendment received little support in Rhode Island. With the entire population keyed to defend state sovereignty and individual liberty from the threat of an expansive Congress, there was little hope that an Impost would pass. Rhode Islanders spoke glow-

49. Howell to Foster, Philadelphia, October 12, 1782, Correspondence, Foster Collection, Mss., R.I.H.S. Howell's success may be measured by articles published in the *Freeman's Journal* (Philadelphia), November 6, 13, 20, December 4, 18, 1782; *Pennsylvania Packet* (Philadelphia), December 7, 12, 14, 19, 1782. Some of Howell's "Farmer" series was also printed in the *Independent Chronicle* (Boston), July 25, 1782; other anti-Impost essays appeared on August 1, 8, 15, 22, 24, 1782.

50. Howell to Foster, Philadelphia, November 11, 1782, Correspondence, Foster Collection, Mss., R.I.H.S.; William Gordon to James Manning, Jamaica Plains [Boston], September 2, 1782, Brown Papers, Mss., J.C.B.L.; Howell to Abraham Yates, New York, July 12, 1785, Abraham Yates Papers, Mss., N.Y.P.L.

51. Elliot, *Debates*, V, 40–41, 49; Ford, *Journals of the Continental Congress*, XXIV, 97–99, 126–28.

52. "Address and Recommendations to the States, By the United States in Congress assembled," *Newport Mercury*, June 14, 1783; and Alexander Hamilton to Governor George Clinton, Burnett, *Letters*, VII, 165.

ingly of the successful war that had been won by a weak Congress, lamenting the nationalistic amendments which represented a radical break from the virtuous days of the American Revolution. The new Impost was caustically denounced as a "deformed, aristocratic brat, Proteous like, changing its shape but not its nature, and again crying, with worse than crocodile tears to receive our embrace." [53] Almost to a man the majority in Rhode Island upheld a federal system in which the states were supreme.

The Impost of 1783 suffered the same fate as its predecessor. From Philadelphia the delegates in Congress, Jonathan Arnold and John Collins, gave witness to the state's unyielding opposition by attacking the plan when it was revived.[54] David Howell and William Ellery, completing the congressional delegation, also took an intractable position. As a fixed and general rule, they recommended, changes in the federal constitution should be studiously avoided. "One alteration in the Confederation may be a precedent," and the first amendment might lead to another "until that system, founded in the republican principles of the eastern states, shall be utterly annihilated." [55] The General Assembly shared these apprehensions. Ellery addressed the legislature on the subject of the dangers involved in admitting the slightest changes in the federal system; he declared that any nationalist advance would be a step toward the loss of liberty.[56] On July 1, 1784, the General Assembly again refused to ratify an Impost amendment. This time the vote was 52 to 12 in the lower house.[57]

An Overview

In this manner, on two separate occasions, Rhode Island was unwilling to strengthen the Union by enlarging the power of the central government. The fundamental motives which led the state to reject the Impost amendments were clearly revealed in the campaign used to de-

53. Letter from "The Plain-Dealer," *Providence Gazette*, May 10, 1783.

54. Collins and Arnold to Governor Greene, Philadelphia, April 23, 1783, Staples, *R.I. in the Continental Congress*, p. 435.

55. Ellery and Howell to Governor Greene, Princeton, February 8, 1783, *ibid.*, pp. 452–53.

56. Nathanael Greene to Robert Morris, July, 1783, quoted in George Washington Greene, *The Life of Nathanael Greene*, 3 vols. (New York, 1871), III, 524.

57. Bartlett, *Records*, X, 44–45; *Providence Gazette*, July 10, 1784; *Newport Mercury*, July 3, 1784.

feat the proposals. Rhode Islanders were convinced that the federal system, balanced under the Articles of Confederation in favor of the sovereignty of the states, was best designed to secure a free society. The road of nationalism, it was argued and believed, would end in despotism. Critics of the Impost amendments secured the support of the freemen with their imaginative political propaganda against the plans, stressing states' rights and appealing to the traditions of democratic and local self-government that characterized the structure of politics in Rhode Island. The Impost was particularly susceptible to attack because it was a revenue amendment that transferred the power of taxation in some degree from the states to the nation. Given the colony's experience during the Ward-Hopkins controversy and the lengthy quarrel with Great Britain, Rhode Islanders would not lightly alienate their power of the purse. In the town of Providence there was a maxim concerning taxation which stated: "Mankind are not to be trusted where they are interested against you." [58] This applied automatically against the national government, in whose interest it was to gain an independent and growing revenue; Rhode Islanders were simply not willing to trust the Congress. This explains why the townsmen responded with alacrity to the repeated invocation of the anti-Impost forces: "The power of the purse is the touch-stone of freedom in all the states. If the people command their own money they are free; but if their sovereign commands it, they are slaves." [59] This was good doctrine in town-oriented Rhode Island—doctrine that was popular, plausible, and sanctified by local experience.

In Rhode Island the merchants led the attack on the Impost amendments. They perceived that there were special economic advantages to be gained if the state could destroy the federal Impost, and because of this they took the front ranks in blocking the Impost amendments. There was a strong feeling that after so destructive a war, to which Rhode Island had contributed in excess of its just proportion, commerce should be left free to enjoy the profits of peace unburdened by tariffs. When it became certain that a revenue would be levied on trade, the merchants were determined that these funds be used to support the credit of the state. As the largest creditors of Rhode Island,

58. Providence Town Meeting, January 30, 1778, William R. Staples, ed., *Annals of the Town of Providence* (Providence, 1843) , p. 280. The same principle is stated in a letter from "A Lover of Liberty," *Providence Gazette,* January 25, 1783.

59. William Ellery and David Howell to Governor Greene, Princeton, September 8, 1783, Staples, *R.I. in the Continental Congress,* pp. 447–48; letter of David Howell, *Providence Gazette,* April 12, 1783.

they saw distinct benefits in a state Impost whose revenues were pledged to repay the state debts. An added factor in their opposition to the national Impost was the absence of a drawback provision in the proposed amendments, which would return the federal tax when foreign goods were re-exported from Rhode Island; without such a drawback—which was included in the state Impost—the merchants might find themselves forced to bear the entire cost of the tax if it could not be passed on to the consumer. Moreover, since Rhode Island was a port of entry for goods imported into Connecticut and other states, the proportion of a state duty that was borne by the consumer would, in effect, be a tax levied for the credit of Rhode Island on citizens of the United States.[60] This led Alexander Hamilton to charge in a congressional debate that the "true objection on the part of Rhode Island was the interference of the impost with the opportunity afforded by their situation of levying contributions on Connecticut, etc., which received foreign supplies through the ports of Rhode Island. . . ."[61] A final motive for men to oppose the Impost, one the merchants shared with every segment of public opinion, was the determination of Rhode Island to gain part of the revenues that might arise from the sale of western lands. The state claimed a proportion of this fund as its right, won in the common victory of the Revolution, and the state's leaders were resolved never to surrender any potential profits from tariffs until all individual state claims were surrendered to the nation.[62]

60. David Howell to Nicholas Brown, Philadelphia, September 19, 1782, Brown Papers, Mss., J.C.B.L.; "Policy of Connecticut," No. III, *Connecticut Gazette* (New London) , April 23, 1784.

61. Elliot, *Debates*, V, 52; Hamilton to Governor Clinton, Philadelphia, May 14, 1783, *Public Papers of George Clinton*, ed. Hastings, VIII, 179; *Papers of Hamilton*, ed. Syrett and Cooke, III, 261.

62. William Ellery to Samuel Dick, Newport, August 2, 1784, Burnett, *Letters*, VII, 575; letter from "An Old Son of Liberty," *Newport Mercury*, October 26, 1782; William Ellery to [Benjamin Huntington ?], Annapolis, April 3, 1784, Ellery Letters, Mss., R.I.S.A.

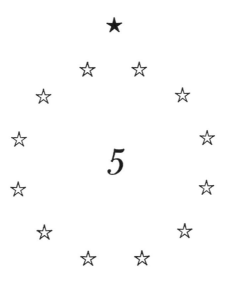

5

A Revolution in Rhode Island

IN ONE RESPECT the Impost struggle represented a high-water mark in Rhode Island's relationship to the Union. Never again during the Confederation era would the state be unified on the question of the national government. This did not mean, however, an end to Rhode Island's growing alienation from the United States. The depression which followed on the heels of independence after 1783 brought a deep and enduring split in Rhode Island politics; men divided over what to do about the crisis. The majority party in the state, the country party, hoping to sustain and protect its program of public relief, not only continued to refuse to strengthen the federal system, but it carried Rhode Island entirely out of the Union in 1789.

When peace came to the United States, an unparalleled prosperity was expected to succeed upon independence. This had been one of the main articles of the Revolutionary faith—to cast off the bonds that tied the colonies to Great Britain and receive a future of plenty in return. But prosperity did not come with peace; instead, freedom from

Great Britain brought with it dangers to the new nation's economic structure. Being unexpected, the economic decline was undoubtedly more dangerous.

The hard times of the first years of independence were the result of a commercial and agricultural depression that gripped the young country at the end of the Revolution. In large measure this depression was a commercial phenomenon.[1] It took little time after hostilities ceased for Great Britain to regain its dominant position in trade with the United States. This was not entirely to the disadvantage of the Americans. Apart from the quality and variety of British goods, which were highly esteemed by American consumers, British commercial firms had close ties with the leading American merchants and were able to provide favorable credit terms in order to encourage business with the former colonies. A tremendous expansion of trade with Great Britain occurred, with serious though predictable consequences for the new nation. Imports from Great Britain soared to £7,591,935 in the period from 1784 to 1786; exports, unhappily, lagged far behind at £2,486,058. The trade gap facing the United States exceeded £5,000,000, a sum beyond the ability of the Americans to sustain.[2] Ironically, the newly independent nation found itself reliving the colonial experience with the mother country. The United States was burdened with a severely unfavorable balance of trade. This dried up sources of capital at home and abroad, forced the American merchants into debt in Great Britain, and drained the states of their meager supplies of hard money.

The shortage of specie had a sharply deflationary impact upon the general price level in the United States. The conclusion of the war and the end of the extraordinarily high demand for goods and services had resulted in declining prices. Likewise, in adjusting to a world price level considerably below that of the United States in 1783, the collapse of domestic prices was speeded.[3] The flight of gold and silver abroad

1. The most recent accounts of the economic history of the Confederation are Merrill Jensen, *The New Nation: A History of the United States During the Confederation 1781–1789* (New York, 1950), pp. 177–244; Curtis P. Nettels, *The Emergence of a National Economy 1775–1815* (New York, 1962), pp. 45–64; and Gordon C. Bjork, "The Weaning of the American Economy: Independence, Market Changes, and Economic Development," *The Journal of Economic History*, XXIV (1964), 541–60.

2. Nettels, *Emergence of a National Economy*, p. 49.

3. Bjork, "Weaning of the American Economy," pp. 549–59.

also hastened the trend. In 1785, the wholesale price level was less than half what it had been in 1781,[4] bringing hardship to anyone who counted on a postwar boom. The downward plunge of prices held out a bleak future for American farmers, especially those in debt and those who sold on the world market. Mercantile interests were also endangered by the absence of specie and the downward spiral of the price level. Inadequate supplies of hard money, the most reliable medium of exchange, meant a contraction of the nation's credit network, upon which the merchants depended for sales and for financing their own ventures. Almost as distressing was the thought of future emissions of paper money. Mercantile debts abroad, especially those owed by New Englanders to British firms, were made wholly unmanageable by the drop in prices. Payment of these debts required that American shipments abroad increase greatly in order to achieve the former value of exports, which had been calculated at higher prices. This was not an easy task in a time of credit restriction, depression, and economic decline.

The depression fell with great impact upon Rhode Island. In the absence of an extensive back country producing a salable surplus, the economy of Rhode Island was precariously dependent on trade; without its earnings from commerce, the state's economic health was seriously threatened. For this reason the economic crisis of the United States appeared in Rhode Island with unwelcome harshness.[5] The first symptom that all was not well was the disappearance of hard money in 1784, the result of excessive foreign purchases by Rhode Islanders and inadequate earnings outside the state. So complete was the flight of specie abroad that in some instances internal business transactions reverted to barter, with merchants paying their laborers in commodities while they were obliged to accept the produce of Rhode Island farms in payment for purchases and debts. Business stagnated because of the

---

4. Anne Bezanson, *Prices and Inflation During the American Revolution: Pennsylvania, 1770–1790* (Philadelphia, 1951), traces the fluctuation of commodity prices throughout this period and provides an important insight into business and monetary conditions. The price level during the Confederation is given a detailed presentation in G. F. Warren and F. A. Pearson, "Wholesale Prices for 213 Years, 1720–1932," *Cornell University Experimental Station*, Memoir 142 (1932), pp. 6–10.

5. The most important and revealing study of the Rhode Island economic picture during the Confederation years is the work of James B. Hedges, *The Browns of Providence Plantations: Colonial Years* (Cambridge, Mass., 1952), pp. 287–305. Chapter 15 is appropriately entitled: "Back to London."

insufficiency of a circulating medium.[6] Merchants in Providence and Newport were particularly buffeted by falling prices, reduced margins of profit, declining sales, and huge debts owed to European firms; they found themselves facing an era of uncomfortable stringency. The merchants pleaded with their foreign creditors for further time and extensions before being required to meet their obligations. European factors, however, demanded prompt payment and refused to send more shipments to Rhode Island on credit. They were compelled, however, to bide their time until the Americans might again consolidate their affairs.[7]

On their part the Rhode Island merchants pleaded with those who owed them money in New England to supply the funds desperately needed to make overseas remittances. But American debtors merely echoed the same refrain of hardship and hard times which the merchants themselves had already given their European counterparts. One Massachusetts farmer, after receiving two requests for payment from his creditor, Moses Brown, wrote sadly that he would willingly pay what was due if he could collect his own debts.[8] The depression was thus a danger to creditors and debtors alike, for most men, regardless of their wealth or status, were one or the other in some degree. Even the General Assembly could not blind itself to the shortage of specie and the economic doldrums which that phenomenon represented. Rhode Island law held the town treasurer responsible for the amount of the general taxation laid upon his community; should the town default in meeting its assessment, the treasurer became liable to imprisonment until the tax was paid. Throughout 1784 and 1785, town treasurers petitioned the General Assembly for exemption from these penalties, insisting that their deficiencies were "owing to the great scarcity of money . . . and the inability of the delinquent individuals to pay without taking their stock." Many treasurers took the part of

6. Letter from "A.Z.," *U.S. Chronicle* (Providence) , September 22, 1785; Arthur R. Ross, *A Discourse Embracing the Civil and Religious History of Rhode Island* (Providence, 1838) , pp. 73–74.

7. Moses Brown to Champion and Dickinson, Providence, June 25, 1785; Benjamin Howland to Moses Brown, East Greenwich, January 9, 1785, Moses Brown Papers, Mss., R.I.H.S., Vol. V, Nos. 1275, 1204; John Brown to Moses Brown, Providence, November 27, 1786, Peck Collection, Mss., R.I.H.S., Vol. VIII, p. 10; Protheroe and Claxton to Christopher Champlin, Bristol, January 23, 1786; Lane, Son, and Fraser to Christopher Champlin, London, March 30, 1786, Wetmore Collection on Rhode Island Commerce, Mss., M.H.S.

8. Jacob Stafford to Moses Brown, Adams, May 6, 1784, Moses Brown Papers, Mss., R.I.H.S., Vol. IV, No. 1137.

their fellow townsmen. They complained that because of the drop in prices any man who was obliged to sell under the duress of tax collections would receive for his property, especially land, a sum hardly equal to its true worth in normal times.[9] In some cases, the returns from forced sales were still far short of what the taxpayer owed to the state. A feeling of injustice began to take hold of the countryside.

Paper Money Is Proposed

The depression of 1784–86 was not a unique experience in Rhode Island history, for the colony and state underwent several trying periods of economic stagnation during the colonial years. Most severe was the crisis of the mid-1760's. The depression of the Confederation period came with added hardship for two special reasons. The freemen had accumulated a relatively heavy private debt, and the state was burdened with the largest public debt in its history. The two problems, moreover, were interrelated.

For the people of Rhode Island the American Revolution was a mixed blessing, because prosperity went side by side with the war. Demand for the small amounts of agricultural and processed goods produced in Rhode Island was very strong, and the agricultural communities freely expanded their indebtedness, a particularly easy process in a period of rising prices. Few men thought that peace would bring hardship in its train; fewer still believed that anything but prosperity would be their reward for sacrifice. "With these prospects," wrote an observer, "the enterprizing and thoughtless undauntedly accumulated debts, pledged their lands, etc. without knowing what scenes of distress they were involving themselves and their families in." [10] The luxury of wartime became the bane of peace when the depression arrived, be-

9. John Russell Bartlett, ed., *Records of the Colony of Rhode Island and Providence Plantations in New England*, 10 vols. (Providence, 1856–65), IX, 441–42, 483, 497–99, 511, 593; X, 34, 43, 65, 124–25, 146–47. The scarcity of hard money was so marked that the treasury bills of Rhode Island, issued in anticipation of tax collections, circulated at great discounts. It was found that many town treasurers took advantage of the situation by using whatever specie they took in to purchase these bills at less than nominal values in order to submit them in lieu of hard money to the General Treasurer, pocketing the discount in the process. The legislature was forced to forbid this practice by statute (*Newport Mercury*, May 21, 1785; Bartlett, *Records*, X, 104).

10. Letter from "Brutus," *Newport Mercury*, August 21, 1786.

cause the private debt had been contracted at inflated prices and was never scaled down in value. For many the outcome was lawsuit and execution for breach of contract, which took away needed stock and lands at greatly depressed prices. These proceedings were denounced as the "inhumane extortions of rapacious creditors." [11]

Much more onerous, in this respect, was the public debt, which carried with it a relatively heavy peacetime tax load for the average freeman. War had been expensive. In doing its part during the Revolution, Rhode Island accumulated a large public debt, to say nothing of its financial obligations to the federal government. The internal debt of Rhode Island stood at more than $500,000 in 1786,[12] a large sum for a state with pre-Revolutionary expenses that averaged less than $5,000 yearly and whose citizens enjoyed their ante-bellum days practically free of taxation.[13] The burden of taxation weighed heavily during the lean years of the Confederation. Two youthful English travelers to North America, Robert Hunter, Jr., and Joseph Hadfield, on a debt-collecting mission and gentleman's journey for pleasure and experience, recorded that farmers in Rhode Island were "miserably poor" and generally in debt. They told of one farm, esteemed among the best in the state, where taxes were greater than profits drawn from the land.[14] Just as foreboding, in view of the hard times and grinding taxation, was the fact that the funds raised by the General Assembly were

11. *Ibid.*

12. An estimate of the state debt was made in 1787 by William Ellery, a knowledgeable Newport politician and commissioner of the loan office in Rhode Island. He calculated the total at £153,047 15s. 9½d., about $492,000 (Channing-Ellery Papers, Mss., R.I.H.S., Vol. IV, p. 13). Governor Arthur Fenner, Jr., approximated this estimate in 1790 when he put the figure of the state debt at slightly under £161,000, or nearly $545,000. For Fenner's calculations see General Treasurer's Accounts 1781–1792, Alphabetical Book No. 7, Mss., R.I.S.A., p. 321; and Bartlett, *Records*, X, 451–53. Another estimate, based on the dollar value of securities redeemed in paper bills and the sum confiscated by state law, yields a figure of $587,312.75. This is the final total which I have used in this book. For an earlier figure of £130,000 by Governor Greene in 1784, see *The Papers of Thomas Jefferson*, ed. Julian P. Boyd et al., 17 vols. (in progress; Princeton, 1950—), VII, 337.

13. John B. MacInnes, "Rhode Island Bills of Public Credit 1710–1755" (Doctoral dissertation, Brown University, 1952), pp. 149–50; Allan Nevins, *The American States During and After the Revolution 1775–1789* (New York, 1924), p. 539.

14. *Quebec to Carolina in 1785–1786: Being the Travel Diary and Observations of Robert Hunter, Jr., a Young Merchant of London,* ed. Louis Wright and Marion Tinling (San Marino, Calif., 1943), pp. 127–28; *An Englishman in America: Being the Diary of Joseph Hadfield,* ed. Douglas S. Robertson (Toronto, 1933), pp. 216–19.

insufficient to service the internal debt of the state and amortize its principal; and payments on the principal were scheduled to begin in 1786. Although the treasury drew in more than $70,000 each year in revenue, the state, after meeting administrative expenses and obligations to the federal government, had less than $18,000 for other uses.[15] Interest on the state debt alone was probably at least $25,000.[16] The years 1785 and 1786 were going to be decisive for Rhode Island. The state was compelled by the circumstances of the debt to increase its revenues by further taxation, to repudiate the sum, or to seek other ways of averting bankruptcy.

Pressed by the equally unattractive alternatives of accelerated taxation or repudiation of the public debt, Rhode Islanders turned to a middle way—an issue of paper money. This was nothing new, because Rhode Island had emitted eight issues of paper currency before 1763. The best evidence suggests that the bills gave a needed boost to the colony's economy by substituting for the lack of specie and providing sources of capital and credit for commercial interests.[17] The Anglican missionary of the Society for the Propagation of the Gospel in Foreign Parts, James MacSparran, was not far from the mark when he declared, with tongue in cheek: "Nova Anglia, the Rhode Islanders in particular, are perhaps the only people on earth who have hit on the art of enriching themselves by running into debt."[18] In 1784, when appeals for a paper-money emission were first heard again, it was hoped that similarly beneficial results would come from more paper currency. A recent precedent for paper bills was the American Revolution, when hundreds of emissions of paper currency served the nation and the states in winning the war. Legal-tender provisions of the Revolutionary emissions were similar to those of Rhode Island in 1786, which provided penalties for anyone who refused to accept the bills on a par with gold and silver.[19] Added encouragement also came from seven pa-

15. Letters to the Governor, Mss., R.I.S.A., Vol. 19, p. 47.

16. This estimate is based upon a state debt of $500,000, composed of $160,000 in 4 per cent notes and $340,000 in 6 per cent notes.

17. MacInnes, "R.I. Bills of Public Credit," particularly pp. 218–19, 237, 497, 554, 562; Bray Hammond, *Banks and Politics in America: From the Revolution to the Civil War* (Princeton, 1957), pp. 17–23.

18. Wilkins Updike, *History of the Episcopal Church in Narragansett, Rhode Island and, including a history of other Episcopal Churches in the State, with an Appendix Containing a reprint of a work now extremely rare, entitled "America Dissected,"* by the Rev. J. MacSparran, D.D. (Newport, 1847), p. 515.

19. For material on the United States consult Worthington C. Ford *et al.*, eds., *Journals of the Continental Congress, 1774–1789*, 34 vols. (Washington, D.C.,

per-money emissions by Rhode Island's sister states during the Confederation period, including three that made the currency a legal tender, indicating that Rhode Island was not alone in its use of a paper-money system to meet financial problems posed by the depression.[20]

A clear indication that the economic crisis would work a revolution in Rhode Island came after the first full year of peace, when the state reversed its position on the ever-present question of a federal Impost. Samuel Vernon, an important Newport merchant, reported to his friends in Philadelphia that there were many who regretted their "error" in twice refusing to strengthen the national government and were suffering for their ill-considered "imprudence and obstinacy." [21] Presumably the financial collapse facing Congress and Rhode Island convinced the merchants that a stronger federal system was one way out of the crisis. In February, 1785, the General Assembly decided to accede to a congressional request for an Impost. The state reserved to itself the appointment of those federal officers who served in Rhode Island. The Assembly also wished to retain part of the revenues to pay its own internal debt and that portion of the federal debt owned by Rhode Islanders. Any excess of money after these payments would go to the national government.[22] The Rhode Island grant was designed to guarantee repayment of the public securities held by Rhode Islanders while strengthening the federal system. The amendment passed in the lower house by 49 to 18, a substantial majority.[23] Soon afterward, the

1904–37) , IV, 149; Albert S. Bolles, *The Financial History of the United States, From 1774–1789: Embracing the Period of the American Revolution* (New York, 1879) , pp. 174–89; and William Graham Sumner, *The Financier and the Finances of the American Revolution,* 2 vols. (New York, 1891) , I, 46, 61. For Rhode Island see Bartlett, *Records,* VII, 370, 374, 584, 591–92; *Providence Gazette,* September 16, 1775. Legal tender provisions in Rhode Island were suspended in May, 1780; the penalty acts were repealed in February 1780.

20. Letter from "A Friend to Good Government," *U.S. Chronicle* (Providence) , June 8, 1786; Jensen, *New Nation,* pp. 313–26; Nettels, *Emergence of a National Economy,* pp. 75–88.

21. Samuel Vernon to Josiah and Samuel Coates, Newport, June 4, November 3, 1784, Gratz Collection, Mss., H.S.P., Case 17, Box 2.

22. Bartlett, *Records,* X, 87–88; *Newport Mercury,* March 12, 1785. For the actions of other states see Ford, *Journals of the Continental Congress,* XXX, 70–72; and the *Newport Mercury,* February 27, 1786. The Rhode Island ratification of the Impost amendment limited the grant to twenty-five years; it provided that the amendment would come into force when all the states voted in its favor and had repealed any duties they might levy in interstate trade.

23. *U.S. Chronicle* (Providence) , March 9, 1786. The eighteen negative votes in the House of Deputies were probably less than a full measure of the sentiment against the Impost in Rhode Island at this time. A Cumberland Town Meeting

General Assembly confirmed its about-face on the Impost by voting to give Congress full authority to regulate foreign trade, a step which the state's leaders hoped might lead to the establishment of an effective system of mercantilism for the United States.[24]

Further confirmation of this growing *rapprochement* between Rhode Island and the Union is indicated by the state's acceptance of an invitation to attend the commercial conference called to meet in Annapolis, Maryland, during the summer of 1786.[25] The difficult economic situation seemed to be turning Rhode Island toward the nation. The Rhode Island commissioners, Deputy Governor Jabez Bowen of Providence and the Newport sea captain Samuel Ward, Jr., son of the former governor, did not arrive in time to attend the fateful Annapolis Convention. On their way south they learned in Philadelphia that the partial representation at Annapolis had already adjourned. But the delegates nevertheless considered it their "duty" to gather for the Assembly as much information as they could concerning the situation of American trade.[26]

Ward and Bowen found to their dismay that the commercial life of the United States was sorely beset by the deepening depression and the inroads of foreign competition. They noted that the commerce of the new nation was dominated by foreigners and, far more alarming, that

---

(Mss., August 12, 1786) still denounced the amendment as a step which "Doth not Harmonize with the second Article of Confederation and perpetual Union." In West Greenwich (April 19, 1786) and Smithfield (April 19, 1786), the town meetings were hostile to the Impost ratification. See Papers Relating to the Adoption of the Constitution, Mss., R.I.S.A., p. 126; William R. Staples, ed., *Rhode Island in the Continental Congress: With the Journal of the Convention that Adopted the Constitution 1765–1790* (Providence, 1870), pp. 558–59.

24. Bartlett, *Records*, X, 130, 180; *Providence Gazette*, March 12, 1785. The state also enacted its own navigation system while awaiting congressional action; this system was designed to favor domestic producers and shippers, and to force Great Britain to end its discrimination against the United States. Bartlett, *Records*, X, 140; *Providence Gazette*, July 23, November 12, 1785; *Newport Mercury*, July 30, 1785.

25. Patrick Henry to Governor Greene, Richmond, Va., February 23, 1786, Letters to the Governor, Mss., R.I.S.A., Vol. 20, p. 20; other manuscript letters pertaining to the Annapolis convention may be found on pp. 27, 31–32, 48, 56; Bartlett, *Records*, X, 203–4. Jabez Bowen and Christopher Champlin, the latter a prominent Newport merchant, were chosen to represent the state. The Assembly declared that the purpose of the meeting was "to consider how far a uniform system in their commercial regulations may be necessary to their [the United States'] common interest and permanent harmony." Champlin resigned his commission and was replaced by Samuel Ward, Jr. (Bartlett, *Records*, X, 206).

26. Report of the Commissioners [Samuel Ward, Jr., and Jabez Bowen] to the Annapolis Convention, October 14, 1786, Reports to the General Assembly, Mss., R.I.S.A., Vol. 41, p. 111.

the carrying trade among the states themselves, from which Rhode Island merchants earned considerable revenue, was being alienated to European shippers. The commissioners were disturbed to see harbors in New York and Philadelphia crowded with foreign vessels to the exclusion of American ships. The basic problem, they contended, was the want of national regulation of international trade. State laws varied considerably, offering little likelihood of a united and effective front against competitors from the Old World. In addition, while the states failed to protect American commerce at home, the United States was powerless to end discrimination against American merchants in foreign ports. The best solution was some formula by which Congress would regulate international commerce and guarantee free trade among the United States.[27]

Controversy

New and radical changes in the regulation of trade, however, could do little to soften the impending financial collapse in Rhode Island and economic hardships that affected the freemen. "Respected friend," wrote a correspondent to Moses Brown, "The people are almost drove to Desparation." [28] Fault for the crisis was fixed on the merchants. The depression was said to have come because excessive purchases abroad by the greedy merchants had glutted markets with foreign goods, driven prices downward, and drained the states of their stock of specie. The shortage of hard money—which most Rhode Islanders believed was the key to the crisis, not its symptom—was thus laid at the feet of the merchant class. Many felt that the state Impost and the proposed reform of mercantile regulation in the United States were only intended to assure, at any cost, repayment of the public securities. The general sentiment for public relief was hardly affected by the reforms envisaged by the General Assembly. Instead demands were heard for an emission of paper money, a time-honored Rhode Island remedy,

27. See also Nicholas Brown to David Howell, Providence, March 6, 1785 [typescript copy], Manuscripts, R.I.H.S., Vol. 14, p. 53; David Howell to Governor Greene, New York, October, 1785, Staples, *R.I. in the Continental Congress*, pp. 537–38; John Brown to Samuel Ward, Providence, September 12, 1786, Ward Manuscripts, R.I.H.S., Box 3.

28. Unknown writer to Moses Brown, 1786, Moses Brown Papers, Mss., R.I.H.S., Vol. 5, No. 1452.

which might be loaned by the government at low interest rates and, as a legal tender, lighten the weight of public and private debts.

The first reaction of the merchants to the proposal was to reject it out of hand. Paper money was said to be a "perversion of Law, of justice, and of humanity." [29] A dangerous political crisis was thus added to the economic problems of the state. An issue of paper bills, one freeman wrote, would be more injurious to his town than "fifty ravenous wolves let loose among our sheep and cattle." Attacks on the plan picked up momentum with charges that paper money would surely depreciate in value and involve Rhode Island in greater troubles than those it already labored to alleviate. Some alleged that every previous Rhode Island paper currency had depreciated, including the most recent Revolutionary issues in the state and the nation. Any loss of value in the money ultimately benefited only parasitical members of society —the speculators and the dishonest. Those opposed to the proposed currency declared that a paper medium would serve no useful purpose in Rhode Island. The very "apprehension" of a forthcoming emission worsened the crisis by hastening the disappearance of hard money in the state.[30] The last word on the subject, as the merchants saw it, was probably best epitomized in a pamphlet by Thomas Paine, extracts of which were published in the state's newspapers. "Money is money and paper is paper," said Paine simply. "All the inventions of man cannot make them otherwise. . . . Gold and silver are the emissions of nature; paper is the emission of art." [31] The only real way to end the economic crisis was individual self-sacrifice, the elimination of luxury, and a willingness to root out immorality and serve the public good. Financial success and sanity required a harsh regime.[32]

Advocates of the paper medium in the country towns were probably dismayed by the acrimonious tone of the merchants on the paper-money question, but they were not dissuaded and launched a counterattack against the recriminations of their opponents. Repeatedly they insisted that the burden of taxation was unbearable and that the depression amounted to an economic calamity. Only an emission of paper money would give hope to the freemen. Critics of the mercantile

29. Letter from "A Bushman," *Newport Mercury*, January 24, 1786.

30. Letters from "A.Z." and "Zeno," *Providence Gazette*, February 22, 1785 and February 25, 1786; letters from "A Farmer" [Benoni Pearce] and "A Friend to the State" in *U.S. Chronicle* (Providence), March 3, 1785, March 2, 1786.

31. *Newport Mercury*, May 15, 1786; *U.S. Chronicle* (Providence), May 18, 1786; *Providence Gazette*, May 20, 1786.

32. Letter from "A Real Friend to the Public," *Newport Mercury*, March 12, 1785.

stand argued that paper money was not an innovation in New England; it had been virtually the only currency throughout the colonial period. One advocate of the plan contradicted statements that the money would depreciate by asserting that "this government has known paper money that did not depreciate, that brought the possessor as many silver shillings as were expressed on its face." [33] Obviously, Rhode Island's experience with paper money was clearly remembered by both its proponents and antagonists, though with different interpretations.

Partisans of the proposed emission seemed particularly aroused by warnings concerning the fate of orphans and widows who, living on fixed incomes, faced destitution because of possible fluctuations in the value of paper money. This argument was denounced as unfounded, hypocritical exaggeration. Paper-money men claimed that greater suffering would be caused by lawsuits and executions for debt than might ever follow from a depreciated paper currency. Reassuring in this regard were the emissions of other American states, which were praised as opportune examples of justice and good fortune. Six American states, besides Rhode Island, showed how false and self-serving were the mercantile prophecies. "Are the people of Pennsylvania all rogues, has the divine wrath burst upon their heads?" asked an adherent of the currency. "We are told they have paper money." [34] The paper-money forces confronted their critics with the thesis that paper bills were far better than the absence of any medium of exchange. Paper money was not desired in preference to silver, "but merely in preference to none at all." [35]

Those who demanded paper money also considered the problem of the state debt and the burden of taxation that accompanied it. Some argued that the debts should be redeemed at less than their nominal values, possibly in depreciated paper currency.[36] When counterarguments were presented that holders of the debts were entitled to receive full value for their securities, paper-money spokesmen did not object in principle; but they believed this standard was equitable and valid only where "no cheat, fraud, error, or mistake had intervened . . . in obtaining a security." [37] Letters in the newspapers asserted that specu-

33. Letters from "A Friend to the Public," *ibid.*, January 30, February 13, 27, 1786.
34. *Ibid.*, January 30, 1786.
35. *Ibid.*, February 13, 1786.
36. Dialogue signed, "A.B.," *U.S. Chronicle* (Providence), August 10, 1786.
37. *Ibid.*

lators had accumulated the greatest proportion of the Rhode Island state debt at inflated prices; to repay them in paper money was felt to be an act of justice, even if the bills depreciated.[38]

A particular point of grievance was the transfer to speculators at less than face value of the securities issued to Revolutionary soldiers in place of pay and bonuses. The combatant "Soldiers' Soliloquy," printed in the Rhode Island press, summarized in doggerel verse a conviction which contributed great moral force to the paper-money movement:

> In times of war, we fought and bled,
> For fine times which they promised;
> And since the jewel we did gain,
> We'll bleed again, or it sustain.
>
> Stock-jobbers did not fight at all,
> Hawkers and sharpers got our all;
> And now we'd rather die like men,
> Than be slaves to such as them.[39]

In response, there were suggestions that the loss in value for soldiers and other creditors of the state was the responsibility of the General Assembly, not of honest purchasers who advanced desperately needed funds to those who despaired of repayment.[40] The great merchant, John Brown, reputed to be a speculator in soldiers' certificates, was cursed because of it when he ventured forth one day in a magnificent new carriage. As he passed by a cooper's shop, a workman called out in an audible voice: "Soldiers' blood makes good varnish." Brown never used the carriage again.[41]

Evidence that exists today does show that contemporary concern over the accumulation of the state debt by a small number of persons,

---

38. Letters from "Q.Z.," "A Real Farmer," "Lycurgus," all, respectively, in *ibid.*, September 22, 1785, February 23 and March 2, 1786, March 13, 1788. See also the letter from "A Warm Friend to the Liberties of Mankind," *ibid.*, April 12, 1787.

39. *Ibid.*, August 1, 1786.

40. Letter of "Cassius," *Newport Mercury*, August 21, 1786. "Cassius" wrote: "It was not the *purchasers* that occasioned it [the sale of the soldiers' securities] but the *necessity* they were under of selling them. What would the Soldiers have done if no body had appeared to purchase. Would not their case have been worse? . . . You have only mistaken the *effect* for the *cause*. The people at large would neither provide a fund by taxation nor the five per cent. impost. Therefore *all* the credit they had was by the *purchasers*."

41. Isaac Putnam Noyes, *Reminiscences of Rhode Island and Ye Providence Plantations* (Washington, D.C., 1905), pp. 3–5.

chiefly merchants, had a real basis. A substantial proportion of the Rhode Island securities was in the hands of a few men and companies —gathered up, everyone presumed, at attractive prices.[42] In 1784, when the state debts were consolidated and refunded, they were divided into two major categories of securities: £50,665 3s. 1¾d. carried interest at 6 per cent; £46,071 4s. 6d. bore interest of 4 per cent.[43] The 6 per cent

42. Concentrated ownership of Rhode Island securities by a small group of people is reasonably well established by the evidence given above. This evidence, however, is not at all conclusive with regard to speculation. Inasmuch as the debts were negotiable instruments of credit and the largest state creditors were merchants and businessmen with constant and changing needs for capital funds, it would have been amazing if some speculation had not occurred as a normal function of economic life. The problem of speculation, therefore, resolves into a matter of *degree* and *price*. Here firm conclusions are hazardous because the evidence is incomplete. It can be inferred, on the basis of the financial records which I have examined, that there was moderate speculation and profits made by those who held the Rhode Island state debt after 1790. One might qualify this further by noting E. James Ferguson's finding that there was a relatively low rate of transfer of federal securities in Rhode Island compared to other states. Here, again, this should suggest that the *degree* of speculation in Rhode Island was perhaps less than elsewhere and that profits were also less, not that speculation did not occur (E. James Ferguson, *The Power of the Purse: A History of American Public Finance, 1776–1790* [Chapel Hill, 1961], p. 281).

43. Lists of Notes Issued for Consolidating the Securities Issued from the General Treasurer's Office, Sept., 1782–June, 1784, Mss., R.I.S.A. These records include account books documenting the last consolidation of the Revolutionary war debts of Rhode Island and lists of those who owned the federal debt in Rhode Island. The information and tables above are derived from tabulations in these materials. This period between 1782–1784 represents the last consolidation of the state debts initiated by the General Assembly—if one does not include the paper-money system of 1786 as an effort to accomplish this end. There were many attempts to devalue and consolidate the securities of Rhode Island before 1782; between 1777 and 1782, the manuscript records of the legislature document nineteen separate attempts by the state to refinance and reduce its indebtedness. A number of other classes of securities were later added to the sum owned by the state, bringing the total debt to just under £161,000. There were as many as twenty different types of Rhode Island securities; each classification had its own generic and descriptive title, and bore interest at either 6 or 4 per cent. These titles, which give the genesis of each debt classification, may be examined in An Act making Provision for the transfer of the Stock of the United States, belonging to this State, to individual Creditors thereof, Rhode Island Records, Mss., R.I.S.A., Vol. 14, p. 613; Abstracts of the State Debt, Nos. 1 and 3, R.I.S.A.

The tables that follow are patterned after those developed by E. James Ferguson in *Power of the Purse*. A comparison with Ferguson's table of ownership of the federal securities in Rhode Island indicates (despite dissimilar monetary amounts and units of account) that the concentration of ownership of the 6 per cent Rhode Island notes follows the general distribution of the federal securities; the 4 per cent Rhode Island notes had a distinctly less concentrated ownership in the highest amounts. When similar studies of other state debts are available, a further comparison among all the state and federal debts may be possible.

TABLE 1. OWNERSHIP OF THE 6 PER CENT
RHODE ISLAND SECURITIES, 1784

AMOUNT OWNED	NUMBER OF PERSONS	PER CENT OF TOTAL PERSONS	COMBINED VALUE OF HOLDINGS	PER CENT OF TOTAL HOLDINGS
£500 and Over	16	3.6	£24,220	47.8
£100 to Under £500	81	18.2	15,747	31.1
£50 to Under £100	66	14.8	4,600	9.1
£20 to Under £50	149	33.5	4,856	9.6
£1 to Under £20	133	29.9	1,242	2.4

(All holdings have been rounded off to the highest £.)

TABLE 2. OWNERSHIP OF THE 4 PER CENT
RHODE ISLAND SECURITIES, 1784

AMOUNT OWNED	NUMBER OF PERSONS	PER CENT OF TOTAL PERSONS	COMBINED VALUE OF HOLDINGS	PER CENT OF TOTAL HOLDINGS
£500 and Over	7	.7	£ 5,416	11.7
£100 to Under £500	90	8.6	17,078	37.1
£50 to Under £100	125	11.9	8,526	18.5
£20 to Under £50	273	26.1	4,417	9.6
£1 to Under £20	551	52.7	10,634	23.1

(All holdings have been rounded off to the highest £.)

securities were owned by 445 creditors, the overwhelming majority of whom held amounts over £20. A few big claimants held the bulk of the 6 per cent notes. The 97 largest owners held more than three-quarters of the entire sum; 10 individuals and companies, including the most important Rhode Island merchants, owned £20,149, almost 40 per cent of the 6 per cent notes. (See Table 1.) The 4 per cent securities were held by 1,046 creditors of the state, making for a wider distribution than in the case of the 6 per cent notes. There were 949 persons who held less than £100, 551 less than £20, with only 7 creditors who owned more than £500. Mitigating this pattern of a broadly based creditor class were the seven largest owners of the 4 per cent securities, including John and Nicholas Brown and Clark and Nightingale, who held more than one-tenth of the total amount. (See Table 2.)

Similarly, the assumption of the Rhode Island state debt by the United States after 1790 revealed a concentration of securities in the hands of a few creditors, most of whom were either merchants or mercantile firms.[44] The full amount of the Rhode Island debt presented to the Treasury Department came to $344,282.78. The Brown family of Providence, or companies with which it was connected, owned $70,881.86 of this debt, slightly over one-fifth of the entire sum. Fifteen subscribers made individual claims for over $5,000, totaling $172,365.50, more than half of all the debts assumed by the United States in Rhode Island. Moreover, the financial records of the assumption operation gives evidence of speculation in Rhode Island securities. The Providence firm of Brown and Benson owned no securities in 1784, but they subscribed $6,036.73 in 1790; Welcome Arnold, the prominent Rhode Island entrepreneur, held £320 15s. 9d. in 1784 (about $1,068) and increased his investments to $17,813.21; John Smith of Johnston added $8,400 to his holdings by 1790; John Brown's totals rose from £2,272 14s. 5¼d. (approximately $7,369) to $26,943.82 in 1790.

The relationship between the paper-money movement and the problem of Rhode Island's securities was direct. Paper-money spokesmen intended to redeem the state's entire debt in paper bills. The possibil-

44. All the records of the funding and assumption of the federal and state debts in Rhode Island may be found in Rhode Island Records, Accounts for the Loan of 1790, 1790–1835, 32 vols., Mss., "Old Loans" Records of the Bureau of Public Debt, Records Group 53, N.A. The tabulations above are taken from the summary lists in Vol. 454.

ity (or even probability) that the paper money would depreciate did little to blunt the force of this movement for public relief. Depreciation made the plan all the more equitable, because the securities were said to be worth more in 1786 than the goods and services exchanged for them at inflated prices in the Revolution; besides, the freemen were alarmed over the supposedly unreasonable profits which speculators would win if the debt was paid at face value in gold and silver. Paper-money exponents suggested that the state debt be liquidated in four quarterly payments with the new currency; the usefulness and value of the money would be protected by its legal-tender status and acceptability in payment of taxes.[45] In this way, if each quarterly assessment by the General Assembly was more than the value of the securities redeemed, a single emission of paper bills might serve to liquidate the entire state debt.[46]

The Struggle in the Towns

The contest over the proposed paper-money emission dominated the public press and political councils throughout 1785 and early 1786. The most important dimension of the controversy took place in the towns, for the town meeting was the real fulcrum of political power in the state of Rhode Island. Should enough of the towns favor the widely agitated plan to print paper money, the General Assembly would have to pass into law an emission of paper currency.

The battle commenced as early as 1784, when the southern towns of Westerly and Hopkinton appealed to the state legislature to authorize a new issue of paper money.[47] This call coincided with the Washington County conventions that met to discuss the question of an equal representation for all the towns in the General Assembly. The issue of

45. Johnston Town Meeting, Mss., February 17, 1787; "A Dialogue between Obadiah and Timothy," and letters from "A Tradesman" and "A Friend to the Present Administration," in the *U.S. Chronicle* (Providence), February 16, 1786, February 12, March 12, 1789.

46. An appraisal of the Rhode Island paper-money system and the first to develop its relationship to the public securities is Forrest McDonald, *We the People: The Economic Origins of the Constitution* (Chicago, 1958), pp. 328–30; see also Ferguson, *Power of the Purse*, pp. 243–44. MacInnes, "R.I. Bills of Public Credit," p. 239, reveals that in 1729 a similar plan was suggested to redeem the British national debt in paper money, and later to recall the bills by taxation.

47. Hopkinton Town Meeting, Mss., April 24, 1784; Westerly Town Meeting, Mss., February 20, 1784.

paper money was thus put squarely before the representatives of the
southern, agricultural towns and was doubtless debated by the delegates, who in turn carried the suggestion back to their own constituents. While this first demand for a paper medium found little support
in 1784, the idea gained favor as the economic crisis of the Confederation worsened in 1785. By the spring of 1786, a majority of the towns
and a majority of the members of the state legislature were convinced
that paper money was a necessity.[48] A paper-money emission was now
inevitable.

Arguments for the paper-money proposal in the town meetings
usually began with a recital of the economic hardships brought by the
depression and the absence of specie in Rhode Island. Joined in importance and emphasis was the problem of the state debt and the tax
burden which the debt required. The freemen seemed sure the state
was on the verge of collapse.

In a formal petition to the General Assembly, the town of Cumberland declared that the disappearance of hard money made it impossible for the people to meet their financial obligations. In order to
ameliorate the crisis, the town recommended a paper emission as "the
only means, in the opinion of your Constituents, of relieving them from
their present distress." [49] The town of Smithfield was much aroused
about the public debt, state and federal, especially the so-called
"Heavy and Unjust Taxes" collected to pay the interest on these secu-

48. In addition to the towns cited above, Hopkinton and Westerly, the following
communities also favored the paper-money emission according to their manuscript
records and information in Papers Relating to the Constitution, Mss., R.I.S.A.:
Cranston, February 18, 25 (all of these citations are for 1786) ; Cumberland,
February 25; Gloucester, February 4; Smithfield, February 14, April 19; Tiverton,
March 6; Foster, February 6; Middletown, February 27; West Greenwich, April 19;
Little Compton, February 17; Coventry, February 25; Portsmouth, January 28; and
Warwick, February 26, making a total of fourteen towns and thirty votes in the
lower house that were without any question ready to approve a paper-money issue.
Five towns were opposed: Richmond, February 17; Newport, March 4; Providence,
March 4; Charlestown, February 17; and South Kingstown, February 20. The latter
two towns soon changed their opinions, because Charlestown was in favor of all the
plans to liquidate the state debt and opposed every attempt to abolish the
legal-tender status of the paper currency; while South Kingstown, in a series of votes
(July 31, September 30, October 27, 1786, April 18, 1787) , became a firm advocate of
the paper-money system. There can be little doubt that other towns, such as
Scituate and Exeter, whose delegates in the legislature and whose votes in the town
meetings consistently supported the paper-money system, were strongly won over to
the paper-money side.

49. Cumberland Town Meeting, February 25, 1786, Papers Relating to the
Adoption of the Constitution, Mss., R.I.S.A., p. 42.

rities. Particularly galling were taxes levied to service an inflated debt that was worth as little as 20 per cent of the unconscionable repayments made in postwar years. Indeed, the Smithfield freemen insisted that one year's interest payment in specie was often more than the original value of the principal when the loan was contracted.[50] Other towns complained of economic "Calamitys" in the state "for want of a circulating Medium sufficient to Carry on Trade and Settle our Just Debts without being Involved in Lawsuits, [the freemen becoming] Consequently the prey of Sheriffs Lawyers and Gaolers." [51] Everywhere hopes were fixed on paper money.

50. Smithfield Town Meeting, April 19, 1786, *ibid.,* p. 53. At an earlier town meeting on February 24, 1786 (*ibid.,* p. 50), the freemen of Smithfield gave another pointed summary of their thoughts on the public debt: "That the Whole of the Public Securities by means of the Scarcity of Circulating money, Promises to the Holders of them a much Larger Sum Than in Justice they Ought to have as it is Well Known that at Present [it] will take Double the Quantity in Produce [in 1786] to pay them Securities That would have paid them When Liquidated [at the end of the Revolution]." For further concern about the debts and taxation see Exeter Town Meeting, Mss., April 21, 1786.

Smithfield was the only town to focus attention on Rhode Island payments to support the loan interest certificates of the federal government. Forrest McDonald has given major importance to this development, asserting that Rhode Island "abandoned" holders of the loan office certificates when it adopted a paper-money system. Presumably, merchants who owned the loan office certificates opposed paper money because it indicated that Rhode Island no longer held itself responsible for these federal debts. (For McDonald's comments, see *We the People,* pp. 327–28, and *E Pluribus Unum: The Formation of the American Republic 1776–1790* [Boston, 1965], pp. 125–26.) I have attributed merchant opposition to other causes: the unwillingness of the merchants to accept depreciated paper currency for their state securities, opposition to the legal-tender articles of the emitting act, and an attempt to redress the political reversals of 1786 by opposing the country party program. McDonald's implication that Rhode Island had virtually assumed the congressional obligation for the loan office certificates is misleading. The General Assembly paid interest on the loan office certificates only in direct response to acts of Congress. Moreover, no one in Rhode Island doubted that any interim payments would later be refunded by the federal government. (See on this point, especially, Accounts with the United States, Ledger "A" 1776–1782, Mss., R.I.S.A., pp. 272 and 274, where auditors note that interest payments on the loan office certificates are "accounts of Rhode Island against the Union.") Given the foregoing, it seems most improbable that the hard-nosed Rhode Island merchants expected the General Assembly to go on supporting federal securities indefinitely, particularly in view of the state's own financial problems, of which they were aware. For the printed record of legislative action consult Bartlett, *Records,* IX, 716–17, 727–28, 736, 739–40, 744–45; X, 79, 106, 124, 145; the authoritative general account is Ferguson, *Power of the Purse,* pp. 179–241.

51. Tiverton Town Meeting, March 6, 1786; Middletown Town Meeting, February 22, 1786; Coventry Town Meeting, February 25, 1786, all in Papers Relating to the Adoption of the Constitution, Mss., R.I.S.A., pp. 58, 60, 63.

Although the majority of towns were staunch supporters of the proposed emission, an implacable opposition developed in the two major commercial centers of Rhode Island, Providence and Newport. In a special "Memorial and Remonstrance" submitted to the General Assembly on February 28, 1786, 300 freemen living in and around Providence denounced the plan to print paper money.[52] The petitioners declared that after a "fair and candid" examination of the proposal, no sensible man would ask willingly for a paper emission. Attention was called to the probability that the state's neighbors would never accept or circulate the currency, an eventuality that would disrupt trade and commerce with the adjacent regions. Lacking its own hinterland, this trade was vital to Rhode Island's economic health and would likely be diverted into other markets. In addition, queried the petitioners, "might it not be expected that the best of our own produce, allured by the charms of silver and gold, would take the same route?" A second allegation was the prediction that paper money would not substitute for specie in Rhode Island nor ease the burden of taxation. The petitioners asserted that the very shortage of hard money had come about because of foolish panting for a paper medium, bad money driving out good money precisely as laid down in the famous law of Sir Thomas Gresham. The petitioners pointed out that as long as the paper money was supposed to be retired at some future date, the freemen were not avoiding taxation but merely postponing it. Moreover, if the bills were permitted to depreciate, a financial sacrifice would still be required of those who were forced to accept the money at par. This would in effect be a tax, indiscriminately and "unjustly levied from the people."

The petition concluded with a forthright attack on suggestions that the paper money be made a legal tender in all contracts. "In this point of view," the petitioners foretold, "it would relax business, cut the sinews of industry, and enable sharpers and speculators to thrive on the plunder of the innocent and incautious." A similar prophecy came from Newport.[53] There another petition saw the ruin of Newport's credit and commerce in the event the money was printed.

Despite these predictions of disaster, those unfavorable to paper money were not oblivious to the impending financial crisis in Rhode Island and the problems facing the farmers; a minority were willing to

52. Petitions to the General Assembly, Mss., R.I.S.A., Vol. 25, Pt. I, p. 59. The Providence petition was printed in the *Providence Gazette,* March 4, 1786, and the *U.S. Chronicle* (Providence) , March 9, 1786.

53. *U.S. Chronicle* (Providence) , March 9, 1786.

admit that they also recognized the economic distress of the Confederation period.[54] Those who fought against the paper bills were ready to offer an alternative program. The Providence "Memorial and Remonstrance" publicized a plan that included an increase in the state Impost, excise taxes, a tax on horses, bounties for selected Rhode Island products, and discriminatory duties on foreign imports. These steps would raise needed revenues and discourage the use of foreign as against Rhode Island products. Another relief measure that received wide support was a plan to permit payments in kind at current market values for state taxes. Somewhat less favorably received was a proposal to make real and personal property a legal tender in the satisfaction of judgments rendered in suits for debt. The compromise proposals gave witness to the sincerity and power of the paper-money agitation, for even its adversaries recognized that something had to be done.

The General Assembly responded to these demands for public relief at its last session before the spring elections of 1786. In March the legislature passed a series of laws in an attempt to forestall an emission of paper money, a measure bitterly opposed by the merchants and their professional allies. A compromise package, it was hoped, would take some steam out of the paper-money powerhouse. Inadvertently, these laws also represented an implied admission that the Confederation crisis necessitated legislative action. The most important relief measure was an act enabling debtors to submit real and personal property when they were sued for nonpayment of debts; it was expected that this statute would make it possible for debtors to meet their obligations without too great a hardship, just as it was believed this law would invite creditors to postpone ill-considered legal action.[55] This concession to the demand for governmental help was accompanied by a system of bounties for a variety of Rhode Island products, a fiscal reorganization that included state excise taxes, authority for Congress to levy an Impost, and a grant of power permitting Congress to regulate

54. The Providence petitioners attributed the depression to "the desolations of the late war, and the heavy debt thereby incurred, as well as the embarrassments of the trade in foreign countries, and some impolitic restraints [such as state tariffs and internal navigation laws] among our selves. —To these causes may be added the almost total shortage of the hard money . . . occasioned by the apprehension of an emission of paper."

55. Rhode Island Records, Mss., R.I.S.A., Vol. 13, pp. 215, 224–29; *Providence Gazette*, March 25, 1786; *Newport Mercury*, March 27, 1786; Bartlett, *Records*, X, 180–82. This act was repealed at the June, 1786, session of the General Assembly, after the paper money had been issued. See Bartlett, *Records*, X, 205.

international trade. A resolution to print paper money, however, was easily defeated in the lower house.[56]

This halfway program was spurned by the freemen of the state. A report in the *New-York Packet* told of the Assembly's accomplishments and called them a compromise package which did not satisfy the people, although it was "full as bad" as the panacea of paper money. New York readers were warned that advocates of paper money in Rhode Island were greatly increasing their ranks and that it was not unlikely that within twelve months the legislature would bend to their will; what was more, "they have even talked of cancelling the public debt." [57] The merchants who controlled the state of Rhode Island had not moved quickly enough to contain the public clamor for relief. Now they had acted, but their program was not what the people had demanded—paper money. The state's leaders ran against a tide of popular discontent which would not down and which they had failed to comprehend.[58] Hence from a position of undisputed dominance in 1784, the mercantile coalition lost ground in 1785 and was turned out of office in May, 1786, with a completeness that only an aroused and effective electorate could achieve.

The Freemen Decide

In the elections of 1786 the incumbent mercantile administration of Governor William Greene and Deputy Governor Jabez Bowen was opposed for re-election by a newly organized country party. The formidable new party campaigned under the platform slogan *"To Relieve the Distressed"*—relief, of course, meaning paper currency and an attack on the problem of the state debt. Nominal leaders of the country party were its candidates for the state's highest offices, John Collins of Newport, a minor merchant and sea captain, and Daniel Owen of Glouces-

56. Rhode Island Records, Mss., R.I.S.A., Vol. 13, pp. 199–201, 216–17; *Providence Gazette,* March 11, 25, April 1, 1786; Staples, *R.I. in the Continental Congress,* p. 541.

57. May 4, 1786. It should be noted that before the paper money was printed and had depreciated, or before plans were put in motion to pay the public debts, charges were heard that the intent of the paper-money system was to repudiate the Rhode Island securities. Obviously, the new currency was designed, in part at least, as a way to avoid bankruptcy—which would have meant no payment whatever, even in paper money.

58. Letter from "A Farmer." *Providence Gazette,* August 12, 1786.

ter, a politician and blacksmith. Effective leadership of the country coalition lay, however, in the town-oriented politicians who brought it into being. These men included such town luminaries as Jonathan J. Hazard of Charlestown and South Kingstown, a local attorney with considerable political and financial experience; Joseph Stanton of Charlestown, a wealthy farmer and politician; Elijah Cobb of Portsmouth, a farmer and small-time merchant; Samuel Allen of Barrington, an influential local politician and merchant; Job Comstock of East Greenwich, a powerful local politician and farmer; Nicholas Easton of Newport, a wealthy landholder, opposed to the merchants of his town for personal reasons; Arthur Fenner, Jr., of Providence, an ambitious politician and merchant who would take control of the party in 1790; and Abraham Barker, a Little Compton farmer and politician. The country party was thus dominated by the traditional leaders of the state's towns: farmers, lawyers, merchants, and the sons of Rhode Island's most distinguished families. Its support and electoral power came from the mass of farmers, still predominant in Rhode Island, who sought legislative action on their behalf in the face of an economic and financial emergency.

Balloting in the elections of 1786 brought out the largest vote of the Confederation period in Rhode Island. The country party candidates were specifically pledged to an emission of paper money and a solution of the financial debacle promised by nonpayment of the state debt. In the towns the vote favored John Collins over the incumbent governor, William Greene, as the tide of rural discontent completely overwhelmed the mercantile party. Thereafter, the merchants and their party were a hopeless minority.[59] Those who backed the country party were bitter in appraising the economic crisis and the government's failure to soften its severity. Publicists wrote in the newspapers that mer-

59. This conclusion is based on a survey of the manuscript records of the towns. Some indication of the scope of the country triumph may be derived from the following figures: In 1785 Governor Greene secured all the 61 votes of West Greenwich; in 1786 he gained the votes of only 13 freemen, while John Collins received 149. In Coventry, Greene received 90 out of 91 votes in 1785; the year 1786 saw a startling reversal, as John Collins won a majority of 104 in the balloting. The story was much the same in Foster. Governor Greene had a unanimous vote of 61 freemen in 1785, but the next year only 6 voters favored him as against 178 who backed John Collins and the country party. In addition to electing its entire slate of state officers, the country party also won a substantial majority in the General Assembly. After 1786, so overwhelming was the country victory that contemporaries often referred to the mercantile party as the "minority," and to the triumphant paper-money party as the "majority."

chant rule was crass and hardhearted, wholly without regard for the people of the state.[60] Rhode Islanders repudiated their government and merchant class, convinced that the state had been badly served in the past and poorly led in the present.

At the first session of the newly elected General Assembly, in May, 1786, the legislature authorized a paper-money emission of £100,000.[61] The money was issued as part of a land-bank scheme, with the state providing capital in the form of £100,000 of paper bills, on a par with gold and silver, lending the currency to its citizens on the basis of a real estate mortgage twice the value of each loan. Every loan carried an interest charge of 4 per cent; the principal was repayable after seven years in seven annual installments, bearing interest only for the first seven-year period. Crucial to the success of the plan was the stipulation of the emitting act that made the paper bills a legal tender in all contracts—past, present, and future. Refusal to accept the money extinguished a debt in contrast to the common law, where rejection of legal tender merely suspended further interest charges until the creditor was willing to take the offered payment. The statute outlined a legal process whereby the debtor might lodge the money with a court when a tender had been made and refused. If upon citation the creditor persisted in spurning the "lodge money," as it was termed, the law required public notification of the tender in the newspapers for three consecutive weeks—the famous "Know-Ye" citation. If, after three months, the lodged money had not been claimed, it was forfeited to the state.

Although it was certain beforehand that the General Assembly would approve an emission of paper money, the mercantile minority girded itself for a vigorous battle in the lower house. A motion to print the paper currency was offered by deputies from the agricultural communities over the heated objections of men from the commercial towns.[62] The opposition, led by members from Providence and New-

60. Letter of "Brutus," *U.S. Chronicle* (Providence), September 21, 1786.

61. Rhode Island Records, Mss., R.I.S.A., Vol. 13, pp. 262–66; *U.S. Chronicle* (Providence), May 11, 1786; *Providence Gazette,* May 13, 1786.

62. Scattered reports on the Assembly session may be obtained in the *U.S. Chronicle* (Providence), May 11, 1786; *Providence Gazette,* May 13, 1786; *Pennsylvania Packet* (Philadelphia), May 25, 1786; *American Herald* (Boston), May 15, 1786; *The Essex Journal and the Massachusetts and New-Hampshire General Advertiser* (Newburyport, Mass.), May 15, 1786; *State Gazette of South-Carolina* (Charleston), June 3, 1786; and the *Worcester Magazine,* May 1786, p. 96. (This last-mentioned journal was a continuation of Isaiah Thomas's influential *Massachusetts Spy* which Thomas, the founder of the American Antiquarian Society, refused

port, denounced the emission as inadvisable, suggesting also that the legal-tender provisions of the statute were an unconstitutional infringement on the rights of private property. Representatives from Providence in the lower house entered a formal protest against the emission with a statement that it was designed to further the special interests of a small number of unnamed "certain persons" in the state, claiming the new money would bring economic chaos.

Shortly after the paper money was authorized, the bills began to depreciate in value relative to gold and silver. By the end of the summer of 1786 the discount was three to one, reaching six to one in the spring of 1787 and seven to one in August, 1787.[63] The country party leaders, fearful that headlong depreciation of the money would destroy its value and threaten their administration, charged that the declining value of the currency resulted from the intransigence of the merchants.[64] Resolute in its program, the country leadership attempted to arrest the depreciation and to harass its political foes by the passage of two penal laws that would force the circulation of the paper on a par with hard money.

Early in June, 1786, the General Assembly passed a law subjecting anyone who refused to accept the paper money at its nominal value to a fine of £100; upon a second conviction, the offender was rendered ineligible to hold elected office.[65] The purpose of these penalties, the statute related, was to keep the currency in good credit, an objective inhibited by "a certain Class of Men, who from Mistaken Principles, suppose the said Currency to be injurious to their Interests." This unusual law, which, in addition to the confiscation of the debts owed a

---

to publish because of a Massachusetts stamp tax on newspapers. When the tax was removed, Thomas returned to his old format.) According to these incomplete newspaper accounts, deputies from Providence, Newport, Bristol, and Portsmouth opposed the emission. Only the first three commercial towns consistently opposed the country party.

63. Copy of a Certificate Relating to the Paper Medium of this State [Rhode Island], August 1787, Wetmore Collection, Mss., M.H.S.; Welcome Arnold to Wilt Delmestre and Company, Providence, February 17, 1787, Welcome Arnold Papers, Mss., J.C.B.L. An official scale of depreciation, adopted by the General Assembly in 1790, is printed in the *Providence Gazette*, January 16, 1790.

64. William Ellery to the Commissioners of the Treasury of the U.S., Newport, June 27, 1786, William Ellery, Loan Office and Customs House Letter Book, 1786–1794, Mss., N.H.S.; letter from "A Friend to the Laborious Poor," *Newport Mercury*, April 16, 1786.

65. Rhode Island Records, Mss., R.I.S.A., Vol. 13, pp. 279–80; Bartlett, *Records*, X, 205; *U.S. Chronicle* (Providence), July 6, 1786; *Providence Gazette*, July 8, 1786.

creditor, added new penalties for refusing to accept the paper bills, passed by a reduced majority of six votes in the House of Deputies. Once again, the opposition was led by members from Providence and Newport.[66] The Providence delegation entered another formal protest that was unacceptable to the upper house, "because it was drawn up in disrespectful terms." The Providence censure spoke openly of the repugnance of the "Largest Proportion of the Property within the State" to the paper-money system. An attempt to restore the protest as part of the freedom of debate customary in the Rhode Island legislature was defeated in the House of Deputies. A member from Charlestown, probably the country party chief, Jonathan J. Hazard, taunted the merchants and said that, if they were dissatisfied with the new regime and wanted to leave Rhode Island, "he could not help it." Hazard wished them a more profitable existence elsewhere, but he warned that, if they stayed, the government must not be obstructed. The country leaders obviously meant business.

This first addition to the original emitting act had little effect. The merchants continued to oppose the paper-money system with all their power. Consequently, a second and more stringent penal statute followed quickly upon the first. Governor John Collins, troubled by what he believed was an impending disaster in Rhode Island, convoked the General Assembly into special session in August, 1786. Addressing the legislators, Collins declared that action was necessary to inhibit further depreciation of the currency and economic instability, problems "arising from a Combination of influential men against the good and wholesome Laws of this State." [67] The new statute set up a more

66. The *U.S. Chronicle* (Providence), July 6, 1786, reported that Newport, Providence, Bristol, Westerly, and Johnston were unanimously opposed to the law, with a partial representation from Portsmouth, Warwick, New Shoreham, Charlestown, Exeter, Tiverton, Little Compton, Richmond, Cranston, North Providence, and Barrington joining the opposition. But North and South Kingstown, East and West Greenwich, Jamestown, Smithfield, Scituate, Gloucester, Coventry, Foster, Middletown, Hopkinton, Cumberland, and Warren were unanimously in favor of the law. This meant that five towns with 16 votes were unanimously opposed, eleven towns with 26 votes were divided, and fourteen towns—two short of a majority—with 28 votes were unanimously in favor. From this distribution of the votes in the House of Deputies we are able to gain a rough but very important estimate of the hard-core strength of the country party: 28 votes, just 8 short of an absolute majority, which could be easily made up from among the eleven divided towns.

67. *Providence Gazette,* September 2, 1786; *U.S. Chronicle* (Providence), September 7, 1786; *Connecticut Gazette* (New London), September 1, 1786; *Pennsylvania Journal* (Philadelphia), September 13, 1786; *State Gazette of South-Carolina* (Charleston), October 19, 1786.

speedy process of law that would confront enemies of the paper-money system. The second penal statute provided that if a regular term of one of the Rhode Island courts was not in session when a case arose concerning the new money, a special court might be convened, consisting of three or more members of the bench, to try the suit immediately. Any litigation heard under the second penal statute—whether by a regular term of a state court or a specially organized court—would be tried without a jury, and no appeal was permitted to a higher jurisdiction.[68]

The second penal statute clearly reflected the concern of the country leaders that depreciation of the currency might bring their relief program into disrepute and endanger the success of the paper-money administration. Drastic measures were thought necessary. As a result, this statute limited the traditional right of Rhode Islanders to enjoy the privilege of trial by jury. In the legislature, members elected by the commercial towns blasted the bill as a patent and ugly violation of the Rhode Island constitution, because it took away "the natural and constitutional rights of the citizen." [69] A formal remonstrance against the statute was introduced into the Assembly, signed by thirteen prominent deputies from the commercial centers. Their protest was rejected in the lower house. The dissenting members took the opportunity to attack the entire paper-money system as partial and class legislation before turning their attention to the legislation under consideration. The bill was denounced in a ringing declaration as a denial of the very civil and natural rights which the Revolution had been fought to secure, "the foremost of which was Trials by Jury." [70] The philosophy which had served to justify a revolution against Great Britain for home rule was thus invoked to protect a minority against the democracy which ruled at home. An influential shift in the utility of the natural-rights philosophy was taking place in Rhode Island.

68. Rhode Island Records, Mss., R.I.S.A., Vol. 13, pp. 296–99; Bartlett, *Records*, X, 212.

69. Ellery to the Board of Treasury of the U.S., Newport, August 29, 1786, Papers of the Continental Congress, 1774–1789, Letters of the Board of Treasury, 1785–1788, 2 vols., Mss., N.A., Vol. II, pp. 319–20.

70. *Newport Mercury*, August 21, 1786; *Providence Gazette*, September 2, 1786.

6

The Paper-Money Tangle

ENACTMENT of the paper-money system and penal laws designed to force the circulation of the new currency did not arrest the deepening crisis in Rhode Island. Political divisions were now added to economic and financial controversies. Greater pressures on the mercantile and professional minority only served to stiffen its resistance. A continuing theme throughout the spring and summer of 1786 suggested that "more complaints" were heard during the Confederation era than ever "during the late distressing war." Business conditions were uncertain as Rhode Islanders, town and country alike, awaited and pondered the impact which paper money would have. The merchants believed that commercial life would be fatally injured by laws which permitted any contract to be terminated by a tender of depreciated paper bills.[1]

1. *Providence Gazette,* April 17, 1786; Moses Brown to Champion and Dickinson, Providence, September 6, 1786, Moses Brown Papers, Mss., R.I.H.S., No. 1418; Brown and Benson to John Murray and Co., Providence, May 24, 1786, Brown Papers, Mss., J.C.B.L.; letter from "A Lover of Justice," *Providence Gazette,* July 22, 1786; Lane,

For many observers the heart of the paper-money tangle was not the economic implications of the emission of legal-tender currency; the true danger was the subtle attack on private property which paper money represented, insofar as an individual was obligated by law to surrender his goods and services upon an offer of depreciated money. A citizen could not refuse the money without the threat of penalties that could take away his property and liberty.[2] The paper-money system was thus believed to be an infringement upon the natural rights of man. Another complaint of the minority was directed against the one-sided operation of the governmental system in the state. Many feared that the country party's domination of political life was a danger to freedom and liberty in Rhode Island. The power of the majority was so strong, asserted the merchants, that in the absence of any checks or controls it had become a virtual despotism. The course of events appeared to confirm this, for the General Assembly no longer expressed both majority and minority viewpoints. It had become a tool of the country party, whose members were strictly disciplined and voted the party line without regard to, or respect for, the mercantile interest. Every important measure was part of a party program and was decided outside the regular channels of lawmaking. The country party majority made any decision of its leaders a state law. For this reason, whenever objections to a proposed statute were made in the Assembly, they received scant consideration. The country leaders might say, with aplomb, "it is in vain to dispute, for we, who are the majority, are determined."[3] The mercantile minority was convinced that democratic power might itself be an instrument of tyranny and oppression, and it began to search for remedies.

Confronted by the powerful and united country majority, ready and able to make full use of the authority of the state to bring about the success of its program, the effectiveness of the mercantile members of the General Assembly was very limited. The power of their opposition had to be exercised outside the normal course of politics. This took the

---

Son, and Fraser to Christopher Champlin, London, October 16, 1786, Charles Francis Adams *et al.*, eds., "Commerce of Rhode Island 1726–1800," *Collections of the Massachusetts Historical Society,* 7th ser., IX–X (1914–15), 295; *American Herald* (Boston), July 17, 24, 1786.

2. Letter from "A Friend to Justice," *U.S. Chronicle* (Providence), August 10, 1786.

3. *American Mercury* (Hartford), September 18, 1786; *Daily Advertiser* (New York), September 14, 1786.

form of a concerted refusal to accept paper bills throughout 1786, which intensified the issues in dispute. In order to avoid the grip of the penal laws, retail sales were temporarily suspended when merchants failed to open their shops for business.[4] The rural communities reacted bitterly to this strategy of the merchants. In retaliation, farmers stopped bringing their agricultural produce into the town markets, causing a shortage of grain that necessitated a special town meeting and emergency measures to prevent hardship in Providence.[5] These developments reinforced the conviction of those who favored the country party that "a certain class of people" in Rhode Island was stubbornly determined to wreck the policies supported by the state's freemen in overwhelming numbers. The "class" in question was the merchants, "stripped of the reigns of power in so unexpected, and so extraordinary a manner," explained a paper-money adherent, that "they are now determined to disapprobate every measure adopted by the new administration which is not perfectly agreeable to their own private interests." [6] A further test of strength was in prospect between the contending parties.

Judicial Review

Into this maelstrom of controversy came the celebrated decision in the case of *Trevett* v. *Weeden,* which added fuel to the intense fire of contention that divided Rhode Island.[7] The circumstances leading up to this famous trial were ubiquitous in Rhode Island in 1786, where, in countless similar situations, one party to a commercial transaction refused to accept the paper bills. The unique aspect of the Trevett

4. Solomon Drowne to Rev. James Manning, Providence, June 23, 1786, and Drowne to Dr. E. Richmond, Providence, July 18, 1786, both in Drowne Collection, B.U.L.; *Newport Mercury,* August 7, 1786.

5. "Report of a Providence Town Meeting," July 24, 1786, *Providence Gazette,* July 29, 1786; William R. Staples, ed., *Annals of the Town of Providence* (Providence, 1843), p. 304; letter of "Juvenal," *U.S. Chronicle* (Providence), August 3, 1786; letter from "A Citizen of the United States," *Providence Gazette,* April 19, 1786.

6. *U.S. Chronicle* (Providence), July 27, 1786; *Providence Gazette,* August 7, 1786.

7. This discussion of the *Trevett* case is adapted from my article, "Trevett vs. Weeden and the Case of the Judges," *Newport History,* XXXVIII (1965), 45–69.

case was that it was the first and last to be tried under the provisions of the second penal statute, which made litigation concerning the currency recognizable by special or regular courts that could sit without impaneling a jury. The suit of John Trevett, a Newport cabinetmaker, against John Weeden, a Newport butcher, was only one of several actions in progress under the law in question; at least three other cases were under way when the Trevett litigation was heard. All the suits were against Newport butchers, indicating prior agreement among these tradesmen and probably strong support from the mercantile community. The Trevett cause was not the earliest of the four suits, but it was the first to be tried. Since the defense plea in each action was identical, one among these cases was expected to be a test for all litigation under the paper-money system. If this suit could be successfully defended, the whole fabric of the paper-money structure might be rent.[8]

On September 25, 1786, the trial of *Trevett* v. *Weeden* was heard before a regular term of the Superior Court of Judicature, the state's highest court. In accordance with the second penal statute, there was no jury. That day the courthouse in Newport was packed to overflowing, as citizens of the state's only city vied to attend the session. The importance of the case was obviously known to everyone; it seemed almost certain before the trial began that the constitutionality of the paper-money laws would be contested.[9]

8. Papers relating to these suits may be examined in the newly catalogued miscellaneous manuscripts of the Newport Historical Society, Box 43, Folder 12.

9. The case was a *cause célèbre* in Rhode Island and the United States. The first reports of the trial and decision came in the Rhode Island newspapers, beginning with the *Providence Gazette,* September 30, October 7, 1786; *Newport Mercury,* October 2, 1786; and the *U.S. Chronicle* (Providence), October 5, 1786. The official transcript of the litigation and decision is printed in John R. Bartlett, ed., *Records of the Colony of Rhode Island and Providence Plantations in New England,* 10 vols. (Providence, 1856–65), X, 218–20. Because of the great interest in the case and the defense arguments favoring judicial review, John Carter, printer of the *Providence Gazette,* urged the principal defense attorney, James Mitchell Varnum, to publish the history of the suit and its aftermath. Varnum complied in the now rare volume, *The Case, Trevett against Weeden: On Information and Complaint, for refusing Paper Bills in Payment for Butcher's Meat, in Market, at Par with Specie, Tried before the Honourable Superior Court, in the County of Newport, September Term, 1786. Also the Case of the Judges of said Court, Before the Honourable General Assembly, at Providence, October Session, 1786, on Citation for dismissing said Complaint. Wherein the Rights of the People to Trial by Jury, etc., are stated and maintained, and the Legislative, and Executive Powers of Government are examined and defined* (Providence, 1787). Excerpts from this volume are printed in Peleg W. Chandler, *American Criminal Trials,* 2 vols. (Boston, 1841–42).

Henry Marchant and James Mitchell Varnum appeared as counsel for the defendant, John Weeden. Tradition has it that both men accepted the case without fee, because the butcher Weeden—soon to appear on the relief rolls in Newport—was unable to pay the costs of his own defense. Marchant was a well-known Newport advocate who later played an important role in Rhode Island's ratification of the federal Constitution in 1790, but it was James Mitchell Varnum, then an East Greenwich attorney, who bore the brunt of the defense that day in Newport.

The defense problem in the Trevett case was unprecedented. Varnum and Marchant had to demonstrate that an act of the General Assembly might be unconstitutional. They also had to convince the judges that it was their obligation to bar the enforcement of such a statute. Both tasks were equally monumental in Confederation Rhode Island.

Throughout the colonial period the General Assembly had been virtually supreme. Except for the direct intervention of Parliament or indirect appellate jurisdiction of the King in Council, the Rhode Island Assembly had full power in governing the colony. Inevitably, after 1776, the General Assembly was all-powerful, subject only to the vote of the freemen in the semiannual spring and fall elections. It was not limited by a bill of rights, as were most other American states, for the charter of 1663 contained no such document. In the absence, therefore, of any customary or institutional check on the laws of the legislature, the assertion that an act of the Assembly might be unconstitutional was an unprecedented claim in Rhode Island. The prospect for judicial review as a remedy for unconstitutional laws was slight. In the Rhode Island structure of government the judiciary was not independent. The judiciary was a creature of the General Assembly. It existed to enforce the law, not to judge the law's validity. Under the charter there had been no provision for a separate judiciary, and in the early years of the colony the legislature served as the only higher court in Rhode Island. Later, when the burden of judicial work became too heavy, separate courts were organized. But the Assembly never surrendered its appellate authority, and in certain cases it retained original jurisdiction. The courts were subject to the General Assembly and could not do more than they were authorized to do by either legislation or tradition.[10] The courts also labored under other handicaps.

10. See Edward S. Stinnes, "The Struggle for Judicial Supremacy," in Edward Field, ed., *State of Rhode Island and Providence Plantations at the End of the*

The members of the bench were annually appointed by the Assembly; their tenure in office was completely dependent on the will of the legislature. A further weakness of the judiciary—one that followed from its brief and imperfect tenure—was the political nature of the annual appointments and the fact that judges who held office were generally beholden to the party in power. As Thomas W. Dorr later explained, "the Judiciary is the creature of the legislature, and the places of most of the Judges are annually distributed by the prevailing party among political friends." [11] Independent judgment, especially in political matters, was not to be expected of the judiciary in Rhode Island.

James Mitchell Varnum dominated the proceedings of the defense in the trial. Henry Marchant spoke only briefly, permitting his fellow attorney to carry the cause of John Weeden. Varnum began by affirming the "illegality of the new-fangled jurisdictions erected by the General Assembly," a pointed reference to the second penal statute.[12] He averred that the act of legislation permitting a special court to hear paper-money complaints without a jury trial violated the fundamental law of Rhode Island and was unconstitutional. The country leaders aimed at a "summary process" of law by their measures, said Varnum, "flattering themselves that the Judges, being elected by the legislators, would blindly submit to their sovereign will and pleasure."[13] Here were the two key aspects of the defense case: the claim that the second penal statute was unconstitutional, and the hope that the judges would repudiate that law.

Varnum continued his exposition with an elaborate analysis of the fundamental law of Rhode Island, placing trial by jury among its essential prescriptions. He rested his contention on the great precedents of English history—Magna Carta, the Petition of Right, and the Bill of Rights—in an attempt to prove that trial by jury, though not secured in the charter, was an integral principle of the British constitution predating the Rhode Island compact. For this reason, trial by jury might not be denied by the Assembly without violating the fundamen-

---

Century: A History, 3 vols. (Boston, 1902), III; and Thomas Durfee, "Gleanings from the Judicial History of Rhode Island," Rhode Island Historical Society Tracts, 1st ser., No. 18 (Providence, 1883).

11. Reform Resolutions Presented by Thomas W. Dorr, January 13, 1837, Rejected January 21, 1837, General Assembly, Acts and Resolves, Miscellaneous Mss., Folder XII, R.I.S.A.

12. Varnum, Trevett against Weeden, p. 3.

13. Ibid., p. 11.

tal law, carried over from England, that embodied the natural rights of man.

Before ending his presentation, Varnum again discussed the role of the judiciary, knowing that he had to convince the judges that it was their duty to exercise the power of judicial review. Though Varnum necessarily paid lip service to the doctrine that the legislature in Rhode Island had what he termed "supreme power," he asked, who was to judge when it violated the rights of the people. He maintained that it must be the judiciary. "The true distinction lies in this," explained Varnum, "that the legislative have the incontroulable power of making laws not repugnant to the constitution:—The Judiciary have the sole power of judging of those laws . . . but cannot admit any act of the Legislative as Law, which is against the constitution." [14] In the event the judges found the law in conflict with a litigant's privileges and unreasonable in nature, Varnum concluded, it was their obligation to assume the power of judicial review.

Varnum's development of the defense position extended over a period of hours. The force of his arguments carried conviction and reportedly had a profound impact upon his audience in the crowded courthouse.[15] The state's attorney, Henry Goodwin (who became Attorney General of Rhode Island in the subsequent election), had his work cut out for him. He spoke briefly in behalf of the second penal statute under which the Trevett case was heard. Goodwin stated that the charter of 1663 was the only fundamental law of Rhode Island and that in accordance with its terms the General Assembly had been given complete legislative and judicial power. Furthermore, Goodwin insisted, the state was governed under a constitution that contained no guarantee of a jury trial. The statute under scrutiny, if it had been duly passed into law by the Assembly, was constitutional.[16]

After hearing Goodwin's case for the state, the court adjourned until the next day while the judges considered the arguments in this remarkable trial. But the decision was a foregone conclusion, for Varnum's or-

14. *Ibid.*, pp. 26–27.
15. John Carter reported in the *Providence Gazette,* October 7, 1786, that Varnum "displayed the oratorical strength of a Demosthenes, and the eloquence of a Cicero."
16. The press took little notice of Goodwin's pleadings. Most wrote deprecatingly: "Mr. Goodwin spoke for the informers, but could not say much" (*Newport Mercury,* October 2, 1786; *Independent Chronicle* [Boston], October 5, 1786). The account in the *U.S. Chronicle* (Providence), October 5, 1786, usually the paper most favorable to the country party, said Goodwin spoke "as well on the subject as could be expected." The best source is the *Providence Gazette,* October 30, 1786.

atory and persuasion had carried the day. The decision was for the defendant, John Weeden, on the grounds that the second penal statute was unconstitutional and unenforceable by the courts because it failed to offer the accused the benefit of trial by jury. The verdict was unanimous, with four of the judges—David Howell, Thomas Tillinghast, Joseph Hazard, and Gilbert Devol—participating. The Chief Justice, Paul Mumford, who had a reputation for trimming, failed to vote in the case.[17] David Howell spoke vigorously from the bench in rendering his judgment. He declared that as a judge he was independent of the Assembly, asserting also that the contested law was flagrantly unconstitutional. Judge Tillinghast stressed the repugnancy of the wording of the statute. The law permitted trial without a jury, "according to the laws of the land," observed Tillinghast, but the laws of the land mandated the ancient custom of trial by one's peers. It was his opinion that a contradictory statute should not be enforced.[18] The verdict and statements were greeted with joy in the overflowing courthouse and, according to one account, with "a universal clap." [19]

In light of the traditions and customs of Rhode Island, the decision of the judges was a courageous one, and, indeed, the Trevett verdict brought an immediate retort from the General Assembly. In this context, the deviation from precedent involved in judicial review should not be mistaken for a living principle of the Rhode Island constitution. Dissent without firm precedent was a dangerous course during the Confederation years.

The country party and its numerous supporters were enraged by the decision of the court in the Trevett case. An alarm was sounded because the decision struck down an important part of the paper-money system, and it was especially feared in view of the assumption of authority by the judiciary to declare an act of the Assembly unconstitutional. This arrogation of power by the judges might endanger the en-

17. Just why Mumford failed to vote is uncertain. He was in poor health during the trial and this might explain his absence on September 26. Most probably he failed to join the majority because he wanted to keep his position, for it was certain that the verdict would engender a political storm. The *Newport Mercury*, October 2, 1786, reported that, while Mumford did not participate in the decision, he was always a "good Whig and therefore a friend of Trial by Jury and in Agreement [with his fellow judges]."

18. *Newport Mercury*, October 2, 1786; *Providence Gazette*, September 30, 1786.

19. *Independent Chronicle* (Boston), October 5, 1786; *Massachusetts Gazette* (Boston), October 3, 1786.

tire program of public relief. The depth of feeling on the issue was illustrated by the consideration which the agricultural town of Coventry gave to the *Trevett* decision. The townsmen recorded in their meeting-book that the Superior Court had exceeded its jurisdiction by deciding on the constitutionality of a statute; they asserted that the only power the Superior Court possessed was to decide whether or not Weeden had broken the law of the state.[20] According to the freemen of Coventry, the judges had no business to rule on the legality of an act of the Assembly.

The General Assembly was also disturbed by the Trevett decision. A resolution was introduced into the House of Deputies calling for the judges to come before the legislature to declare the reasons for their decision, "if any they have in order that this Assembly on proper information may adopt such measures as may be agreeable to Right & Justice." [21] This insulting summons was set aside, but the Assembly did adopt a strongly worded resolution summoning all the judges to appear before it to defend and explain their judgment, which, in the opinion of the legislators, was "absolutely unprecedented in this state and may tend directly to abolish the legislative authority thereof." [22] The judges' offense seemed grave, for it threatened the paper-money program and gave aid and comfort to enemies of the paper-money system.

Only three of the judges answered the call of the General Assembly. The Chief Justice, Paul Mumford, pleaded illness, as did Gilbert Devol; this left David Howell, Joseph Hazard, and Thomas Tillinghast to face the wrath of the hostile legislature.[23]

Doubtless the judges blanched at the peremptory tone of the legislative summons. David Howell began the hearing with a firm declaration that the courts of the state were not responsible to the legislative branch of government for their decisions. The judges, Howell protested, were independent of any power on earth in their judicial capacity. They were "accountable only to God, and to their consciences." [24] Howell willingly affirmed his belief in the doctrine of judicial review,

20. Coventry Town Meeting, Mss., October 28, 1786.
21. General Assembly, Acts and Resolves, Mss., R.I.S.A., Vol. 25, p. 61.
22. Rhode Island Colony Records, Mss., R.I.S.A., Vol. 13, p. 309; Bartlett, *Records*, X, 215.
23. *Providence Gazette*, November 11, 1786; *Newport Mercury*, November 13, 1786.
24. Varnum, *Trevett against Weeden*, pp. 38–39.

which had given offense to the legislature. The judge

> adduced a number of the most respectable authorities to shew the
> power and duties of the General Assembly and those of the Superior
> Court—the principal part of which went to prove—That the General
> Assembly in making laws is bound by certain lines drawn by the con-
> stitution;—one of the most capital of which is [trial by jury]. . . .
> That when the General Assemblies attempt to overleap the bounds of
> the constitution, by making laws contrary thereto, the Superior Court
> have Power, *and it is their duty*, to refuse to carry such laws into effect.[25]

A second jurist, Joseph Hazard, a country party stalwart strongly in
favor of the paper-money emission, said it gave him pain as a judge to
oppose a specific measure of an administration he supported. "But
their obligations were of too sacred a nature to aim at pleasing . . . in
this line of duty," he declared. Hazard lamented the turn of fate that
found him convinced that the law in dispute was unconstitutional,
and he declared with feeling that his decision had been motivated by
the great "energy of truth." [26]

The words of the judges fell upon unfriendly ears. The country
leaders and their substantial majority had called the judges of the Superior Court before the bar of the Assembly to receive a public rebuke
and then to be replaced on the bench.[27] In this way the traditional supremacy of the legislature would be confirmed. New candidates for
office were selected before the judges appeared, and a vote removing
them was imminent soon after they were heard. But the judges interrupted the country strategy with a special memorial, again pleading
their cause. The jurists demanded due process of law, asserting "a
mere suggestion of a mere error of judgment" was insufficient reason
for their removal. They asked for a clear accusation of misconduct before removal.

James Mitchell Varnum strongly favored the memorial in the lower
house, where, ironically, he now served as counsel for the judges.
Varnum condemned the plan to fire the members of the court without
any charges of criminality or malfeasance; even a common criminal, he
thundered, had this right to due process. No man should be forced to

25. *Newport Mercury*, November 13, 1786.

26. Varnum, *Trevett against Weeden*, p. 43.

27. *Ibid.*, pp. 43–44. The *Pennsylvania Gazette* (Philadelphia), October 25, 1786,
wrote that the General Assembly intended to appoint new judges who "will
implicitly obey, and prosecute those who will not implicitly obey their arbitrary
mandates, without impertinently calling into question the justice of them."

vacate his office, Varnum remarked, unless found guilty of a breach of law, not merely an unpopular decision. The state's attorney general, William Channing, fully agreed with Varnum's protest. Channing claimed that to remove the entire bench, as the majority intended, with no better reason than politics, would fatally injure the cause of free government.[28]

The country party receded from its determination before the heated objections of Varnum and Channing, perhaps content that all the members of the court could soon be changed when a new Assembly met in the spring. Instead of dismissal, the judges were reproved by an Assembly resolution stating that they had submitted "no satisfactory reasons" for their decision. But because the judges were not convicted of any criminal act, they were excused, with their offices temporarily intact.[29] Within six months all but one of the judges had retired to private life.

The trial of the judges brought a dramatic end to the case of *Trevett* v. *Weeden*. The case is justly famous as an example of the practice of judicial review before the establishment of the federal Constitution of 1787, and it set a precedent for the exercise of that power by the United States Supreme Court. The reasoning of James Mitchell Varnum in the suit was once more a precursor of the political ideas of Alexander Hamilton and the philosophy expounded by John Marshall in the Marbury decision. The fact that the Trevett episode involved an unprecedented assumption of power by a state court functioning in a constitutional system that granted extensive judicial authority to the General Assembly has been overlooked, despite the unique aftermath of the trial of the judges by the legislature. Nor did the Trevett decision mean that the judiciary had established its independence of the General Assembly. Never again under the charter of 1663 did the courts in Rhode Island openly challenge the validity of the Assembly's laws. Thereafter the courts were carefully controlled and the country leaders were far more circumspect regarding their recommendations for the bench. The Trevett case and its circumstances are revealing for another reason. They reflected an important shift in the uses which Americans would make of the natural-rights ideology in future years. In 1776, the natural-rights philosophy had been invoked to secure the independence of the United States against the claims of Great Britain. By 1786, in Rhode Island, the same philosophy was being called upon

28. Varnum, *Trevett against Weeden,* pp. 46–52.
29. Bartlett, *Records,* X, 220.

to uphold the rights and privileges of a decided minority against the constituent power of a democratic majority in the state.

Recrimination and Reaction

Concurrent with the reversal which the country party experienced in the Trevett affair, the agricultural towns began to feel the pinch of mercantile opposition to the paper-money system. The produce of many farms lay unsold, and farmers found themselves unable to buy freely at retail stores in Providence and Newport. A sense of urgency fell over Rhode Island. Responding to the situation, the freemen of South Kingstown met in an emergency session on July 31, 1786, to consider the crisis and possible avenues of relief. The townsmen protested that "there is an unwarrantable Combination of Men, in many parts of this State, who refuse to sell their Goods and Merchandise, to the Country . . . for the Currency . . . intentionally to subvert the promulgated laws of this State." They favored a strict counter-boycott of any transactions with the commercial towns and also suggested that a convention of the towns be gathered at East Greenwich, located in Kent County, to "advise and consult" on other steps that might be adopted. While this was happening, another convention was already in progress in the town of Scituate, in Providence County, with paper money and the penal laws needed to guarantee its stability being the chief items of interest. When the call went out from South Kingstown, the Scituate convention adjourned to meet with delegates from the southern towns at East Greenwich.[30]

The East Greenwich meeting convened on schedule on August 22. Sixteen towns were represented. The conference urged the towns to instruct their representatives in the General Assembly to strengthen the paper-money system with whatever new state action was deemed necessary. A second recommendation was the enactment of statutes against the monopolizing of grain, a real danger if the counter-boycott of the commercial towns was to be effective. The convention demanded the redemption of the public securities of the state as quickly as possible, with the entire sum of the state debt scaled down in value.[31]

30. *Providence Gazette*, August 5, 12, 1786.
31. *Ibid.*, August 26, 1786.

Though these measures were approved by strong majorities, the delegates from Providence were loud in protest. Instead of more laws to support an inherently unstable currency, the men from Providence asked for a compromise on the issues between the parties, a plan that was later pursued by the merchants. The compromise did not envisage withdrawal of the paper money. It sought repeal of the harsher provisions of the penal laws, particularly those relating to disfranchisement, and a revision of that part of the original emitting act which made the currency a legal tender in all contracts. In return for these concessions, the compromisers offered to accept the paper bills as legal tender in future contracts and in any judgment for debt obtained through the courts; in past contracts that called for specie payments, the paper money might no longer extinguish a debt. If these accommodations were agreed upon, the Providence delegates implied that the mercantile community would lend its support to the paper-money system. The country leaders, however, sure of their majority and determined to strike at the heart of the financial crisis by paying off the state debt in paper bills, paid little heed to these entreaties of the minority; they showed little disposition for compromise.

Indicative of the growing unrest in Rhode Island, and increasing lack of restraint in the majority's response to the merchants, was another convention of paper-money forces that met early in the fall in Smithfield, a northern town in Providence County. There were few moderate voices at this conference.[32] The Smithfield gathering, like its predecessors, also told of the "alarming" crisis in Rhode Island because of mercantile opposition to the paper currency. To deal with this recalcitrance, the convention suggested a Draconic plan of action.

The first item of the Smithfield program was a proposal that the legal standing of most forms of promissory notes be ended by statute; this was intended to harass the merchants by destroying an important source of commercial credit. Debts and contracts not formally detailed in a written agreement, which included the majority of all commercial transactions, were no longer to be enforceable in the courts.[33] More

32. Letter from "Z.Y.," *U.S. Chronicle* (Providence), September 28, 1786; *Providence Gazette*, September 30, 1786.

33. *Providence Gazette*, September 30, 1786; William Ellery to the Commissioners of the Treasury Board, September 22, 1786, Ellery Letters, Mss., N.H.S. The towns of Coventry (Town Meeting, Mss., June 24, 1786) and Warwick (Town Meeting, Mss., August 26, 1786) instructed their deputies in the General Assembly before the Smithfield convention to favor steps to prohibit the use of promissory notes in commerce.

radical in its approach was the determination of the delegates to accept the mercantile opposition as formidable and irreconcilable and to destroy it by having the state take over foreign trade in Rhode Island.[34] The convention asked the General Assembly to obtain the funds necessary to buy ships, wharves, and the materials needed to conduct international commerce and then use the profits arising from this enterprise to liquidate the public debt. An enthusiast saw this plan as one which would "harmonize" the true public interest in the legislature and "level all classes of men" in their influence over public policy. Beneficial also, from a political viewpoint, was the way in which the newly strengthened legislature would be empowered to resolve the crisis in Rhode Island "without courting . . . any particular class of men whatever." [35] There could be no mistaking the reference to the merchants.

The discontent represented by these extralegal conventions, as well as by the reaction to the Trevett decision, induced Governor Collins to call the General Assembly into session on October 2, 1786. No one doubted that severe measures would be enacted by the legislature. "They may propose embargoes, tests and I don't know what; but their money will never go into circulation but at a depreciated rate," wrote William Ellery, then commissioner of the Loan Office in Rhode Island. The merchants expected the worst as they waited defiantly. Rhode Island's paper-money system and the disquiet throughout the northeastern states impelled Ellery to exclaim in near disbelief:

> What madness has seized the people of the New England States! I once thought that there was virtue enough in the Eastern States to admit of Liberty in its greatest extent, but from late experiences I begin to think that we do not deserve the privileges which we are possessed of, and that unless power is lodged somewhere to controul the vice and folly of the people we shall soon be involved in all the horrors of anarchy and confusion.[36]

34. *Providence Gazette*, September 30, 1786.

35. Letter of "W.B.," *U.S. Chronicle* (Providence), September 21, 1786. This proposal to have the state monopolize all foreign commerce got nowhere, even among the most ardent country party adherents; it was specifically repudiated in a Cumberland town meeting on September 30, 1786.

36. Ellery to Nathaniel Appleton, Newport, October 2, 1786, Ellery Letters, Mss., N.H.S. See also Solomon Drowne to Mr. Otto, Providence, October 16, 1786, Drowne Collection, B.U.L. The testimony of J. P. Brissot DeWarville, *New Travels in the United States of America: Performed in 1788* (New York, 1792), p. 83, is very revealing on this point. "The State of Rhode Island will never see happy days, till they take from circulation their paper money," he wrote, adding significantly, "and

So spoke the Newport merchant and politician who, in combination with David Howell and a mercantile coalition, had mounted a successful attack against the nationalist movement, between 1781 and 1785, as marking a progress toward tyranny. How they must have lamented their support of the states' rights doctrine that destroyed the Impost, for the same ideas now protected the country party. Ellery's thoughts and those of the mercantile minority turned to the idea of surrendering local power to the national government, a sentiment created during the paper-money tangle in Rhode Island. The American Revolution had secured home rule, but many began to wonder whether home rule would secure liberty.

The business of this October session of the General Assembly was devoted to shoring up the paper-money structure in such a way as to intimidate the opposition. A new penalty act was introduced, greatly exceeding in its severity the most extreme views of paper-money men prior to September, 1786. So drastic were the penalties proposed for those who refused to accept the currency at its nominal value that the country party hesitated to enact the statute without a referendum. The freemen were consulted in their town meetings on the proposed bill, and their voice would decide.[37] The bill required that every freeman take an oath pledging that he would accept the currency on a par with hard money; all public officials were specifically called upon to honor this pledge. Anyone who took the oath and later infringed the paper-money system was guilty of perjury and subject to harsh punishment; those who refused to swear or affirm were rendered ineligible to hold public office in Rhode Island or to vote in any election. As a special stab at the merchants, no resident was allowed to clear a vessel from the state unless he subscribed to the oath.

---

reform their government. The magistrates should be less dependent on the people than they are at present, and members of the legislature should not be so often elected. . . . I doubt not likewise, but the example of Rhode-Island will be a proof, in the eyes of the people, that republican government is disastrous. This would be a wrong conclusion—this example only proves that there ought to be a rotation in the legislative power, and that there ought to be a stability in the executive; that there is as much danger in placing the magistrates in a state of too great dependence on the people, as there is in making them too independent. It argues, in fact, against a pure democracy, but not against a representative democracy; for a representation of six months, is but a government by the people themselves."

37. The proposed statute was officially entitled: "An act to stimulate and give efficacy to the Paper Bills. . . ." It may be consulted in Rhode Island Colony Records, Mss., R.I.S.A., Vol. 13, p. 308; Bartlett, *Records*, X, 217; or the *Providence Gazette*, October 14, 1786.

The extreme penalties prescribed in this proposed law brought a crushing defeat to the country party leaders. The freemen were unwilling to sanction the statute. Opponents of the paper-money system charged that the real intent of the country party was to disfranchise minority voters who would not accept the currency or swear humiliating oaths. This mass disfranchisement was allegedly designed to ensure the continuance of the country party in power.[38] A tour of the southern towns by a Newport merchant, Daniel Rogers, found very few Rhode Islanders who favored "this Galling Bill." [39] A lengthy town meeting in Providence denounced the plan as "unconstitutional, impolitic, and unjust." The townsmen believed the bill was a danger to the survival of liberty and free institutions in the state, something already suspected by the minority. The Providence meeting asserted that the injunction obligating a creditor to accept the paper money under the threat of disfranchisement, even if he was willing to have the debt canceled, was an unprecedented invasion of an individual's personal freedom. To take away a man's civil rights in spite of his willingness to suffer a pecuniary loss was characterized as despotism.[40] The freemen of Newport also assailed the proposed law. They pointed out that the disfranchisement of the minority would give absolute power to the country party and subvert democracy in Rhode Island. The Newporters said the bill was a precedent for other oaths in the future, pledges that might test religious as well as political creeds, forcing men to surrender their personal beliefs in order to conform to the law.[41]

The commercial centers were not alone in their opposition to the proposal. Only three towns favored it.[42] Many of the paper-money strongholds were against the bill. The town of Smithfield, for example, rejected the scheme unanimously. Warwick, one of the leaders in securing the new currency, repudiated the proposal by a margin of 44 votes. In another country party bastion, Exeter, the freemen were ar-

38. Letter from "A Freeman," *Providence Gazette,* October 14, 1786. As early as August another writer, under the pseudonym of "A Farmer," had warned that the country party planned to curtail the number of minority voters (*Providence Gazette,* August 19, 1786) .

39. Rogers to Nicholas Brown, Newport, October 16, 1786, Brown Papers, Mss., J.C.B.L.

40. Staples, *Annals of Providence,* pp. 306–9; *Providence Gazette,* October 24, 1786.

41. *Newport Mercury,* October 30, 1786.

42. *Ibid.,* November 6, 1786; *U.S. Chronicle* (Providence) , November 2, 1786.

rayed 51 to 3 against the bill.[43] The country extremists had gone too far. When the suggested law came to a vote in the lower house, only six deputies voted in its favor.[44] The defeat was overwhelming.

Although the country party suffered a smashing setback on the proposed test act, it was not without new weapons against the merchants. At the December, 1786, session of the General Assembly, the long-standing threat to destroy the most common types of business credit— promissory notes and book accounts—was passed into law.[45] The statute provided for the redemption of all promissory notes and other informal instruments of short-term credit within a period of two years. Ominous for the mercantile minority was yet another line of attack. Once more the country party tried to force a revision of the charter of 1663 in order to gain an equal representation of the towns in the House of Deputies. If this proposal became law, the minority would have lost its chief source of legislative strength in the weighted representation granted to Providence and Newport under the charter.

Failing to win equal representation of the towns at the end of 1786, the country party again sought to amend the charter in the spring of 1787. At the March session of the General Assembly, a bill embodying this reform was sent to the towns for the decision of the freemen directly. The country party, though they had the votes, dared not make such a basic change in Rhode Island's constitution without consulting the people in a referendum.[46] The proposal received an intensive hearing in the towns.

Probably the country party leaders anticipated a powerful ground swell of enthusiasm for an equal representation of the towns in the Assembly, hoping to capitalize on their substantial majority in favor of the paper-money system. But this ground swell did not develop. The argument in favor of the amendment was best expressed by the freemen of Johnston in their instructions to the town's representatives in the legislature. These instructions recalled the early days of the colony,

43. Smithfield Town Meeting, Mss., October 27, 1786; Warwick Town Meeting, Mss., October 21, 1786; Exeter Town Meeting, Mss., October 26, 1786.

44. *Newport Mercury*, November 13, 1786.

45. For the legislative record and text of the bill, see Acts and Resolves of the General Assembly, Mss., R.I.S.A., Vol. 25, p. 82; Journals of the House of Deputies, December 28, 29, 1786, Mss., R.I.S.A.; Bartlett, *Records*, X, 226; and the *U.S. Chronicle* (Providence), January 7, 1787.

46. Rhode Island Records, Mss., R.I.S.A., Vol. 13, p. 366; *Providence Gazette*, March 31, 1787.

when an unequal representation of the four original towns was thought equitable and necessary to ensure the presence of enough deputies to carry on the business of government. Since the seventeenth century, the freemen complained, enough new and populous towns had been incorporated to render the weighted representation an anachronism.[47] In contrast, the town of Providence described the bill as an improper infringement of the state's constitution, explaining that the General Assembly could not lawfully play any part in amending the charter. The Assembly was limited in its legislative power by the charter, reasoned the Providence meeting, and because of this it should not alter the document. Indeed, any change in the state constitution must originate in a special convention called for that purpose alone.[48] New Shoreham's town meeting advised against amending the charter during a period of bitter political contention. The freemen believed any change of "the Constitution at this time would be attended with evil Consequences." [49]

With the division of the towns evenly balanced, the decision in the General Assembly was very close. The equal-representation amendment lost by a single vote in the lower house. Significantly, the weighted representation of the four shire towns of Rhode Island—Providence, Newport, Warwick, and Portsmouth—brought defeat to the country party.[50] But the plan was never long in abeyance during the Confederation years, for, if it had ever been enacted into law, the political power of the merchants in Rhode Island would have been even more badly shaken.

Further evidence of the increasingly combative turn that the paper-money movement had taken was manifested when the country party looked with favor upon a petition to the General Assembly, signed by 107 freemen, calling for the repeal of Newport's city charter and the restoration of the town-meeting form of government. The petition asserted that the city government, established in 1784, which placed legislative and executive power in the hands of a mayor, alderman, and a city council, was unsuitable to a free people.[51] The petitioners pre-

47. Johnston Town Meeting, Mss., June 4, 1787.
48. Staples, *Annals of Providence*, pp. 311–15.
49. New Shoreham Town Meeting, April 18, 1787, Papers Relating to the Adoption of the Constitution, Mss., R.I.S.A.
50. *Newport Herald*, November 8, 1787; *Providence Gazette*, November 10, 1787.
51. Petitions to the General Assembly, Mss., R.I.S.A., Vol. 23, p. 83.

ferred the direct democracy of a town meeting. The document charged that the "undemocratic" city government had been captured by a small group of "influential Men" who used the special powers of the Newport government to enhance their own prestige and purse.

On the face of it, the controversy over the Newport city charter might have been a nonpartisan one, except that Newport was an important center of disaffection from the paper-money system and a major source of strength for the merchants. Added to this was the opposition of Nicholas Easton, a Newport land owner and country party leader, who was an intractable enemy of the city administration. Easton was a direct descendant of an original founder of Rhode Island. He claimed certain tracts of land which the city asserted were public property. A complicated suit over the contested land was adjudicated by a special court of referees, which included Benjamin Huntington, governor of Connecticut, and Oliver Ellsworth, later Chief Justice of the United States Supreme Court. The case was decided against the stubborn Easton.[52] Afterwards he was hostile to the merchants who ran the city government.

When the petition against the Newport city charter was presented to the Assembly late in 1786, it found two important sources of strength in the country party: Nicholas Easton, and the hope that a reversion back to a town-meeting form of government might give greater strength to the small group of paper-money freemen in Newport.[53] At the March, 1787, session of the legislature, Jonathan J. Hazard and Thomas Joslyn of West Greenwich, two key country party spokesmen in the Assembly, urged acceptance of the petition and the vacating of the Newport charter. The General Assembly acted accordingly, and the city of Newport was once again a town.[54] But the expectations of neither the country politicians nor Nicholas Easton were fulfilled. The freemen of Newport reassembled in a town meeting and defiantly approved a resolution of appreciation to the old city administrators, thanking them for their past services to the people. The meeting re-elected many members of the city government to run the town; the

52. Easton's position is analyzed in George C. Mason, "Nicholas Easton vs. the City of Newport," *Proceedings of the Rhode Island Historical Society,* V (1875–76) , 15–18.

53. Letter from "Fidelis," *Newport Herald,* April 12, 1787.

54. Rhode Island Records, Mss., R.I.S.A., Vol. 13, p. 351; Bartlett, *Records,* X, 233–34; *Newport Herald,* March 22, 1787; *Newport Mercury,* March 26, 1787.

merchants still controlled Newport.[55] As for Easton, he was somewhat more successful. The General Assembly intervened in his dispute with Newport and upset the judgment of the court of referees. But the agreement he reached with the town government on the disputed property was still short of what he wanted.[56]

Proposals for Compromise

These increasingly truculent policies of the country party caused the merchants to regret their original attitude of intransigence toward the paper-money emission. They had badly miscalculated when they surmised that political and economic pressures might topple the country party from power. Blind opposition merely engendered blind rage.[57] A publicist put his apprehension into doggerel form for the newspapers:

> When now the mob in lucky hour,
> Had got their enemies in their power;
> For in the ferment of the stream,
> The dregs have work'd up to the brim,
> And by the rule of topsy turveys,
> The scum stands swelling on the surface.[58]

The mercantile minority began to express concern about its future in Rhode Island. After their initial attacks on the paper-money system, the merchants mounted an energetic campaign to compromise the issues in dispute between the parties. A number of proposals were put forward at various sessions of the General Assembly after the currency was emitted. In every instance they were spurned.

In the summer of 1786 the minority first entertained the idea of a compromise by suggesting that a bipartisan committee of the lower house of the legislature be appointed to draw up the terms of a political truce in Rhode Island. These representatives were supposed to meet and "coolly discuss the Subject, and try if possible to agree on

55. *Newport Mercury*, April 2, 1787.

56. *Newport Herald*, June 21, 1787.

57. "An Essay on Discord in the States," *U.S. Chronicle* (Providence), March 16, 1786. See also the letters from "A.Z." and "A Constitutional Republican," *Providence Gazette*, July 7, August 5, 1786.

58. *Providence Gazette*, March 31, 1787.

some middle Line, that more Harmony and Unanimity might take place." [59] Though this initial feeler to the majority was rejected at the June, 1786, session of the General Assembly, John Brown announced in a public letter that the proposal would remain open indefinitely. More specifically, Brown spelled out his compromise in greater detail than the vague suggestions of early summer. He recommended a plan that called for an immediate end to any further paper-money loans, which then totaled about £40,000—less than half the authorized emission. Brown also asked for the repeal of that portion of the emitting act which made the currency a legal tender for past debts. In return for these concessions, which would have restricted the amount of the paper bills and exempted the state securities, as past contracts, from the operation of the tender laws, Brown pledged: "I promise to countenance the money, and do every thing in my power to give it a currency." [60] This initial attempt at compromise was a failure. A paper-money partisan responded to Brown's proposals with a frank appraisal: "A middle line cannot be drawn; because the state securities must, or must not, be paid. If the money is a tender for past contracts it may pay them, otherwise it cannot." [61]

The pressure of the merchants for compromise did bear some fruit in the fall of 1786 when a committee of ten members of the General Assembly, drawn from leaders in both parties, was appointed to consider ways to resolve political differences in Rhode Island and to support the paper emission.[62] This time the merchants offered more in the hope of gaining an accommodation with the country party. They asked that the laws be relaxed to permit a tender of paper money to suspend future interest payments on a debt until the creditor was willing to accept the currency, but not to extinguish the debt entirely. In the case of judgments obtained by court action, the merchants were willing to have the paper bills operate as an absolute discharge on any payments due to a creditor. The merchants also agreed to the liquidation of the state debt in paper money, provided that the legal-tender laws were reformed as they suggested and that sufficient taxes were imposed to create a platform for the stability of the currency. Lastly,

59. Letter from "A Friend to the State," *U.S. Chronicle* (Providence), July 13, 1786.

60. Letter of John Brown, *Providence Gazette*, July 8, 1786. See also the letter from "Persius" in the *Newport Herald*, May 24, 1787.

61. Dialogue signed "A.B.," *U.S. Chronicle* (Providence), August 10, 1786.

62. Letter from "A Well-Wisher to the State," *Newport Mercury*, October 9, 1786.

they insisted that the penal laws be repealed where they infringed upon civil rights. This plan was agreeable to the committee over the objections of two of its country party members, but it was defeated in the General Assembly.[63]

Defeat did not stifle the mercantile hope for compromise. On several occasions after 1786 the merchants attempted to get country party approval of an agreement to end the political divisions in Rhode Island. At the March, 1787, session of the legislature, the earlier plans were refurbished, with the additional understanding that the paper money should circulate as a legal tender for all debts, past as well as present and future, but at a discount of four to one, though the rate then current was more than six to one. The minority pointed out that this proposal would allow the state securities to be redeemed in paper bills, and the merchants would support this liquidation. By now the opposition knew that the hold of the country party on the freemen was unshakable, and they sought to compromise by accepting the circulation of the currency at a depreciated rate. Under these circumstances, they believed, the state's economic life would again return to some semblance of stability. The compromise plan, however, was rejected in the House of Deputies by a majority of seventeen. A resolution of the merchants to send the proposal to the town meetings in a referendum was set aside without a vote.[64]

When all attempts at conciliation had failed, the merchants prepared for the political campaign of 1787. They had faint hope of victory. Their purpose in entering the contest was not to score an electoral triumph, for such expectations were chimerical, but with the expectation that, if they secured a substantial vote in opposition to the country policies, their chance for a compromise settlement would be enhanced. For this reason the spring elections were hard-fought.

Governor John Collins and Deputy Governor Daniel Owen sought re-election at the head of the country party's slate of candidates. They ran on a platform that called for "Perseverance" in the paper-money system. The country party pledged to be steadfast in supporting the

63. *Providence Gazette,* October 14, 1786.
64. *Newport Herald,* March 22, 1787. Important aspects of the mercantile attitude may be seen in a letter from "Sidney," *Newport Herald,* April 12, 1787; and letters from "Plato," *U.S. Chronicle* (Providence), April 12, 19, 1787. There were continuing mercantile entreaties aimed at compromise as late as the summer of 1789. But then, as before, the country leaders declared "they will not repeal, or make any alteration in the present law, till such time as all the State notes are carried into the Treasury and cancelled" (*Gazette of the United States* [New York], July 1, 1789).

currency and promised to act as quickly as possible to pay off the state debt in paper money. The country appeal to the mass of farmers also asked for unity and cautioned Rhode Islanders to be suspicious of the mercantile propositions for compromise. One country slogan proclaimed: *"Landholder! Beware; be firm and persevere: For United we stand, divided we fall."* [65]

The mercantile coalition ran William Bradford, an attorney from the commercial town of Bristol, as its candidate for governor. Bradford's platform was one of moderation. The fundamental theme of the mercantile candidates was the belief that the paper-money system had done nothing to relieve the state's economic and financial crisis and was a disgrace to Rhode Island. Every mercantile spokesman declared that the country party had not succeeded in its promised program of public relief, implying that things were worse in 1787 than in the years before. The incumbent government was also denounced for having embittered relations between Rhode Island and the Union. Minority candidates charged that the country administration had alienated the United States Congress by attempting to pay its federal bills in paper money and by refusing to provide needed revenues to protect the territories in the West. Good citizens everywhere in the Union had held Rhode Island in disrepute since the beginning of the paper-money system. To be a resident of Rhode Island, said critics of the government, had become a synonym for villain.[66] A vote for the mercantile party was hailed as the only way to escape infamy.

There was no comfort for the mercantile minority in the balloting at the end of April, 1787. The country party received an unprecedented vote of confidence from the freemen. John Collins was re-elected governor of Rhode Island by a vote of 2,969 to 1,141, receiving more than twice the ballots given his opponent, William Bradford. Similar majorities were given other country party candidates; every one of its nominees for office was elected. The incumbent attorney general, William Channing of Newport, who applauded the Trevett decision and was hostile to the various penal laws, was turned out of office by a margin of 1,152, losing to the state's attorney in that case, Henry Goodwin. James Mitchell Varnum, also associated with the Trevett

65. Eighteenth Century Election Proxies, R.I.H.S., Nos. 2045, 2043, 1447, 1464. This pledge of "Perseverance" was used by the country party in the campaigns of 1788 and 1789.

66. Letters of "A Freeman," and "An Independent Elector," *Providence Gazette,* April 7, 14, 1787.

case and marked by his well-known nationalism, was beaten in a race for Congress by 1,558 votes. In another congressional contest, Jonathan J. Hazard tested his popularity and won by 1,516 votes.[67] Only in Providence and Newport did the mercantile minority attract sizable numbers of freemen. It was not nearly enough to win in Rhode Island.

Culmination

The country party triumph in the spring of 1787 set the stage for the culmination of the principal relief measure promised the year before —the redemption of the state's debts in paper money. Already at the end of 1786, the General Assembly had established a committee of four of its members to investigate and analyze the problem of the internal debt of Rhode Island and to report on its findings to the legislature. In anticipation of the committee's report, in December, 1786, the General Assembly ordered the payment of one-fourth of the state securities in paper money.[68]

The report of the committeemen—the country party leaders Oliver Durfee, John Sayles, Thomas Joslyn, and the ever present Jonathan J. Hazard—was presented at the March, 1787, session of the Assembly. The long-awaited analysis of the state debts found that the bulk of the securities had originated during the American Revolution at real values far less than their nominal worth in the Confederation period, corroborating the widely held opinion that appreciation of the state debt made devaluation of the securities a matter of justice. But the committee made no recommendation for a reduction of the principal of the debt, except for the 4 per cent notes, which it believed should be redeemed at a rate of forty to one.[69] By now everyone understood that forcing depreciated paper money upon the state's creditors would be the same as a reduction of the principal without formal governmental action; and insofar as the merchants had brought about this depreciation by not accepting the currency on a par with specie, they were responsible for their own misfortune. The General Assembly voted its

67. *U.S. Chronicle* (Providence) , May 10, 1787.
68. Rhode Island Records, Mss., R.I.S.A., Vol. 13, pp. 314–15, 341, 345; Bartlett, *Records*, X, 218, 230.
69. Bartlett, *Records*, X, 236–37. The report also appeared as a broadside entitled: "*State of Rhode Island,* etc. To the Honorable the *General Assembly* of the State of Rhode Island, etc." Broadsides, 1774–1795, R.I.H.S., No. A–1084.

approval of the committee report, excluding only that part of the findings relative to the 4 per cent notes. In the upper house there were objections to the forty-to-one rate for this class of debts. Several members of the Assistants asserted that in many instances the 4 per cent notes had been secured in hard money. Consequently, the General Assembly continued the committee's investigation into these notes in order to determine their original value and to be certain that no creditor holding these claims against the state suffered undue injury.

With the committee report confirming what the majority of Rhode Islanders already felt was true, and with the electoral victory of 1787 providing a vote of confidence, the government proceeded to redeem the internal debt of Rhode Island. In four installments the 6 per cent notes were ordered liquidated in paper money by the fall of 1789. Anyone who refused to accept the paper bills had the whole sum of his state securities voided. After much dispute and controversy, the 4 per cent notes—which rumor incorrectly suggested were mostly owned by the paper-money leaders—were repaid in paper bills during the spring and winter of 1789. There was no reduction in the nominal value of this class of Rhode Island securities.[70]

By the end of 1789 the country party administration managed to redeem the full amount of the Rhode Island state debt. Rhode Island was now in the enviable situation of complete freedom from any debts. The money to pay those willing to accept the depreciated currency was obtained through taxation. Between August, 1785, and June, 1789, the General Assembly authorized over $400,000 in taxes; the state also collected nearly $60,000 in interest on the paper-money loans of 1786. The total fund came to $486,000.[71] Of this amount, $243,053.26 was used to liquidate the debts of the state. This redemption succeeded only over the massive opposition of the merchants. Defeat in the election of 1787 convinced the merchants that a continuing struggle against the country party was necessary to bring its leaders to reason; compromise, they knew, was improbable. As a result, when the General Assembly ordered the repayment of the state securities in paper money, the merchants refused to accept any of the currency. In accordance with the law, they forfeited their holdings—$344,259.49 of the

70. The legislative record of the repayment of the state debts may be traced in the Rhode Island Records, Mss., R.I.S.A., Vol. 13; Acts and Resolves of the General Assembly, Mss., R.I.S.A., Vol. 25, pp. 98, 120, 140; Vol. 26, pp. 14, 25, 27, 48; and Bartlett, *Records*, X, 266, 280, 293–94, 305–6.

71. Report on the Registered State Debt, Ms., R.I.S.A., pp. 43–44, 100.

total state debt of $587,312.75.[72] The mercantile stand against the proffered payments was nearly complete, and those merchants with the largest sums of the state debts—Nicholas Brown, John Brown, John Smith, John Jenckes, and the firm of Clark and Nightingale—were unwilling to accept depreciated money in exchange for their securities.[73] The vast number of notes voluntarily redeemed were owned by those who held the smallest amounts of the debt. Approximately 750 persons took the paper currency in payments from the state. Of the 3,117 Rhode Island securities liquidated in paper money, only 118 exceeded £100 in value; 1,174 were in amounts from £10 to £50; 1,566 were in notes from £1 to £10; and 67 were under £1.[74] Similarly, each quarterly repayment of the 6 per cent securities was dominated by the small creditors of Rhode Island. Among the average of 742 subscribers to the third and fourth quarterly subscriptions, 17 persons received over £100; 143 accepted from £20 to £100; with the remaining number of 583 creditors claiming from £1 to £20.[75] The same was true of the liquidation of the 4 per cent securities. Only 14 out of a total of 515 subscribers claimed more than £200 in principal and interest, while there were 273 subscriptions under £20.[76] In light of the mercantile noncompliance and the depreciated value of the paper-money payments, Governor Arthur Fenner, Jr., estimated that the liquidation payment between 1786 and 1789 was equal to one-sixth the nominal specie value of all the Rhode Island securities.[77] This sum redeemed the entire amount.

A second important aspect of the paper-money system in Rhode Island was the way in which the currency was used to liquidate private debts. As noted earlier, the paper bills were made legal tender in all commercial transactions under the original emitting act of 1786. This

72. The figure of $344,259.49 was the amount of Rhode Island securities subscribed in the federal loan of 1790. Because the merchants did not surrender their securities for paper money, they were permitted to subscribe this amount to the loan that was part of the Hamiltonian assumption of the state debts. The sum of $243,053.26 liquidated in paper money, added to the $344,259.49 that was not, gives a figure of $587,312.75 for the total Rhode Island state debt.
73. The document labeled Description of Notes (on which the State have paid a part) agreeable to an Act of Assembly passed at June Session A.D. 1791, Ms., R.I.S.A., contains a list of every person who was willing to accept paper money. None of the above-mentioned merchants were included.
74. Report on the Registered State Debt, Ms., R.I.S.A., p. 35.
75. General Treasurer's Accounts, Book No. 7, Mss., R.I.S.A., pp. 265–304.
76. An Account of the Persons who have Received the First Quarter Part of the Principal & Interest of the 4 pc Notes, Ms., R.I.S.A.
77. Bartlett, *Records*, X, 451–53.

enabled Rhode Islanders to tender depreciated paper money in the payment of their debts, prompting charges of fraud and cheat which have ever since characterized Confederation Rhode Island. Naturally, whether such tenders were truly fraudulent would depend on the real value of each debt at the time it was incurred. Had these debts appreciated in real value because of the deflation of the postwar period? If so, a reduction of the principal of a debt by an offer of depreciated paper bills may well have been fair and equitable. Most Rhode Islanders believed this was the case and saw no greater injustice in such payments than the unreasonable demands of their creditors for full compensation.

During the paper-money era approximately £17,000 was tendered in the satisfaction of private contracts and, when refused by creditors, was lodged with the courts as allowed by the paper-money statutes.[78] Upon the continued refusal of a creditor to accept the money so lodged, the funds were forfeited to the state. The actual total of forced payments was probably higher, for the £17,000 figure does not account for tenders that were accepted by creditors under the threat of forfeiture to the state. Most Rhode Islanders considered these tenders an act of necessity. Interestingly, many individuals who tendered paper money during the Confederation period later compensated their creditors a second time. Obviously, for these people the offer of paper bills was not an escape from financial difficulties into fraud. The operation of the paper-money system with respect to private debts was similar to that of "stay laws" which suspended the completion of contracts. The full amount of money lodged with the courts that was surrendered to the state came to £13,515 1d. Between 1788 and 1798 there were more than 50 petitions to the Assembly requesting the return of forfeited money to debtors who had reached an "amicable settlement" with their former creditors. Before 1792, £845 7s. 9d. was given back to debtors by order of the General Assembly after they presented evidence of having worked out another financial arrangement with their creditors. In 1808 only £6,869 14s. 10½d. remained in the treasury of the total sum of money forfeited to the government. This was just over half the funds confiscated in the forced satisfaction of private debts.[79]

78. This is the tabulation of Forrest McDonald in *We the People: The Economic Origins of the Constitution* (Chicago, 1958), p. 332.
79. General Treasurer's Accounts 1714–1737 [and] Auditor's Reports 1732–1815, Mss.; Petitions to the General Assembly, Mss., Vols. 24–31; and Reports to the General Assembly, Mss., Vol. 6, p. 107; all are in the Rhode Island State Archives.

Notwithstanding the absence of a desire to defraud their creditors, many debtors found themselves hard-pressed to explain why they had taken this step. It was often difficult to avoid the imputation of cheating when such an interpretation might easily fit the circumstances of most debts liquidated by a forced tender of paper bills. In consequence a tender of paper money was an act of disrepute that had to be explained and defended. A perfect example of this was provided by a lodgment of paper bills by William West of Scituate, justice of the Superior Court and a country party leader. After offering the currency to his creditor, who would not accept it, West lodged the tender with the courts. He then found himself obliged to enter into a lengthy and public explanation of his action.[80] West's story of a hard-money debt contracted many years before at inflated prices, his repeated offers of real property twice the value of the loan in repayment, and his difficulties in accumulating the specie needed to satisfy the letter of his obligation, was offered as justification for a tender of paper bills. West's tale of woe was little different from those of other debtors who forced paper money upon their creditors.[81] But it is important to note that justification was believed necessary.

The advent of the paper-money era brought tremendous problems for the merchants in the course of their normal business affairs. As creditors, of course, they found it almost impossible to collect what was due them without the danger of being forced to take paper bills. As debtors themselves, the merchants found it difficult to meet their own obligations. Generally it was prudent not to extend new credit to anyone or even to bring new merchandise into the state; thus one could never be forced to accept the paper currency.[82] The merchants and other creditors were driven to a series of ingenious artifices to avoid having a tender made which might extinguish a hard-money debt. One method was to sign over estates and securities to out-of-state residents, with the knowledge that those not on hand could not be penalized

80. Advertisement of William West, *Providence Gazette*, December 3, 1789.

81. See, for example, the document entitled, "Col. Cooks proposals to his Creditors," in which Cook says he will tender paper currency despite the "Great Sensure of being a Designing paper Money man" (Miscellaneous Manuscripts, N.H.S., Box 43, Folder 12).

82. Lane, Son, and Fraser to Christopher Champlin, London, October 16, 1786, and William Greene to Christopher Champlin, London, January 24, 1787, both in Wetmore Collection, Mss., M.H.S.; letter from "A Lover of Justice and Peace," *Providence Gazette*, July 22, 1786.

with paper money.[83] The public-spirited Brown family also moved to save the endowment of the university in Providence from depletion because of payments in depreciated currency. They sponsored an act in the General Assembly that excluded incorporated bodies from the operation of the legal-tender laws, so that their future incomes would be fully protected.[84]

			COMBINED	
AMOUNT LOANED	NUMBER OF PERSONS	PER CENT OF TOTAL PERSONS	VALUE OF LOANS	PER CENT OF TOTAL AMOUNT
£500 and Over	8	.4	£ 7,969	8.3
£100 to Under £500	199	10.6	33,250	34.6
£50 to Under £100	320	17.1	21,404	22.2
£1 to Under £50	1,351	71.9	33,524	34.9

TABLE 3. PAPER MONEY LOANS, 1786

(All loans have been rounded off to the highest £.)

The manuscript records of the paper-money administration in Rhode Island show that 1,878 loans were contracted during the period when the paper bills were available to citizens of the state. This meant that almost 25 per cent of the freemen took advantage of the low-interest loans made possible by the government. Of these loans, the greater number were for small sums. (See Table 3.) Only 207 persons borrowed over £100, while the number of loans under £50, 1,351, was

83. Benjamin Bowen to Thomas Worthington, Providence, June 2, 1786, Peck Collection, Mss., R.I.H.S., Box VIII, p. 12; Brown and Benson to Hewes and Anthony, Providence, October 2, 1789, and "John Brown's Memo for Mr. John Francis," both in Brown Papers, Mss., J.C.B.L.; William Rodman to William Ellery, Bensalem, May 14, 1787, November 15, 1790, April 9, 1791, February 22, 1792, Miscellaneous Manuscripts, N.H.S., Box 1, Folder 6.

84. Copy of an Act to prevent paper money being a tender to any of the incorporated bodies in the state, May 6, 1786, Brown Papers, Mss., J.C.B.L. A notation by Nicholas Brown said by "this act the College fund was saved from being paid in paper money." See Bartlett, *Records*, X, 199, for the statute.

71.9 per cent of the total figure of 1,878 loans made by the state.[85] For the most part, therefore, the paper emission was initially a supply of credit for real-property holders and those in need of small amounts of money. Despite this general observation, there also tended to be a concentration of the amounts borrowed in the hands of a smaller number of persons, especially in certain towns. The 207 individuals who borrowed the highest sums took 42.9 per cent of the entire amount. Although in only a few instances were the paper bills taken by the most important merchants and commercial firms, there were enough large farmers and smaller merchants everywhere in Rhode Island to subscribe a substantial proportion of the paper money funds. Examined on a town-by-town basis, the commercial centers saw the greatest concentrations in the amounts of money borrowed. In Newport, 15.9 per cent of the number of borrowers took 73.1 per cent of the total amount; in Providence, tabulations reveal that 20.7 per cent of the number of subscribers borrowed 69.6 per cent of the currency available to the town. A similar pattern developed in several of the influential farming communities. For example, in Charlestown, more than half the paper money available was lent to 17.1 per cent of all the borrowers. Of course, these concentrations were to some extent offset by the pattern of loans in other parts of Rhode Island, particularly the inland agricultural towns. The best case was in West Greenwich, where only 1 person received more than £100 while the remaining 79 borrowers took more than 95 per cent of the full sum.

As might be expected, opposition of the mercantile minority to the paper-money system did not prevent some of the merchants from making use of the new state credit fund. The largest single loan was granted to the commercial firm of Clark and Nightingale—£2,625. (The other loan of more than £1,000 was contracted by the wealthy Newport landowner, Nicholas Easton.) Such important mercantile leaders as Theodore Foster, Benjamin Bourne, and John Malbone borrowed funds in varying amounts. The reasons for the loans made to prominent opponents of the paper-money system was the value of the paper money in trade, especially after it began to circulate unofficially at depreciated rates, and the fact that the currency might always be used to meet any tax obligation to the towns or the state. Indeed, even some of the great merchants who did not borrow the paper currency

85. These figures and those which follow are tabulated from two manuscript volumes of the paper-money administrators labeled Grand Committee Office, Account Books A. & B., 1786–1803, R.I.S.A.

began to use it in trade and accumulated it at depreciated rates.[86] Virtually all the towns, whether commercial or agricultural, subscribed close to the full amount of their allotted proportion of the paper money. In many instances, moreover, merchants were not loath to tender the depreciated currency in satisfaction of debts they owed. One estimate finds that merchants, almost as frequently as farmers, tendered the currency to their creditors.[87] All of which seems to indicate that the paper-money system may not have been so dastardly a scheme as the relentless condemnation of the mercantile minority had made it seem.

Repeal

The redemption of the state debts was the final work for which the paper-money emission had been created, and its reason for being had now disappeared. A movement to repeal the legal-tender laws gained new strength early in 1788 as the discharge of the state securities proceeded to an end, picking up steam in 1789 when all of Rhode Island's debts were liquidated by the government. Before the year was out the legal-tender provisions of the paper-money system were repealed.

The most important step on the road to repeal was a forceful petition presented by the Society of Friends at the February, 1788, session of the General Assembly. The Quakers denounced the paper-money system and urged that the legislature reconsider its vindictive act abolishing most forms of short-term business credit. The petitioners called attention to the depreciation of the paper money, asserting that its legal-tender status on a par with gold and silver was unjust. Since the Society of Friends was a large and powerful denomination in Rhode Island, the petition received a respectful and patient hearing in the General Assembly. Instead of voting it down immediately—a likely thing, because the discharge of the public securities was incomplete—the legislators sent the petition directly to the freemen for consideration in their town meetings.[88] In the towns the Quaker demands were

86. Thomas Rumreil to Welcome Arnold, Newport, March 23, 1786, Welcome Arnold Papers, Mss., J.C.B.L.
87. McDonald, *We the People*, p. 333.
88. Rhode Island Records, Mss., R.I.S.A., Vol. 13, p. 438; Bartlett, *Records*, X, 268· *Providence Gazette*, March 1, 1788; *Newport Herald*, March 6, 1788.

given a surprisingly favorable reception. Although the legal-tender provisions of the paper-money statutes were upheld, the request for the repeal of the act restricting business credit was approved.[89] When the General Assembly again convened in April, 1788, the statute limiting instruments of private credit was repealed. The tender laws were retained.[90]

The Quaker petition gave a powerful moral impetus to the revision of the paper-money system. Its disapproval of forced tenders of depreciated paper money quickened the tides of change in Rhode Island. With all the public securities paid off in 1789, repeal was only a matter of time. A positive signal came in the spring of 1789 when the town of Warwick, one of the initial sponsors of a paper-money medium, came out in favor of repeal. Earlier, on March 24, 1788, when the Quaker petition had been reviewed, the freemen rejected it by a vote of 98 to 24; in April, 1789, they were in favor of repeal.[91] Late in the summer of 1789, Governor John Collins called the General Assembly into special session, and rumor had it that he would ask for the withdrawal of the legal-tender statutes.[92] The Assembly confirmed the rumor when it suspended the legal-tender articles of the paper-money system. In October, 1789, these provisions were fully repealed, and an official scale of depreciation for the currency was set up by statute.[93] The paper-money system in Rhode Island had quietly come to an end.

89. Charlestown and Westerly, for example, voted to continue the tender laws, but their manuscript records show they agreed to repeal the statute limiting business credit. More significantly, the town meeting manuscripts show that several hitherto paper-money communities, such as Cumberland, Middletown, and Little Compton, supported the entire petition, Little Compton unanimously.

90. *Newport Herald,* April 10, 1788; *Providence Gazette,* April 12, 1788.

91. This is based on the town meeting manuscripts of Warwick. A similar change of sentiment may be seen in the town of Warren, where the freeman adopted an official town discount rate for the paper bills. Moreover, the country party itself revealed that repeal was on hand when in May, 1789, the Assembly agreed to pay the salaries of the Justices of the Superior Court of Judicature at the rate of six to ten to one (*Newport Herald,* May 14, 1789) . The establishment of a discount showed the country leadership was ready to change the legal-tender provisions of the paper-money system, which nominally required the acceptance of the paper bills on a par with specie.

92. William Ellery to Benjamin Huntington, Newport, September 8, 1789, Ellery Letters, Mss., R.I.S.A.

93. Rhode Island Colony Records, Mss., R.I.S.A, Vol. 13, pp. 664, 671–72, 675–83, 694; Bartlett, *Records,* X, 355, 366; *U.S. Chronicle* (Providence) , September 24, October 22, November 5, 1789; *Providence Gazette,* September 26, November 7, 1789.

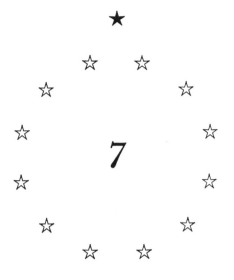

Rhode Island and the Union

SUCCESS CROWNED the policies of the country party in Rhode Island. Its primary objective, redemption of the state debt in paper currency, was achieved without concession to the mercantile opposition. Despite charges to the contrary, liquidation of the state securities in paper bills was proposed as an alternative to nonpayment or unacceptable levels of taxation. Of secondary importance as a motive force behind the paper-money movement was the burden of private debts. The wide dispersal of paper-money loans and the willingness of farmers and non-farmers to make use of the currency gives evidence of the value of the money as a source of credit in satisfying private debts and in meeting tax obligations to the state.

The country party success was not without its costs. Rhode Island was divided into two hostile political camps. Unlike the colonial factional struggles, the Confederation contest was tied to important issues and eventually took on ideological characteristics in the battle over the federal Constitution of 1787. On the question of using paper money to pay off the state debt, the political struggle arrayed the largest merchants against the majority of farmers throughout the state; from the point of view of geography, the commercial centers of Providence, Newport, and Bristol, with occasional support from other commercial towns, opposed the rural communities still predominant in Rhode Island. More complex is the problem of the private debt and the use of the money in paying taxes and other commercial transactions. With the exception of Clarke and Nightingale, a Providence commercial firm, the largest merchants did not subscribe to the paper-money loans or tender the bills in the execution of private contracts. But many who were opposed to the country party did utilize the money. The paper currency, in other words, was not without value, even to its enemies. This did not signify, however, any lessening of mercantile opposition to the paper-money system, nor did it modify political divisions within Rhode Island. The merchants had aimed at total victory; they achieved instead total defeat. Reduced to impotence in the popular elections of 1786 and 1787, they denounced unsparingly the paper-money system. These denunciations had an important impact on public opinion in the United States. Everywhere Americans were convinced that the Rhode Island situation showed the dangers inherent in state control of the nation's future and was symptomatic of the crisis of the Union.

Despite the fact that six other American states emitted paper money during the Confederation years, Rhode Island bore the brunt of interstate attacks on these emissions, even from those other states that printed paper money. The reasons for the calumny that fell upon the state were its unorthodox origins and its controversial paper-money issues during the colonial period. The entire nation knew Rhode Island's reputation and was sensitized to expect the disreputable from the Narragansett state. Of greater importance were the legal-tender provisions of the paper-money statutes. Only in Rhode Island was a creditor obliged to accept the money under the threat of forfeiture of the debt and penalties if a tender was refused. No other state emission contained these stipulations, giving credence to mercantile accusations that the Rhode Island system was rooted in dishonesty and confiscation. The ensuing political struggle gave the Rhode Island conflict a focus it did not attain elsewhere, with the exception perhaps of the less publicized situation in North Carolina. The fact that the other paper-money systems were supported from the start by some of the most powerful merchants precluded the unyielding political battles of Confederation Rhode Island. Pennsylvania and South Carolina, particularly, had notable examples of paper-money programs that elicited mercantile cooperation and were able to succeed without undue acrimony and depreciation.[1] In Rhode Island there were no holds barred during the abusive mercantile campaign against the paper-money system.

Infamy

The unsavory reputation of Confederation Rhode Island, therefore, originated largely in the state itself, for the mercantile minority refused to acknowledge publicly that the policies of the country party were justified in any degree, despite its willingness to recognize that a crisis existed and privately to accept parts of the country program if a compromise was possible. For public consumption the merchants held that the Confederation period "was the worst time that the inhabitants of Rhode Island ever saw." [2] In a steady stream of complaints, the minority alleged that trade and commerce had been recklessly disrupted by the policies initiated in May, 1786.[3] Worrisome also were the political implications of these excesses. Opponents of the country party asserted that liberty and freedom were threatened by a tyrannical majority that knew no bounds. Mercantile domination of the press and contacts outside the state caused this image to be propagated throughout the United States.

The mercantile caricature was repeated as unqualified truth in the nation's newspapers, the most important medium of information and a primary influence in the formulation of public opinion. Innumerable articles and exhortations about Rhode Island's condition were printed, each declaring that paper money had been issued as a substi-

1. The best accounts of the Confederation paper-money emissions may be found in Merrill Jensen, *The New Nation: A History of the United States During the Confederation 1781–1789* (New York, 1950), pp. 313–26; and E. James Ferguson, *The Power of the Purse: A History of American Public Finance, 1776–1790* (Chapel Hill, 1961), pp. 228–50, which is especially illuminating on the relationship between the public debts and paper currency. A somewhat less sympathetic commentary is offered by Curtis P. Nettels, *The Emergence of a National Economy 1775–1815* (New York, 1962), pp. 75–88.

2. Letter from "Poor Old Honesty," *Newport Mercury*, March 29, 1787; "History founded on Facts—Chap. 2nd," Carter-Danforth Papers, 1770–1790, Mss., R.I.H.S.

3. *Newport Mercury*, September 4, 1786.

tute for honesty and justice. News reports informed the American people of the disaster that had overtaken the Rhode Island economy. An estimate of the monetary loss to the state during the first year of the *"Paper Influenza"* was given as £100,000 specie.[4] Unhappy correspondence from Rhode Island reported the "melancholy fact that since the accession to office of our present rules—our commerce hath astonishingly declined—our *Honest Mechanics* and our lands and houses have sunk in value; in addition to which, we have to lament the loss of public and private credit, the only basis of a commercial nation." [5] Other items recounted the supposed disorders that tore at the vitals of Rhode Island because of the paper emission. Eyewitness accounts of travelers—predating the reporters of today—told of the state's doleful outlook, with little business being done amid scenes of political havoc and confusion.[6] A much reprinted dispatch pleaded for a Hogarth, to "Try his graving tools, / On such an odious group of *Knaves* and *Fools*." [7] Even Thomas Paine found it once more necessary to bear witness to the "errors and evils" that disgraced the state so that other members of the Union might guard against Rhode Island's errant behavior.[8]

The full measure of the state's obloquy, after months of hyperbole, was represented by an article that appeared in a New York City newspaper, the *Daily Advertiser,* edited by Francis Childs. Childs reprinted an item that had originated in the bitterly anti–country party journal, the *Newport Herald,* published by Peter Edes. Edes's paper was openly hostile to the party in power; he was in no way an objective observer of the passing scene in Rhode Island. Edes printed a valuable series of articles purporting to record for posterity the proceedings of each session of the Rhode Island General Assembly during the paper-money era. Although informative and unique in the material they contain, Edes's reports presented a frankly biased and prejudiced account of

4. The phrase *Paper Influenza* is taken from the *Virginia Independent Chronicle* (Richmond), June 20, 1787; the figure of the monetary loss to the state may be found in the *American Herald* (Boston), April 22, 1786.

5. *American Mercury* (Hartford), April 23, 1787; *Pennsylvania Gazette* (Philadelphia), June 28, 1787.

6. *Daily Advertiser* (New York), September 16, 1786; *Massachusetts Advertiser* (Boston), September 16, 1786; *Massachusetts Centinel* (Boston), September 21, 1786.

7. *Independent Journal* (New York), June 29, 1786; *New-York Packet* (New York), July 27, 1786; *Virginia Independent Chronicle* (Richmond), July 4, 1786; *American Herald* (Boston), July 17, 1786.

8. *Pennsylvania Packet* (Philadelphia), August 21, 1786.

the legislature and of the country party's policies. Nevertheless, newspapers throughout the United States republished the pieces with regularity, and these "proceedings" were a major source of the subsequent image of Rhode Island's infamy.[9]

Francis Childs reproduced one of Edes's "proceedings" under the provocative title "Quintessence of Villainy." [10] His purpose, Childs announced, was to show "a State verging into anarchy and ruin from democratic licentiousness, while her Representatives are actuated by the most dangerous sentiments of usurpation and despotism." The extreme nature of Child's remarks drew a prompt retort from Rhode Island's congressional delegates, James Mitchel Varnum and Peleg Arnold, who represented both parties. The Rhode Islanders protested to Governor George Clinton and the New York Assembly. They declared that Childs's publication was unfair and cast dishonor upon a state of the Union. The congressmen asked that Francis Childs and the *Daily Advertiser* be censured, a request that was not heeded.[11] The Rhode Island protests led only to suspicions that the nefarious state on Narragansett Bay now sought to add to its catalogue of evils curtailment of freedom of the press. "It is wisest and best, that they who cannot be restrained by the laws of religion and morality, should be roused by a sense of shame," said newspapers in Connecticut and elsewhere.

> Let any man of . . . common honesty examine the measures of the last [Rhode Island] *General Assembly* and then say . . . whether ever a sovereign power . . . so totally broke down all fences of property, and let loose *Villains* to prey upon the innocent, and whether it can be presumed that a just God will continue to such a society much longer the forms of government.[12]

9. There were seventeen sessions of the General Assembly between March, 1787, when the first of Edes's articles appeared, and January, 1790, when they ceased. All but one of these meetings was covered in the *Newport Herald* in a report giving a detailed account of the activities of the Assembly. A discussion of Edes's publication and the text of each legislative account is given in Irwin H. Polishook, "Peter Edes's Report of the Proceedings of the Rhode Island General Assembly, 1787–1790," *Rhode Island History*, XXV (1966), 33–42, 87–97, 117–29; XXVI (1967), 15–31. Edes's articles were reprinted in newspapers throughout the United States, an indication of the kind of news America's journalists believed was important for their readers.

10. *Daily Advertiser* (New York), April 9, 1787.

11. Varnum and Arnold to Governor Collins, New York, April 7, 1787, John R. Bartlett, ed., *Records of the Colony of Rhode Island and Providence Plantations in New England*, 10 vols. (Providence, 1856–65), X, 245–46.

12. *Connecticut Gazette* (New London), April 20, 1787; *Connecticut Journal* (New Haven), April 25, 1787; and *Massachusetts Centinel* (Boston), April 25, 1787.

Childs and his publications were defended as accurate, and Rhode Island branded as shameless.

Probably the most famous single blast against Rhode Island was supplied by the *Anarchiad,* a long political satire in verse which recounted the crisis of the Confederation era. In it the reputed apostasy of Rhode Island from civilization was denounced with style and grace:

> Hail! realm of rogues, renow'd for fraud and guile,
> All hail, ye knav'ries of yon little isle.
> There prowls the rascal, cloth'd with legal pow'r,
> To snare the orphan, and the poor devour;
> The crafty knave his creditor besets,
> And advertising paper pays his debts;
> Bankrupts their creditors with rage pursue,
> No stop, no mercy from the debtor crew.
> Arm'd with new test, the licens'd villain bold,
> Presents his bills, and robs them of their gold.
> . . . .
> New paper struck, new tests new tenders made,
> Insult mankind, and help thriving trade.
> Each weekly print new lists of Cheats proclaims,
> Proud to enroll their knav'ries and their names;
> The wiser race, the snares of law to shun,
> Like Lot from Sodom, from Rhode Island run.[13]

The complex origins of the paper-money system in Rhode Island and its many-sided development were not reported during the Confederation period. The state became a subject of disrepute and a source of wonderment thereafter. There was rarely a word about the economic and financial crisis that brought the paper bills into being or about the burdens of public and private debts they were created to lessen. The use of the paper money by farmers and nonfarmers was never mentioned. In no instance were the advantages of the paper-money system publicly discussed outside the state.

The traditional picture of stagnation and economic decline in Confederation Rhode Island must be carefully evaluated before firm conclusions are reached. It is impossible to determine the extent to which the depression in trade and commerce antedated the paper currency.

13. This diatribe was written by four of the group later known as the "Connecticut Wits," which included John Trumbull, author of the popular *McFingal;* Joel Barlow, diplomat and poet who composed the nationalistic *Columbiad;* David Humphreys; and Lemuel Barlow. The selection above is taken from Abe C. Ravits, "Anarch in Rhode Island," *Rhode Island History,* XI (1952), 117–24.

Nor is the role of the new money in the economic and financial crisis altogether clear. Other things being equal, had the paper money produced a mildly inflationary effect on the price level and acted as a source of credit and capital, its influence would have been salutary. There can be no dispute that the lightened burdens of taxation and private debts were sensible alternatives to bankruptcy and civil disorder. Doubtless, the unsettled business conditions after May, 1786, did little to encourage an economic upturn; the depreciation of the currency certainly inhibited the revival of commerce in Rhode Island. But whether this instability and depreciation were the result of an overissue of paper money and a loss of confidence in the future, or whether these conditions were an outgrowth of mercantile opposition to country policies, is beyond precise determination. This much is probable. The financial difficulties of Rhode Island after 1786 were doubtless abetted by the political and economic opposition of the mercantile community. On the whole, the weight of evidence would seem to discount a large part of the mercantile criticism of the paper-money system.

Furthermore, the customary appearance of economic contraction must be weighed against evidence that all was not misfortune in the period between 1786 and 1790. Despite the genuine problems which the paper money entailed, especially in 1786 and 1787, Forrest McDonald calculates that there was a yearly increase in Rhode Island's interstate and foreign commerce during the Confederation.[14] In addition, the state's economic development saw changes occur which were to be of prodigious importance for the future growth of Rhode Island and the United States. At this time Moses Brown and others were experimenting with the first stages of cotton manufacturing in North America; in 1790, while Rhode Island was separated from the Union, Samuel Slater established his celebrated factory at Pawtucket, an enterprise of great daring and cost.[15] Rhode Island was moving away from an un-

14. McDonald, *We the People: The Economic Origins of the Constitution* (Chicago, 1958), p. 335, reaches this conclusion after an examination of the data on ship clearances in the Rhode Island State Archives. Other manuscript evidence, such as the records of Impost revenues for the Confederation period, corroborates McDonald. McDonald comments further on this point in *E Pluribus Unum: The Formation of the American Republic 1776–1790* (Boston, 1965), p. 127.

15. A full account of Moses Brown and his enterprise is given in Mack Thompson, *Moses Brown: Reluctant Reformer* (Chapel Hill, 1962), pp. 203–33. The irony of the initiation of the industrial revolution in Rhode Island during the paper-money years intrigued Samuel Slater's son; see William B. Weeden, *Economic and Social History of New England, 1620–1789*, 2 vols. (Boston, 1894), II, 912–13. Additional

differentiated mercantile economy into a new world of industrial and entrepreneurial capitalism. Probably the new supplies of credit represented by the paper-money loans assisted this transformation, despite the opposition of the merchants; indirect evidence drawn from material on speculation in both Rhode Island and national securities supports this conclusion. At the end of this period the Rhode Island merchants had invested significant amounts in these securities, indicating that risk capital was encouraged to find other profitable outlets besides mercantile activity. Moses Brown's cotton mill is a good example of the movement of capital into manufacturing. These revolutionary developments were taking place at the very moment when many in America awaited the depopulation and extinction of civilization in the notorious state of Rhode Island.[16]

Distorted also were the incessant claims that anarchy reigned along the shores of Narragansett Bay. Every incident of civil conflict in Rhode Island was exaggerated into riot and discord, threatening life and property with equal menace. Such was the governing impression throughout the United States. Actually, this impression was far from the truth. The state government was in firm control of the affairs of Rhode Island throughout the period—perhaps in too firm control to suit those who opposed the paper-money administration. There was little need for the majority to use force or extralegal means to gain its will, since country party support was absolutely dominant. The merchants understood their weakness too well to resort to anything more than random attempts at passive disobedience. They were humble in their affliction throughout these years, satisfied that it was wiser to wait.

Lessons to be Learned

Whatever the truth may have been, the Rhode Island experience during the paper-money era was portrayed in odious and deplorable

information on the burgeoning cotton manufacture of Rhode Island is printed in the *Salem Mercury* (Mass.) , July 15, 1788; *Massachusetts Spy* (Worcester) , July 17, 1788.

16. Changes in Rhode Island's economic life after 1790 are fully explored in Peter J. Coleman, *The Transformation of Rhode Island 1790–1860* (Providence, 1963) . For predictions of Rhode Island's economic collapse see *Independent Journal* (New York) , July 29, 1786; *Middlesex Gazette* (Middletown, Conn.) , November 15, 1786.

terms throughout the United States. There is no evidence to indicate that this image was not accepted by the citizens of the new nation. Everyone believed Rhode Island had gone bad, if not mad. Starting with this understanding, arguments were drawn from the Rhode Island situation to warn the people of other states to guard against the same road to ruin. In this way the history of Rhode Island during the Confederation period became an instrument of propaganda against the use of paper money in all the other states of the Union. More importantly, it was also utilized to demonstrate the need for a reformed federal system. "The rogues of every other state blush at your exhibition," wrote Oliver Ellsworth about events in Rhode Island in an influential series of anonymous essays, "and say you have betrayed them by carrying the matter too far." [17]

The most significant conclusion drawn from the Rhode Island story was the evidence it offered in favor of a new federal constitution, one able to control the excesses of the members of the Union by transferring sovereignty from the states to the nation. Inevitably, this became quickly apparent in Rhode Island itself. There the mercantile minority, sensing that it had no hope of reversing the paper-money country party within the confines of Rhode Island politics, sought help outside the state. In a letter to Levi Hart, a Philadelphia friend and merchant, Henry Marchant admitted that the country party would never be concerned with the protests of the merchants. "But from the Union at large," Marchant observed, "I think we may flatter ourselves that Heaven hath not defeated us, but will bring good out of Evil, Order out of Confusion, and give Strength and Energy to our Weakness." [18] The Federal Convention and the Constitution of 1787 were godsends to the minority in Rhode Island. The proposed federal Constitution promised to affect fundamentally the paper-money policies of the country party. For this reason the leadership behind the cause of the Federalists in Rhode Island was supplied by the merchants.[19]

If the mercantile community in Rhode Island perceived the connection between escape from its troubles and a powerful national govern-

17. "Landholder," No. 12, reprinted from the *American Mercury* (Hartford), in the *U.S. Chronicle* (Providence), March 27, 1787; and the *Newport Mercury*, March 17, 1787.
18. Marchant to Hart, Newport, October 30, 1787, Dreer Collection, M.O.C., Mss., H.S.P., Vol. 7, p. 117.
19. *Gazette of the United States* (New York), September 12, 1789; *State Gazette of North Carolina* (Edenton), October 8, 1789.

ment, others in the United States could do likewise. A short stay in Providence in 1786 was enough to lead the American lexicographer, Noah Webster, to reproach his fellow citizens with the discovery that state sovereignty was the work of the devil. The only remedy for the disease was a strong national government. "Believe me my friends, *You lose rights,* because you will not give your magistrates authority to *protect them,*" declared Webster. "Your [state] liberty is despotism, because it has no control; your power is nothing, because it is not united." [20] Other observers were just as explicit. The cornerstone of the federal system must not be the states, Jeremiah Wadsworth of Connecticut noted in a letter to Samuel Ward, Jr., a delegate to the Annapolis Convention. Sovereign power must be found in the nation, where it can "check the Caprice & absurdity of Local prejudices & give Vigor & permanence to National resolves." [21] Another Connecticut notable, Benjamin Huntington, was of a similarly gloomy mind, believing that state sovereignty and democratic power were apt to "run into confusion & anarchy & consequently fall under despotism in a short time." He confided to William Ellery that "our men of public virtue are taking advantage of the distress they see their Neighbours in & preach up terror to the people at large. . . ." [22] The unheavals that were reported in Rhode Island induced uneasiness among those of property and power, giving rise to the sentiment that "some general and permanent system may be established, which will restore the wonted tranquility to this distracted country." [23] In Pennsylvania, an anonymous writer, after contemplating what was reputed to be happening in Rhode Island, beseeched God that the power of the states be eliminated and a consolidated government set up in their place. "That idol of the people, state sovereignty will forever disappoint any hopes we entertain of peace, happiness and responsibility, and prevent any sovereignty at all," he reasoned. Only a radical cure would insure a "flourishing and

20. Letter from "Tom Thoughtful" (Noah Webster), *U.S. Chronicle* (Providence), September 28, 1786; *American Herald* (Boston), October 9, 1786; *New-York Packet* (New York), October 12, 1786; *Columbian Herald* (Charleston), November 13, 1786.

21. Wadsworth to Ward, Hartford, August 13, 1786, Ward Manuscripts, 1784–1793, R.I.H.S., Box 3.

22. Huntington to Ellery, Norwich, July 16, 1787, Miscellaneous Manuscripts, N.H.S., Box 1, Folder 6.

23. *Massachusetts Centinel* (Boston), June 28, 1786; Oliver Bowen to Enos Hitchcock, New York, November 20, 1786, Enos Hitchcock Papers, Mss., R.I.H.S.

happy" future for the United States.[24] Once the ratification struggle began in earnest, Rhode Island served as a favorite weapon for those who supported the Constitution. "Many powerful arguments have been used in favor of the proposed constitution," said a Federalist in the *Connecticut Courant* on November 10, 1788, "but the arguments drawn in its favour from the proceedings of Rhode-Island are the most powerful and uncontradictory of any that may have been hitherto suggested." The very fact that Rhode Island was opposed to the new Constitution was taken as an "infallible sign of the justice and utility" of that frame of government, because it was unacceptable and obnoxious to the "rogues" and "villains" who ruled the state.

Congress, the States, and Rhode Island

The paper-money system of Rhode Island also resulted in untoward complications in its relations with the Continental Congress and its New England neighbors. These difficulties grew out of the legal-tender status of the paper money issued by the state.

Shortly after the paper money was authorized in May, 1786, an interesting controversy developed between the financial agents of Congress and the General Assembly. This controversy was not unexpected. Anticipating trouble, the receiver of federal taxes in Rhode Island, Joseph Clarke, resigned his office. He explained to the Board of Treasury in New York City that his salary of $200 per annum would no longer suffice in view of the forthcoming paper-money overturn in the state and the certainty that the execution of his office "will be attended with great Labour & pains." [25] He was right. The General Assembly, acting in pursuance of the statutes which made the paper currency a legal tender in all business transactions, insisted that these bills be accepted in fulfillment of Rhode Island's share of the continental requisitions. This was flatly refused by William Ellery, commissioner of the Loan

24. Letter from "Nestor," *Pennsylvania Packet* (Philadelphia), February 2, 1787; *Independent Journal* (New York), February 14, 1787.

25. Clarke to the Board of Treasury, Newport, April 13, 1786, and Jabez Bowen to the Commissioners of the Treasury, Providence, April 13, 1786, both in the Papers of the Continental Congress, 1774–1789, Letters of the Board of Treasury, 1785–1788, Mss., N.A., Vol. II, pp. 193, 197.

Office, who was fully supported by Congress.[26] A minor crisis in state and federal relations was the result.

Both Ellery and the congressional Board of Treasury believed that Congress could not accept depreciated state currencies without endangering the financial health of the United States, already beset with chronic—if not fatal—symptoms. They knew very well that the financial and political implications of this controversy were dangerous to the Union. What if all the states duplicated Rhode Island's stubborn course? Hoping to intimidate the Assembly, Ellery informed Governor Collins that unless Rhode Island altered its position he would issue no more federal acknowledgments of interest due on the national debt—certificates known as indents. Such an act would deprive Rhode Island citizens of all future claims of arrearages in interest on the federal debt. Disregarding Ellery's threat and his assertion that chaos would result if Congress accepted the currency of the states, the General Assembly stood firm in its determination that its paper bills be received in discharge of Rhode Island's financial obligations to the Union. Congress upheld Ellery and ordered federal officials to reject any payments in state currency.[27]

This standoff between Congress and Rhode Island was clearly indicative of the fundamental problem of the federal system organized under the Articles of Confederation, namely, the sovereign power of the states in matters of taxation. It was very evident in this clash of wills. As in the case of the Impost amendments, Congress came out second best.

William Ellery had been hopeful that a deadlock would not occur, but in this hope, he wrote to the Board of Treasury, he was disappointed. When called before the General Assembly to explain his position and set a date when he would again authorize indent certificates for Rhode Island, Ellery replied by inquiring as to when the legislature intended to pay its share of the federal requisitions in specie.

26. Commissioners of the Treasury, Samuel Osgood and Arthur Lee, to the President of Congress, Board of Treasury [New York], September 12, October 17, 1786, Letters of the Board of Treasury, Mss., N.A., Vol. II, pp. 309–11, 331–32.

27. Ellery to the Commissioners of the Board of Treasury, Newport, September 22, 1786; Ellery to Nathaniel Appleton, Newport, October 2, 1786, both in Ellery Letters, Mss., N.H.S.; Rhode Island Colony Records, Mss., R.I.S.A., Vol. 13, pp. 295–96, and Acts and Resolves of the General Assembly, Mss., R.I.S.A., Vol. 25, p. 25; Bartlett, *Records*, X, 203, 211–12; Worthington C. Ford *et al.*, eds., *Journals of the Continental Congress, 1774–1789*, 34 vols. (Washington, D.C., 1904–37), XXXI, 662–65.

There was no response. The Assembly peremptorily disposed of the problem by declaring that the commissioner of the Loan Office should issue the indents as justice required. It compounded its error, Ellery remarked in disgust, by failing to order any federal taxes in either specie or paper money. Ellery reported all this to his superiors in New York City with "shame and anxiety," because Rhode Island was his native state. "The only consolation I have is this," he added, "that the neighboring States, warned by our example, may avoid the rock on which we have split." [28] Soon this consolation no longer served to soothe the aggrieved federal official, and he advised cryptically, for the first time: "Perhaps some serious, decided act of Congress might make this state feel that the preservation of the Union . . . depends upon the state's compliance with the requisitions of Congress." [29] There were others who were less subtle in suggesting that force be used to control the malevolent contagion in Rhode Island. After all, the disease might spread.[30]

Another and somewhat ludicrous contretemps in the relations of Rhode Island and the Union was represented by a controversy that developed between Governor John Collins and the federal postmaster in Newport. Here was an episode which revealed the perplexities that could arise out of a paper-money currency.[31]

Jacob Richardson was the federal postmaster in Newport. Like Joseph Clarke, he was worried about the forthcoming emission of paper money in the state. Unlike Clarke, he did not resign his federal post. Richardson wrote to the Postmaster General of the United States, Ebenezer Hazard, asking for advice on what he was to do if Rhode Islanders tried to pay for their mail in depreciated paper money. Should he receive the currency? Could the postal service legally refuse the paper bills without infringing the laws of Rhode Island, which said they were a legal tender in every commercial transaction? No doubt Richardson was well aware of the penalties that might be his reward

28. Ellery to the Commissioners of the Board of Treasury, Newport, August 29, 1786, Ellery Letters, Mss., N.H.S.; see also Ellery to unknown correspondent, Newport, July 20, 1786, Gratz Collection, Mss., H.S.P., Case 1, Box 19.

29. Ellery to the Commissioners of the Board of Treasury, Newport, February 12, 1787, Ellery Letters, Mss., N.H.S.

30. Letter from "Jonathan," *Boston Gazette*, May 22, 1786; *U.S. Chronicle* (Providence), July 6, August 31, 1787; *American Mercury* (Hartford), April 23, 1787; *Newport Herald*, April 12, 1787.

31. I have discussed this incident before in "The Collins-Richardson Fracas of 1787: A Problem in State and Federal Relations During the Confederation Era," *Rhode Island History*, XXII (1963), 117–21.

for intransigence. And who was there to protect him? The Postmaster General was also concerned. In a letter to the President of Congress, he noted: "such money will not answer to satisfy our Contract with the Proprietors of the Stages,—and yet, being a legal Tender in the states which have emitted it the Postmasters in those States conceive they may not refuse it." [32] After instructions from Hazard and the support of Congress, Richardson would not deliver any letter for paper money, and he demanded that the General Assembly pay its outstanding accounts in gold or silver. The Assembly refused. For a time there was a hiatus in relations between the Newport postmaster and the government of Rhode Island.

Soon thereafter, early in 1787, two communications addressed to the governor of Rhode Island arrived at the post office in Newport. Governor Collins, determined to uphold the law of Rhode Island and to receive his mail, sent his son for the letters without the necessary specie payment. Richardson, as instructed, refused to deliver the letters. Thus provoked, Governor Collins went in person to the post office and, finding the postmaster absent, demanded his official mail from Richardson's son, who fearfully acceded to the elderly governor's request. The triumphant Collins, now desirous of a complete victory, ordered the boy to call his father, presumably to chide the man for his unwillingness to respect the authority of the governor's office. Undaunted, the postmaster sullied the triumph and snatched the letters from Collins's hand, upbraiding the governor with the congressional request that he pay his bills in hard money.

John Collins, though nearing seventy, was a man of some temper when aroused. He was irritated beyond endurance by Richardson's recapture of the now coveted letters. The governor offered to break every bone in Richardson's body should he accept a challenge and step out of his office into the street. The postmaster agreed quickly, but upon reconsideration apparently thought discretion the better part of valor and stayed safely behind his counter. The governor, deprived of success, not only in obtaining the letters but also in winning satisfaction, eventually left the shop in a rage.

The controversy between the governor and the postmaster immediately became the talk of the town. Collins reported the incident to the

32. Hazard to the President of Congress, General Post Office [New York], June 19, 1786, Papers of the Continental Congress, 1774–1789, Letters from Bache and Hazard, Postmasters General, 1777–1788, and Committee Reports on the Post Office, 1776–1778, Mss., N.A., p. 255.

General Assembly, telling of the insult he had received from the federal postmaster and of the detainment of possibly important letters. Richardson was ordered to come before the bar of the legislature to justify his alleged insult to the governor and the state.[33] When the postmaster appeared, he was still roused by the heat of battle and determined not to give in, though threatened with confinement by the assembled legislators. Richardson defended his stand by saying that Rhode Island was already past due for several letters and that he would no longer trust it because "my account has been lying before the Assembly Three Sessions, and they will not pay it without I will take Paper Money. . . ." [34] But the urging of the Newport deputies and the prospect that the Assembly really meant business brought moderation in Richardson's position. He apologized for his rudeness to Governor Collins, paid the costs of his summons before the legislature, and in a written statement formally asked for pardon.[35]

The importance of this affair was readily apparent to contemporaries. Ebenezer Hazard took special care to inform Congress of Richardson's imbroglio with Rhode Island. He sent Richardson's communications to the President of Congress with the explanation that they contained matters of vital concern to the Union.[36] The contest was clearly one between the nation and a state, and the state was evidently a victor. "It seems the misconduct of the postmaster," announced a report in the press, "was his obedience to the resolves of Congress in not being willing to receive the *paper* of that state for the postage of a letter." [37]

By now the letters in question were almost forgotten as Rhode Island pursued its federal postmaster; they were, however, to prove an added embarrassment for the state. One of the letters zealously withheld by Richardson contained a request from Governor Bowdoin of Massachusetts regarding a proclamation for the seizure of fugitives from Shays's Rebellion, an event that shocked the nation and sup-

33. Rhode Island Records, Mss., R.I.S.A., Vol. 13, p. 350; Bartlett, *Records*, X, 233.
34. Richardson to Ebenezer Hazard, Newport, March 20, 1787, Letters from Bache and Hazard, Mss., N.A., p. 307.
35. The fracas between Collins and Richardson was reported by Peter Edes in his *Newport Herald* on March 29, 1787. It was carried by newspapers in many states from New Hampshire to Virginia. After his encounter with the General Assembly, Richardson was obliged to accept the paper bills.
36. Hazard to the President of Congress, General Post Office [New York], Letters from Bache and Hazard, Mss., N.A., p. 303.
37. *Middletown Gazette* (Middletown, Conn.) , April 16, 1787.

planted Rhode Island as the bête noire of public opinion. Naturally, Rhode Island was unable to act for a time upon the Massachusetts request because Bowdoin's communication lay incarcerated in the Newport post office until the state paid its accounts in hard money. In a message to Bowdoin, Governor Collins excused Rhode Island's inaction by placing the blame on the "misconduct" of a federal postmaster.

Meanwhile, at the March, 1787, meeting of the General Assembly, the lower house refused to cooperate with Massachusetts in the apprehension of any participants in the rebellion. Rumor had it that many of the insurgents found safety in Rhode Island. In fact, one of the rebels, Dr. Samuel Willard, attended a session of the legislature and gained further notoriety when he afterward became involved in a tavern brawl.[38] Rhode Island's unwillingness to help in bringing the Massachusetts rebels to trial merely certified for many Americans the inevitable association between paper money and sedition. Reflecting this sentiment, several newspapers published a mock dispatch asserting:

> The University of Rhode-Island have . . . lately conferred the honor of L.L.D. (Doctor of Musket, Swivel, and Cannon Laws) upon his Excellency Major-General Shays; and that a Diploma, upon parchment, will be forwarded to the General as soon as the Governor [of Rhode Island] can acquire *Hard Money* . . . sufficiently to pay the postage to Vermont.[39]

Here in one fell swoop were associated three great villains of the Confederation period—Rhode Island, Daniel Shays, and Vermont.

Another aspect of the increasingly difficult relations between Rhode Island and its New England neighbors came when out-of-state residents began to avail themselves of the privilege of paying debts to Rhode Islanders by tendering depreciated paper money. In their session of March, 1787, Rhode Island's legislators passed a statute prohibiting citizens of other states from invoking the legal-tender laws, a violation of the fourth article of the Articles of Confederation, which

38. Jacob Richardson to Ebenezer Hazard, Newport, March 20, 1787, Letters of Bache and Hazard, Mss., N.A., p. 307; *Essex Journal* (Newburyport, Mass.) , March 28, 1787; *Newport Mercury*, March 22, 1787; *Providence Gazette*, March 31, 1787; George R. Minot, *The History of the Insurrections in Massachusetts in the Year MDCCLXXXVI, and the Rebellion Consequent Thereon* (Worcester, 1788) , pp. 151–52.

39. *Daily Advertiser* (New York) , June 5, 1787; *Essex Journal* (Newburyport, Mass.) , July 4, 1787.

guaranteed that each state would allow all Americans the same benefits under its laws as it gave to its own residents. This action was called to the attention of the Connecticut Assembly when an irate freeman protested against the partiality of Rhode Island law and asked for prompt retaliation. The Connecticut legislature responded with an act prohibiting Rhode Islanders from any recovery for debt in a Connecticut court until Rhode Island repealed its discrimination against non-residents.[40]

In a preliminary debate on the proposed discrimination against Rhode Island, the Connecticut Assembly was not anxious to aggravate interstate relations, though its members were bitter toward their neighbor to the east. "Their conduct is little better than that of robbers and pirates," declared a Connecticut representative in the lower house of the General Assembly. The same legislator recalled:

> This is not the first instance of their fraud; they have heretofore cheated us out of large sums by their depreciating paper money. They have now declared war against the property of our citizens who have debts due from them. . . . That state must be chastized. They are at the old game which they have been playing for three hundred years past.[41]

Another legislator suggested that Congress ought to be called upon to bring Rhode Island to account for its anti-federal actions in violating the Articles of Confederation and abusing its neighbors. But, as James Mitchell Varnum remarked, it was futile to consider particular violations of the spirit and substance of the federal constitution. "There is not a State which can throw the first stone," he said. "The evil is radical, and so must be the cure." [42] The cure Varnum had in mind was the Constitution of 1787.

The reaction in the United States to Rhode Island's Confederation history was thus uniformly unfavorable. The logic which impelled the state to resort again to paper money was generally ignored in the pro-

40. Charles J. Hoadly and Leonard W. Labaree, eds., *The Public Records of the State of Connecticut, 1766–1796*, 8 vols. (Hartford, 1894–1951), VI, 383, 500; VII, 175. The prohibitory law was repealed in the fall of 1790 after Rhode Island ratified the federal Constitution of 1787.

41. *Connecticut Journal* (New Haven), June 20, 1787; *Middlesex Gazette* (Middletown, Conn.), June 25, 1787; *Connecticut Courant* (Hartford), June 28, 1787; *Connecticut Gazette* (New London), June 29, 1787.

42. Varnum to Samuel Ward, New York, April 2, 1787, Ward Manuscripts, R.I.H.S., Box 3.

fusion of scorn and abuse that fell upon the state. The country party, in turn, increasingly concerned with its financial program and dismayed at the massive assault on its policies, became rapidly disenchanted with the national government. In this disenchantment were prefigured the events which later took Rhode Island out of the Union.

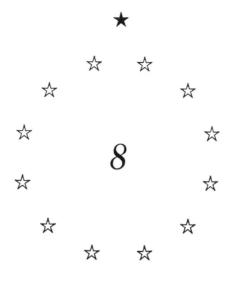

8

A Foreign State

RHODE ISLAND was fully aware of the many problems afflicting the national government. In order to enhance the state's battered prestige, the freemen were not averse to sending some men to Congress with nationalistic points of view. These congressmen were never backward in describing the crisis of the Union as they conceived it. One of them, the Baptist minister and president of Rhode Island College, James Manning, sent a number of letters to Rhode Island in 1786 relating in detail the difficulties of the central government and his fear that Congress might dissolve. Manning's communications painted a grim picture of the country's prospects. Financial, commercial, diplomatic, and territorial embarrassments were destroying the United States, and state indifference was speeding the process. Because of its paper-money system and its disregard of the Union, Manning predicted, Rhode Island would take a "distinguished rank" among those who contributed to the ruin of the United States.[1] "Should not all these considerations reconcile the mercantile and landed interests in Rhode Island," he asked plaintively, "and produce a real concern for a reform of the federal system." [2]

Reform of the federal system did not await the advocacy of Rhode Island. The partial representation of states that met at Annapolis had already started the process of constitutional change in the United States. Despite the congressional call for the Federal Convention early in 1787 and the urging of Rhode Island's congressmen that the state not remain indifferent,[3] the country party stood aloof. The government rejected any participation in the Federal Convention, choosing to repudiate the Union rather than join its sister states in the new federal system. Between 1787 and 1789 Rhode Island became a foreign state.

An indication of Rhode Island's alienation from the Union came in the summer of 1787, when the state's congressional delegation was recalled and no new representatives were sent in its place. The ostensible reason for the withdrawal was the meeting of the Federal Convention and the probability that public attention would be focused on this important conference. Congress, it was assumed, would be suspended until the Convention completed its deliberations and a report was presented. In the interval the General Assembly proposed to save money and asked its delegates to return home. At the termination of the Federal Convention, however, the Assembly failed to send new representatives to Congress.[4] The mercantile minority contended that the Assembly's neglect grew out of the country party's antipathy to a federal Union.

Another revealing episode was the General Assembly's response to a

1. Manning to Governor Collins, New York, May 26, 1786, and Manning to Nathan Miller, New York, June 12, 1786, both in William R. Staples, ed., *Rhode Island in the Continental Congress: With the Journal of the Convention that Adopted the Constitution 1765–1790* (Providence, 1870), pp. 545–47.

2. Manning and Nathan Miller to Governor Collins, New York, September 28, 1786, John R. Bartlett, ed., *Records of the Colony of Rhode Island and Providence Plantations in New England*, 10 vols. (Providence, 1856–65), X, 222–23. See also Manning to Nicholas Brown, New York, June 9, July 15, 1786, and Manning to Jabez Bowen, New York, June 9, 1786, all in Brown Papers, Mss., J.C.B.L.

3. James M. Varnum and Peleg Arnold to Governor Collins, New York, April 24, 1787, Bartlett, *Records*, X, 246–47.

4. *Newport Herald*, May 10, 1787. Rhode Island did not send another delegation to Congress until the spring of 1788. For further information, see *ibid.*, November 8, 1787, March 6, 1788.

request from Congress asking each state to repeal any laws that might be repugnant to the peace treaty with Great Britain.[5] Congress hoped that compliance with its request would facilitate the payment of debts owed to English merchants and alleviate the situation of the American loyalists. In return, Congress anticipated greater attention to American demands that Great Britain leave the West. As an incident to the repeal of such laws, the states would necessarily acknowledge the supremacy of national treaty obligations over the acts of the states.

Governor Collins and the country party leaders first considered the request of Congress in the fall of 1786. Fully occupied with the paper-money experiment in Rhode Island, they gave short shrift to the national appeal. Collins wrote to John Jay, then secretary for foreign affairs, that Rhode Island had every intention of carrying out the letter of the treaty with Great Britain. He saw no reason for special action by the General Assembly.[6] In the following year the legislature again failed to act, asserting it knew of no statute repugnant to the treaty.[7] This did not settle the question, for the national government persisted in its effort to have the states rescind all laws that contradicted the treaty of peace. At the June, 1787, session of the Assembly the upper house was willing to act favorably on the congressional request, but the lower house rejected its concession. Later, when a member of the lower house tried to revive the issue, the country majority withdrew from the legislature, leaving the house without a quorum to carry on business. The country party's power was clearly dominant.

Rhode Island's recalcitrance was closely related to its paper-money system. The treaty opened up the possibility of a breach in the state's program because the supremacy of the agreements with Great Britain might inhibit the legal-tender status of the depreciated paper bills. According to Rhode Island law, the currency was supposed to satisfy any specie contracts, even those with foreign creditors; but the treaty of peace declared that there would be no impediments established by the United States to prohibit the recovery of pre-Revolutionary debts contracted in hard money and owed to British subjects. The apparent clash between state law and the treaty prompted Rhode Island's inaction. Hesitance, however, did not mean obstinate resistance. The coun-

5. Worthington C. Ford *et al.*, eds., *Journals of the Continental Congress, 1774–1789,* 34 vols. (Washington, D.C., 1904–37), XXXII, 177–84.
6. Collins to Jay, Newport, September 4, 1786, Jefferson Papers, Mss., Library of Congress.
7. *Newport Herald,* May 10, 1787.

try party capitulated on the issue in the fall of 1787.[8] Its surrender came in the nature of a minor concession to Federalist sentiment in Rhode Island. The country party gave in, knowing that if paper money could not extinguish foreign specie debts, the major part of these debts were owed by the mercantile minority. Also reassuring was the knowledge that any judicial proceedings for debt in Rhode Island would be heard in state courts, annually appointed by the General Assembly, and almost always composed of judges favorable to the party in power.

The Philadelphia Convention

The struggle over the national government began in earnest in March, 1787, when the resolution of Congress calling for a constitutional convention was considered by the General Assembly. The Antifederalist character of the country party was promptly established when the House of Deputies refused, by a majority of twenty-three members, to send delegates to Philadelphia.[9] This decision was founded, according to the statements of several country leaders, on a professed satisfaction with the constitutional system organized under the Articles of Confederation.[10] At the May and June meetings of the legislature, efforts to send delegates to Philadelphia were again repulsed. At these sessions, however, some country party leaders showed a marked hesitance to embark on a course that might result in Rhode Island's separation from the United States. A residue of national sentiment still existed in the state.

A motion to have Rhode Island represented at the Federal Convention was renewed in May and was urged with great force in the lower house. The resolution was adopted by a margin of two members when it came to a division. The Assistants vetoed the proposal, and the resolution was lost. Within less than a month the upper house reconsidered its veto. Believing now that Rhode Island should take part in

8. *Providence Gazette,* September 17, 1787; *Newport Herald,* September 20, 1787.
9. *Newport Herald,* March 22, 1787; *Providence Gazette,* March 31, 1787.
10. The attachment of Rhode Island for the Articles of Confederation was pilloried in a satirical article in the *Massachusetts Centinel* (Boston), June 24, 1788. In it the defective Articles of Confederation were put up for sale, and to encourage buyers, "the purchaser will have the State of *Rhode-Island* thrown into the bargain."

the historic discussions in Philadelphia, it sent a bill to the lower house authorizing a deputation. On this occasion, however, the House of Deputies reversed itself and by a majority of seventeen refused to concur.[11]

These strange reversals demonstrated that the majority's leaders were split on the issue of the Philadelphia Convention and the larger question of the federal Union. The fact that Governor John Collins, John Sayles, and Oliver Durfee, all country party spokesmen in the upper house, on one occasion favored Rhode Island's attendance at the Philadelphia meetings demonstrates that the country party was not of one mind on how to react to the prospective reform of the federal system. The issue of a constitutional reformation presented a difficult problem. If Rhode Island refused to participate in the Federal Convention and later spurned its recommendations, the state might gain an unwanted independence. Another danger was the possibility of internal disorder, in the event the mercantile minority utilized force to neutralize the political power of the country party and stay within the United States. Nor were rumors from outside the state reassuring. Gossip abounded that the Philadelphia Convention had decided in its secret deliberations to consider Rhode Island as having withdrawn from the Union; there were hints that Congress would never again admit the state into the federal system.[12] Disconcerting also were suggestions by anonymous informants in the nation's newspapers that Rhode Island was lost to reason and only radical measures would succeed in her case. Instead of trying to persuade Rhode Island to act together with the rest of the United States, hotheads were proposing that it be divided among the neighboring states of Massachusetts and Connecticut.[13] This last recommendation was repeated with increasing earnestness throughout the period of Rhode Island's outright repudiation of the Union. It later proved a crucial factor in the state's decision to ratify the Constitution.

These dangers were not disregarded by the men who governed Rhode Island. There was considerable foreboding about Rhode Island's fate if it remained intransigent. One country party official, Paul

11. Journals of the House of Deputies, June 15, 1787, Mss., R.I.S.A.; *Newport Herald*, June 21, 1787; *Providence Gazette*, June 23, 1787; *U.S. Chronicle* (Providence), August 2, 1787.

12. *Independent Journal* (New York), June 13, 1787; *Salem Mercury* (Mass.), June 19, 1787; *Providence Gazette*, July 7, 1787; *Maryland Journal and Baltimore Advertiser*, April 15, 1788.

13. *Providence Gazette*, August 4, 1787.

Mumford, the chief justice of the Superior Court, expressed the hope that there would be no future discrimination against his state because it was unrepresented in Philadelphia. Masquerading in the newspapers under the pseudonym "Euripides," he said unhappily that there was reason to expect the "worst." Mumford was afraid the state might be dismembered by the new government organized as a result of the Philadelphia Convention. He asked in a knowing tone whether Rhode Island could be expected to withstand the combined force of the United States.[14] In view of the veto of the Impost of 1781 and the state's subsequent disrepute, Mumford implied, there would be serious trouble if Rhode Island did not act together with the other members of the Union as soon as practicable.

After the failure to obtain a Convention deputation early in the summer of 1787, the vocal mercantile minority was still hopeful that a favorable decision might be achieved before the Philadelphia meetings came to an end. The merchants, though fully aware of the state's lack of interest in changing the federal government, could see no reason why Rhode Island should not participate in discussing constitutional changes. Perhaps its negative voice might carry more weight inside the Federal Convention than in isolation. The country members of the legislature reasoned otherwise. Not wanting to affront nationalist sentiment by rejecting a convention call again, they permitted a scheduled session of the Assembly to fail late in the summer by their nonattendance.[15]

Despite this setback, Governor Collins convened a special meeting of the General Assembly at the end of September to discuss the constitutional crisis. During the entire period of the struggle over the Constitution of 1787, Governor John Collins was an acknowledged Federalist. His stand represented an important split in the country ranks, for the elderly governor had been converted to the paper-money movement in 1786, out of a conviction that some measure of relief was necessary. Collins had been a sea captain, a minor merchant in Newport, a man of modest wealth and land, and a patriot during the Revolutionary era; he served Rhode Island in many political offices before becoming governor, including membership in Congress. To this background he added an ingrained distrust of the great merchants who dominated Rhode Island's economic and political life. Where the mer-

14. *Newport Herald,* August 23, 1787.
15. *Salem Mercury* (Mass.), August 28, 1787; *Newport Herald,* September 20, 1787.

chants were concerned, Collins declared, "their Religion is trade and their God is gain and they that Expect men to sacrifice their God and their Religion for the Publick will Certainly be disappointed." [16] Collins was not newly attracted to his belief that reform of the federal system was necessary. "I have for several years past," he advised an unknown correspondent, "wished for a General Convention to mend the Confederation and form some General Bond of Union." [17] He may have come to this belief during his early years of service in Congress.

Governor Collins appeared in person before the Assembly. He explained that he wanted the legislature to be on hand when the Federal Convention completed its work and presented its report. Collins also apprised the legislators of an urgent request that Rhode Island send delegates to New York City so that Congress might attain a quorum to consider the work of the Convention. Before a debate could ensue, the country leaders in the lower house secured a two-day adjournment of the Assembly. In the interval they sought to hammer out a plan of action that would unify the country party. The party members in the government caucused and consulted their supporters in all parts of Rhode Island. The subjects of these discussions were the Federal Convention and future relations between Rhode Island and the Union. When the deliberations were finished, the country party once again had a commanding majority in the General Assembly. The country caucusing induced Peter Edes of the *Newport Herald* to wonder why the majority met in extralegislative conventions when it exhibited a distaste for the Federal Convention in Philadelphia. It must be, he observed sardonically, that "they may imagine that this Grand Convention will swallow up their delectable little ones." [18]

When the legislators reassembled, the results of their deliberations became evident very quickly. The country leaders decided to give the paper-money system precedence over everything else, even the reorganization of the federal government. Outside matters would have to wait until the state debts were redeemed in paper currency. The General Assembly sent a letter to the President of Congress, elucidating why the state failed to attend the Federal Convention. The tone of the

16. Collins to Samuel Ward, Newport, July 17, 1774, Gratz Collection, Mss., H.S.P., Case 1, Box 4.

17. Collins to unknown correspondent, Newport, January 17, 1784, Gratz Collection, Mss., H.S.P., Case 1, Box 21; *Daily Advertiser* (New York), June 27, 1787; *Providence Gazette*, July 28, 1787.

18. *Newport Herald*, September 20, 1787.

communication was exculpatory, though unmistakably firm. There was no desire to insult the United States in the state's absence from Philadelphia, explained the legislature. Rhode Island's nonattendance was actuated by a fundamental principle that had "ever been characteristic of this state—the love of true constitutional liberty, and the fear we have of making innovations on the rights and liberties of the citizens at large." The General Assembly wrote that it had no power to alter the fundamental laws of Rhode Island. This power was reserved to the people themselves, and they alone might exercise it, whether directly or through a convention of delegates popularly elected for the specific purpose of writing or amending the constitution. The Philadelphia Convention satisfied none of these conditions. The Assembly attempted to mitigate its refusal to send delegates to Philadelphia by reminding Congress that it had already granted the national government power over international trade and the right to tax this commerce, measures intended to patch up the chief weaknesses of the Articles of Confederation. If these reforms failed to take effect, Rhode Island was not responsible. The state had done its part in strengthening the federal system. Its inability to attend the Federal Convention should be judged in this light.[19]

This feigned lack of power on the part of the General Assembly brought an acrimonious retort from the Providence and Newport deputies in the lower house. They asserted that the legislature's letter was completely transparent; it simply did not want to change the federal system. Members from Providence and Newport said the legislature had never before been chary of constitution-making without a specific grant of power from the freemen. They pointed out that Rhode Island's willing attendance at the early congresses, its ratification of the Articles of Confederation, and the most recent constitutional amendments offering Congress power over international trade and the right to tax foreign commerce belied the Assembly's self-denial in the case of the Federal Convention. In each instance the General Assembly had acted without consulting the people. The deputies averred that it might have been more dignified to lament Rhode Island's failure to at-

19. Governor Collins to the President of Congress, In General Assembly, Newport, September 17, 1787, State Papers of Rhode Island, Mss., N.A., pp. 588, 596–603; Bartlett, *Records*, X, 255, 258–59. See in this regard the excellent discussion by Jackson Turner Main, "The Antifederalist Solution," *The Antifederalists: Critics of the Constitution 1781–1788* (Chapel Hill, 1961), pp. 168–88.

tend the Federal Convention than to fabricate specious and fatuous principles to excuse the state's nonparticipation.[20]

James Mitchell Varnum and other Federalists prepared a lengthy analysis of Rhode Island's recalcitrance which they sent to the president of the Federal Convention, George Washington. They asked Washington and members of the Federal Convention not to confuse the actions of the General Assembly with the true character of Rhode Island. Antifederalism, they declared, was equally distasteful to the commercial classes, learned professions, and the "most respectable" farmers and mechanics in the country party ranks. Anyone who had the best interests of Rhode Island at heart favored reform of the federal system. "The majority of the [country party] administration are composed of a licentious body of men, destitute of education, and many of them void of principle," the Federalists wrote. "From anarchy and confusion they derive a temporary consequence, and this they endeavor to prolong by debauching the minds of the common people, whose attention is wholly directed to the abolition of debts, public and private."[21] Rhode Island's brand of Antifederalism, the Federalist minority announced, was prompted by the country party's expectation that a strengthened central government would interfere with the state's paper-money system.

A New Constitution

The fact was that the problem of a new federal system was interjected into Rhode Island politics little more than a year after the paper currency was emitted. The country party feared that the Federal Convention and the Constitution of 1787 might limit its power and the ability of the state to fulfill the promises of 1786. Consequently, when the Constitution of 1787 was made public, many country politicians wore "long faces." The document outlawed state emissions of

20. The Newport deputies included Henry Marchant, George Champlin, John Topham, and William Tripp; those from Providence were John Brown, Welcome Arnold, Benjamin Bourne, and Joseph Nightingale. This letter to the Continental Congress is found in State Papers of Rhode Island, Mss., N.A., pp. 592–94; and Bartlett, *Records*, X, 259–60.

21. Varnum to the President of the Federal Convention, Newport, June 18, 1787, Updike Papers, Mss., R.I.H.S.

paper money. Moreover, division in their ranks and disunion among the United States were the stark alternatives if the country leaders spurned the work of the Federal Convention. Eventually, however, the need to redeem the state debt unified the country party until the paper-money program ran its course. As a result, Rhode Island would not ratify the new Constitution and became independent of the United States. As William Ellery noted, the "accursed paper-money system" and extended period of time required to liquidate the public securities separated Rhode Island from its sister states.[22]

More vitriolic in pointing the finger of accusation at paper money as the root cause of Rhode Island's Antifederalism were commentators in the nation's newspapers and members of Congress. Rhode Island's pigheadedness was seen as an open avowal of the primacy of the country party's paper-money system. "Not content with perverting the administration of justice, stabbing public faith at its vitals, and introducing poverty among the citizens," a New York publication said of Rhode Island, "they even seem to view a dissolution of the Federal Compact as of no magnitude, when placed in competition with their favorite Paper Money." [23] The General Assembly's reputed concern for states' rights was roundly condemned as a cover for its "diabolical schemes" and "vile plans." Presumably, just as soon as the public debts were paid off, Rhode Island would again embrace the federal Union. Congressional opinion was much the same, giving added evidence of the marriage between paper money and Antifederalism. The current paper-money "madness" in Rhode Island had not yet run its course, complained Edward Carrington, a congressman from Virginia. Until it did, he implied, Antifederalist policies should be expected in the state.[24] James Madison, the chief architect of the Constitution of 1787, made the same point. He said of Rhode Islanders: "Paper Money is still their idol." [25] And there was little that could be done until the false worship passed.

22. William Ellery to Ebenezer Hazard, Newport, October 16, 1787; January 12, 1789, Ellery Letters, Mss., N.H.S.; Ellery to Benjamin Huntington, Newport, March 10, 1789, Ellery Letters, Mss., R.I.S.A.

23. *Daily Advertiser* (New York), November 30, 1787; *Maryland Gazette* (Annapolis), December 6, 1787; *Massachusetts Centinel* (Boston), October 7, 1789; *Virginia Independent Chronicle* (Richmond), August 20, 1788; *Federal Gazette* (Philadelphia), January 29, 30, 1789.

24. Carrington to Colonel Edmund Randolph, New York, April 2, 1787, Edmund C. Burnett, ed., *Letters of the Members of the Continental Congress*, 8 vols. (Washington, D.C., 1921–36), VIII, 569.

25. Madison to Edmund Randolph, New York, April 2, 1787, *ibid.*, p. 570.

The conflict over the Constitution of 1787 centered in the General Assembly. But the Federalist and Antifederalist forces also engaged in a prolonged campaign to win the allegiance of the majority of freemen who controlled the state's political destiny. The Antifederalists won over to their viewpoint an overwhelming number of the people of Rhode Island. In no other state were the Antifederalists so dominant. Of course, the paper-money problem provided the motivation and cohesion that sustained the Antifederalist assault on the new federal system. The Federalist-Antifederalist cleavage followed the pattern of the continuing divisions over paper money.[26] Two main factors underlay the victory of Antifederalism in Rhode Island. The Antifederalist attack on the Constitution rested on a bedrock of local control and states' rights to which the freemen were firmly attached. The vigorous battle against the Impost of 1781 had reinforced the conviction of Rhode Islanders that a powerful central government was dangerous and should be rejected in any form. Of crucial importance also was the vastly more favorable political vantage of the country party, which stood first and foremost as the sponsor of the paper-money system of 1786. The country record contrasted sharply with that of the Federalist merchants, who were bitter enemies of the program endorsed by most Rhode Islanders. The country leaders had already won the support of a predominant majority of voters; they needed only to hold that support in a new but related cause. The Federalists always carried an insurmountable political handicap in the years from 1787 to 1790. Unlike anywhere else in the United States, Federalist control of the press and effective organization had little influence over the Rhode Island situation. The Antifederalists were better organized, propaganda in the newspapers was readily discounted by the average citizen, and the country party leadership was every bit a match for the most astute men in the Federalist camp.[27] A Federalist defeat, considering these circumstances, was virtually unavoidable.

In public attacks on the Constitution, the core of the Antifederalist argument was a condemnation of the strengthened central government. The new federal system was decried as a backward step toward despotism. "The Thing that the Sons of Liberty greatly feared," an-

---

26. See, in this regard, the careful analysis for all the states in Main, *Antifederalists*, pp. 261–81.

27. Compare *ibid.*, pp. 249–55, and the discussion in Robert A. Rutland, *The Ordeal of the Constitution: The Antifederalists and the Ratification Struggle of 1787–1788* (Norman, Okla., 1966).

nounced an Antifederalist, "the conventioners are trying to bring upon them." [28] Even the usually sacrosanct reputations of Washington and Franklin were not beyond the disapproval of the same critic: "Alas!" he exclaimed, "two mighty men are at this time fallen in America." The Constitution of 1787 was repeatedly denounced by its opponents as an "iron government." Antifederalists found dangerous the numerous traps to be laid by the new national government: unlimited taxation, an oppressive bureaucracy, domination by the largest states, and the loss of individual freedom. They bewailed the "impending ruin" of freedom in their country.[29] Of special concern was the vagueness of the document; every grant of power to Congress permitted more than one construction and required "an interpreter" to unravel. This uncertainty was especially disturbing in view of the amplitude of congressional authority, with no reservation of undelegated powers to the states. "For I conceive Sir," wrote an Antifederalist, "that a Constitution ought to be so founded if possible, that the worst of men, entrusted with power, could not use it to the destruction of the liberties of the people." [30]

Insistent and telling were fears raised by the absence of a bill of rights in the Constitution, an almost fatal blunder of the founding fathers. Those opposed to the proposed federal system—and numerous Federalists who favored it—were disturbed that a strong central government was created without specific guarantees of the natural rights of the people. None of the traditional liberties of Americans—freedom of the press, freedom of speech, and trial by jury—were secured in the new Constitution.[31] The reference to trial by jury was a bitter pill for the Federalists. They replied with acerbity that the Antifederalists now crying about the omission of this right in the Constitution were the same politicians who framed the penal statutes that deprived Rhode Islanders of jury trials in paper-money litigation. The Federalists claimed that the state's indifference to the Constitution resulted in one less member of the Union in favor of establishing a bill of rights through amendment.[32] Paradoxically, Rhode Island would not enter the new federal system in order to effect this change. Contemplating

28. *Newport Herald,* January 3, 1788.
29. Letter from "Lycurgus," *U.S. Chronicle* (Providence), April 3, 1788.
30. Letter from "Z," *ibid.,* December 13, 1787.
31. *Ibid.;* and an unsigned letter in the *U.S. Chronicle* (Providence), December 13, 1787.
32. Letters from "Solon, Jr.," and "A Friend to the Union," *Providence Gazette,* August 9, 23, October 18, 1788.

the seeming maze of futility in which Rhode Island found itself, William Ellery blurted out, "She is a foolish slut." [33]

The Antifederalists did not rely entirely on political objections to the Constitution in winning the allegiance of the freemen. They also attempted to mark off the economic and commercial advantages that would accrue if Rhode Island stayed outside the United States. Independence, the Antifederalists asserted, would bring an era of prosperity.

An excellent sample of this type of Antifederalist electioneering was the assurances of Jonathan J. Hazard, one of the most conspicuous country party leaders. Hazard came from a prominent Washington County family and had served the state in many capacities prior to the Confederation period. A patriot during the early days of ferment against Great Britain, Hazard was elected to seats in both houses of the General Assembly at different times, and, in 1778, served on the council of war. He learned something of finance while acting as paymaster of Rhode Island's continental battalion and was among the most influential men in the legislature when matters relating to finance and paper money were discussed. Though educated as a lawyer, Hazard had a genuine gift for politics. He combined this skill with a courtly manner, immaculate dress, and powerful oratory, and he was bitterly denounced by his opponents in precise relationship to his political success. The "Machievel of Charlestown," as Hazard was calumniated by the Federalists, was determined to show that Rhode Island would prosper without the Union.

In his tours of the state, Hazard freely predicted that no economic harm would come if Rhode Island refused to ratify the proposed Constitution. Instead, economic growth would be accelerated by freedom. Besides insulation from national taxes, which the Antifederalists claimed would be crushing, the basic advantage of an independent course would be Rhode Island's security against duties on international trade that stifled commerce. Free from the yoke of inhibiting tariffs, Rhode Island would sell foreign articles "for a song" and become the entrepôt of commerce in North America. If the United States attempted to interdict this trade, Hazard implied, Rhode Islanders were adept at the ancient art of smuggling.[34] Further security against

33. Ellery to unknown correspondent, Newport, October 13, 1788, Miscellaneous Manuscripts, N.H.S., Box 1, Folder 1.
34. Letter from "Rhodoensis," *Newport Herald*, October 23, 1788; *Independent Journal* (New York), November 8, 1788.

the hostility of the United States might be obtained from foreign powers. A parody in a New York newspaper told of Hazard's expectations:

If tonnage is out of the question, tis clear
All Europe will come with her merchandise here,
From duties give up, and no tonnage paid
Rhode Island shall be the emporium of trade.
Then shall we see the effects of our struggling
When our island abounds with the spirit—of smuggling
Not a ship shall arrive but will bring us some booty
By running you [the United States] packages, free of all duty.[35]

The Federalist Argument

On the whole the Federalist argument in Rhode Island largely duplicated the campaigns waged in other states to secure the ratification of the Constitution; the major difference was one of degree. In Rhode Island the Federalists had little success in attracting popular support, and the Constitution was eventually adopted only with the collaboration of the Antifederalists. Perhaps also, economic issues were emphasized by the Federalists in Rhode Island more than elsewhere. They blamed the postwar depression on the government under the Articles of Confederation, hoping thereby to win the support of all parties in Rhode Island politics. In fact, both sides to the constitutional struggle agreed that the national government had to be changed.[36] The basic issue that separated them was the nature of the change recommended by the Federal Convention, particularly the extensive powers given to the national government.

The Federalists asserted that Rhode Island's economy would be greatly benefited by the operation of the Constitution, especially in comparison with the experience under the Articles of Confederation. The most important articles of the proposed Constitution were those which guaranteed free trade among the members of the Union and gave Congress powers requisite to its responsibility in protecting Americans from foreign competitors. These provisions offered Rhode

---

35. "A Rhode Island Meditation," *Daily Advertiser* (New York), July 2, 1790.
36. Letter from "A Rhode Island Man," *Newport Mercury*, February 25, 1788.

Island a rosy future. The disadvantages of remaining outside the Union were incalculable. Rhode Island not only lost the benefits of the Constitution, but, after the new system began to function under President Washington, was also threatened with discriminatory duties. "Can we long exist as a commercial people after being denied entrance into the Union? Does our soil produce the Bread we consume?" asked a Federalist in a pleading tone. "Let us rather confess that the State is shamefully rent by Party and Faction, and that too many of us are fondly attached to a depreciating, destructive Paper Money!" [37]

The seacoast towns were most receptive to Federalist persuasions about the forthcoming spur to commerce if Rhode Island adopted the Constitution. These towns were generally Federalist in sentiment; a chief reason for their support was the state of affairs under the Confederation, including the depression, foreign competition, and European discrimination against Americans, all of which was attributed to the weak government under the Articles. The town of Little Compton, for example, echoed a familiar Federalist plaint of "the extreme need we stand in, of well organized, energetic, national government, and view our new Federal Constitution as a plan of government well adapted to the present critical situation of our national affairs." [38] The appeals of Providence and Newport were more excited, especially after the new government became operative. Newport predicted that, if Rhode Island stayed a refractory state, the United States would end all trade with its merchants, bringing severe hardship to everyone, town and country alike. The townsmen of Providence, in an exceptionally forceful appeal to the General Assembly, summarized the Federalist case for the proposed Constitution. Under the old system, the state's economic life had progressively declined, a situation resulting from the want of congressional power to regulate interstate and international trade.[39] Under the government of President Washington these faults would be remedied.

In and out of Rhode Island the Federalists took special pains to contradict exaggerated expectations that the state might serve as a duty-free entrance into the United States for European goods, a situation

37. *Providence Gazette,* August 1, 1789.
38. Little Compton Town Meeting, January 6, 1788, Staples, *R.I. in the Continental Congress,* p. 589.
39. Newport Town Meeting, April 15, 1789, "Abstracts from the Records of Newport Relative to the Adoption of the Constitution of the United States, 1788–1789," *Newport Historical Magazine,* IV (1883), 98; Staples, *R.I. in the Continental Congress,* pp. 618–19.

that would be guaranteed by European powers. Such pretensions, Federalists declared with disdain, were "too trifling to be told to children." [40] A newspaper dispatch informed Rhode Islanders that the United States would never permit them to offer a haven for smugglers. Furthermore, the United States would never allow foreign powers to gain a foothold among the thirteen original states through a diplomatic alliance or military presence. Such an eventuality would be considered a threat to the security of the new nation. The so-called "harpies" who governed Rhode Island were warned to avoid talk about foreign entanglements offensive to the United States. Foreign adventures would bring instant retaliation. Sooner than permit Rhode Island to enter into dangerous commitments, it would be invaded and divided among its neighbors. This was no idle threat. Another anonymous publication said that there could be "no medium" for Rhode Island. "Enemies they must be, or fellow citizens, and that in a very short order." [41]

Rhode Island Federalists tried to counteract the apprehension and suspicion that their opponents were able to instill in the freemen of the state. Innumerable tirades against the power of a central government, before and after the American Revolution, were volatile fuel for Antifederalist engines.[42] The Federalists endeavored to show that the new Constitution provided a safe repository for the power of the United States; it offered an admirable structure whose vital parts were put together with a view toward the preservation of freedom. There would be strength in the new system, but also guarantees against the abuse of power by the nation.

Federalist spokesmen pointed to the built-in protective devices of the Constitution of 1787. The states still retained full control over local affairs and kept those powers not specifically given to the national government. Security against abuse of authority was attained by separating the powers of the national government into three coequal parts. This resulted in an artful balance of authority among the executive, legislative, and judicial branches, in which each checked the power of the others. Indeed, some Federalist commentators argued, the new Constitution offered a better shield for American liberty than the

40. Letter from "Solon, Jr.," *Providence Gazette,* August 4, 1788.
41. *Norwich Packet* (Conn.), October 8, 1789; *Salem Mercury* (Mass.), January 15, 1788; *Pennsylvania Packet* (Philadelphia), February 9, 1788; *Massachusetts Centinel* (Boston), April 26, 1788.
42. For a good example, see the exchange between "An Honest Man" and "Civis" [William Ellery] in the *Newport Mercury,* December 14, 21, 1786, January 8, 1787.

Continental Congress, "a single body, without a head possessing and exercising . . . legislative, judicial and executive powers, blended and confused in an indistinguishable mass." [43] If concentration of power was criminal in a constitution, the Articles of Confederation was guilty in the greatest degree.

The Struggle in the Legislature

Try as it did, the Federalist minority gained little acceptance in Rhode Island. The freemen were largely unaffected by the Federalist persuasions. Indicative of the Federalist failure was the ease with which the Antifederalists controlled the General Assembly, and the unity maintained by the country party caucus, at least until the public debts were redeemed in 1789. The solidarity of the Antifederalists resulted in the prolonged refusal of the legislature to call a ratifying convention to consider the proposed Constitution. This was tantamount to a veto. On many different occasions the General Assembly rejected Federalist resolutions to convene a ratifying convention. The record of this effort is the story of Federalist tenacity in the face of continuing defeat.

The proposed federal Constitution arrived in Rhode Island early in the fall of 1787.[44] At the October, 1787, session of the General Assembly, the report of the Philadelphia Convention was read, and a lively debate took place. Henry Marchant, representing Newport in the lower house, said that the issue of a constitutional convention was the most important question ever considered by the legislature. He introduced a resolution sending the Constitution to the towns, with an added proviso that the town meetings be instructed to select delegates to a ratifying convention. This motion was defeated by a substantial majority. The country members denounced the new frame of government, while the Federalist deputies suggested that this opposition derived from the fact that the plan did "not quadrate with their darling privilege of managing paper money." [45] Instead of authorizing a ratify-

---

43. Letter from "A Freeman," *Newport Herald,* March 13, 1788.

44. The constitution and accompanying documents were printed in the *Providence Gazette,* September 29, October 23, 1787, and the *Newport Mercury,* October 8, 27, 1787.

45. *Newport Herald,* November 8, 1787.

ing convention, the Assembly agreed to print 1,000 copies of the document and send them to the towns. The struggle to ratify the Constitution started in defeat.

The next meeting of the General Assembly saw little abatement in the country party's adamant opposition. In order to steal a march on the Federalist campaign to secure a ratifying convention, the majority proposed that the Constitution be submitted directly to the people in a referendum. Sponsors of the resolution in the House of Deputies were Jonathan J. Hazard and Thomas Joslyn of West Greenwich, indicating that this strategy was developed at the highest reaches of the country party leadership. The majority members argued that, since the new federal system would deprive the freemen of many of their former privileges, they should be offered the opportunity of judging the Constitution directly without the intercession of a ratifying convention. Moreover, the Antifederalists maintained, the town meetings were the best forum in which to test the true sentiments of the people. They contended that in other states the use of ratifying conventions had resulted in the adoption of the Constitution over the opposition of the majority of freemen, who were "decoyed" into accepting the proposed system against their better judgment. A referendum would prevent this in Rhode Island.[46]

Debate over the referendum was spirited in the lower house. The Federalists denounced the proposal as a completely worthless procedure. No other state had utilized this method, they complained, and, regardless of its outcome, only a convention could act on the Constitution because that was the means prescribed by the Federal Convention. Discounting Antifederalist contentions, the Federalists asserted that a ratifying convention would be the perfect place in which to assess the will of the people. They said the town meetings were dominated by a small group of men who determined in advance how every town would vote on important issues. No real consideration was given any controversial issue in the town meetings. A referendum would merely reflect the decision of the willful men who bossed the town meetings. In contrast, the state-wide convention would represent every shade of opinion in Rhode Island, town as well as country, and provide a forum for conflicting views without the intrusion of party, personality, or pas-

46. The best record of what went on in the General Assembly may be garnered from the *U.S. Chronicle* (Providence), March 6, 1788; *Newport Mercury*, March 6, 1788; and the *Newport Herald*, March 6, 1788.

sion.[47] Notwithstanding the Federalist protests, the General Assembly, firmly controlled by the country party, sent the Constitution to the town meetings by a majority of twenty votes.[48]

Before the towns gathered on March 24, 1788, the Federalists decided to boycott the balloting.[49] Their reasons were plain: defeat was inevitable, and they wanted to avoid a direct confrontation. In this way, regardless of how commanding the Antifederalist majority—and there were estimates of Antifederalist strength ranging to seven-ninths of the population—its true preponderance would never be known.

As expected, the vote favored the Antifederalist position on the Constitution: 2,708 freemen were against adopting the new frame of government; only 237 voted in its favor. The Federalist boycott was nearly complete. Even so, the Antifederalist triumph was clearly overwhelming. Estimates place the number of nonvoting Federalists at 1,200, which, added to the 237 Federalists who did vote, would still have been barely half the Antifederalist majority. Only two towns favored the constitution, Bristol by a vote of 26 to 23, and Little Compton by 63 to 52. The effectiveness of the boycott is illustrated by the balloting in Providence and Newport, the two principal Federalist strongholds. A single freeman voted in Providence, casting his ballot against the Constitution; the count in Newport stood 1 in favor, 10 opposed.[50] Despite their limited numbers, the Federalists did achieve a measure of solidarity.

Providence justified its boycott by presenting a special petition to the General Assembly. The town objected to the referendum as a duplication of effort. Providence repeated the familiar Federalist complaint that only a ratifying convention would provide a proper forum for competing interests in Rhode Island. The worst possible mode of consulting the people of Rhode Island was to have the freemen ballot in the towns, "under an impression of private and local motives only,

47. *Newport Herald,* March 6, 1788.

48. Rhode Island Records, Mss., R.I.S.A., Vol. 13, pp. 465–66; Bartlett, *Records,* X, 271–72; William Allen to Henry Knox, Providence, March 4, 1788, Knox Papers, Mss., M.H.S., Vol. XXI, p. 160.

49. Letter from "A Freeman," *Providence Gazette,* March 15, 1788; letter of "A Rhode-Island Landholder," *U.S. Chronicle* (Providence), March 20, 1788.

50. The vote of the towns and individual balloting of the freemen may be examined in Rhode Island Records, Mss., R.I.S.A., Vol. 13, pp. 465–66; Bartlett, *Records,* X, 275; Staples, *R.I. in the Continental Congress,* pp. 591–606. Further information on the episode may be obtained in the *U.S. Chronicle* (Providence), April 10, 1788, and the *Newport Herald,* April 10, 1788.

uninformed of those reasons and arguments which might lead to the common utility and public good." [51] The Providence petitioners added to their protest a lengthy exposition in favor of ratification. They recapitulated arguments about the abject failure of the Articles of Confederation, predicting that the crisis of the Union would have destroyed the United States but for the intervention of the Philadelphia Convention. A new federal system was an absolute necessity. The petitioners also admonished the Antifederalist Assembly by declaring that Rhode Island could not survive as an independent country. They indicated it would be much wiser to join the new Union as quickly as possible and add one more voice to the movement for amendment.[52]

The petitions from Providence and other Federalist towns had no influence in the legislature. The General Assembly instructed Governor Collins to prepare a letter to Congress defending Rhode Island's singular course in holding a popular referendum on the Constitution; the governor was also told to inform Congress of the Antifederalist result of the poll. In his communication to Congress, Collins explained that Rhode Island's unique proceedings were not meant to defy the United States. They were based "upon pure republican principles, founded upon that basis of all governments originally deriving from the people at large." [53] He expressed regret that Rhode Island was not yet able to assist in the reformation of the Union. On behalf of the legislature, however, Collins declared that the state's leaders recognized the need for a strengthened central government, and would "heartily acquiesce" in granting Congress a permanent revenue and control over international trade.[54]

One thing was very obvious in the country party's approach during these first months after the Constitution of 1787 was presented to the states. Rhode Island promised to forestall the convocation of a ratify-

51. *Providence Gazette*, March 29, 1788; William R. Staples, ed., *Annals of the Town of Providence* (Providence, 1843), pp. 322–27.

52. Staples, *Annals of Providence*, pp. 322–27. The town of Newport, in its petition to the Assembly, complained that the referendum was "unconstitutional, unprecedented, ineffecacious, and inconsistent" ("Abstracts from the Records of Newport," pp. 93–95); see also the petition of Bristol, in Staples, *R.I. in the Continental Congress*, p. 607.

53. Governor Collins to the President of Congress, In General Assembly, April 5, 1788, State Papers of Rhode Island, Mss., N.A., pp. 604 10; Rhode Island Records, Mss., R.I.S.A., Vol. 13, pp. 472–73; Bartlett, *Records*, X, 291.

54. A country party politician, John Sayles of Smithfield, suggested another policy in place of this letter to Congress. He proposed that the General Assembly draft its own constitution and submit it to Congress in lieu of the Constitution of 1787. This idea got nowhere in the Assembly (*Newport Herald*, April 10, 1788).

ing convention as long as necessary to permit the paper-money program to run its course. After that? No one could be sure. Also certain was the fact that this policy would mean months of delay before Rhode Island found the new Constitution to its liking—if ever. More particularly, the forthcoming liquidation of the state debts gave cohesion to the country forces and allowed supporters of the paper-money system to close ranks after an initial period of division. As the months passed, it became apparent that the financial plans of the majority party would not be completed before the proposed federal system came to life under President George Washington. In time, Rhode Island became a foreign state.

The Struggle in the Towns

The popular referendum on the Constitution was meant to reveal the depth of Antifederalist sentiment in Rhode Island. This satisfied several purposes at once. A referendum would smash the small but obstreperous Federalist minority, still troublesome despite its weakness. It would also be useful in warding off criticism of the country party, which stood as the spokesman of the people, executing their will. Furthermore, the size of the Antifederalist majority would be helpful in preventing precipitant action by either internal or external parties to force Rhode Island into the new Union. In consequence the country leaders seized upon several other opportunities to consult the freemen directly on the proposed frame of government. They knew that the majority of voters in Rhode Island were Antifederalists.

Another chance to consult the freemen presented itself in the winter of 1788–89, after New York had ratified the Constitution. This represented a tremendous victory for Federalism and a major defection from the opposition camp, but it was won only by compromise. New York accompanied its ratification with a request that a second Federal Convention be convened to amend the federal system before the new government became operative. This proposal was circulated among the state assemblies, including Rhode Island, in a communication from Governor George Clinton.[55] The movement for another constitu-

55. This subject is discussed by E. P. Smith, "The Movement Towards a Second Constitutional Convention in 1788," in J. Franklin Jameson, ed., *Essays in the Constitutional History of the United States in the Formative Period* (New York,

tional convention was unsuccessful. Once having ratified the Constitution, the Federalists assumed there could be no conditions; besides, there was a general consensus among all parties that the Constitution should be changed to include the most important items demanded by the New York State ratifying convention. These understandings clipped the wings of those who wanted a second Federal Convention. Nevertheless, the country party found the idea to its liking. If the proposal succeeded, it might delay the commencement of the new government and might reconstruct the federal system. Accordingly, the majority caucus decided to accept the suggestion. Jonathan J. Hazard proposed that the Assembly print Clinton's letter and send it to the freemen for their consideration; his motion was adopted by a three to one majority.[56] The General Assembly endorsed the concept of another constitutional convention with the statement that it was required to secure "necessary amendment." The legislature saw its acceptance of New York's recommendation as indicative of its willingness to join in a reformation of the federal system. Indeed, the Assembly declared, "it was the indispensable duty of the citizens of this state to be connected in the Union . . . if it could be done upon the principles of good government." [57] If not, Rhode Island would reject the United States.

The country leaders knew what they wanted when they sent Clinton's letter to the towns. The results of the town meetings showed that most Rhode Islanders were still opposed to the Constitution, in many cases even with amendments. Nine towns instructed their deputies in the lower house to favor New York's proposal; five were opposed. The Federalist towns, caught in a quandary, took no united stand on the issue. Portsmouth supported the plan because it felt that only after radical changes would Rhode Island enter the new federal system. Another community, Barrington, signified it was not unalterably opposed to the revised federal government, provided amendments were added for the "publick good." [58] There were other towns that offered no in-

---

1940) , pp. 46–115. Two recent appraisals are Rutland, *The Ordeal of the Constitution,* pp. 255–66, 283–300, and Linda Grant DePauw, *The Eleventh Pillar: New York State and the Federal Constitution* (Ithaca, 1966) , pp. 257–64, 270–74.

56. Jeremiah Olney to Henry Knox, Providence, November 5, 1788, Knox Papers, Mss., M.H.S., Vol. XXIII, p. 11.

57. Rhode Island Records, Mss., R.I.S.A., Vol. 13, p. 558; Bartlett, *Records,* X, 309–10.

58. Portsmouth Town Meeting, Mss., December 20, 1788; Barrington Town Meeting, Mss., December 5, 1788.

structions upon the principle of opposing any alteration of the Union whatever.[59] In one case, the conflict engendered by consideration of Clinton's letter led to near chaos. On November 25, 1788, an East Greenwich town meeting debated the New York recommendation and voted to approve it in principle. The townsmen selected a special committee to draw up the formal instructions for the representatives in the legislature. When the committee reported on December 22, the Federalists decided to reject the idea of a second Federal Convention. They appeared in strength, and the written instructions were disapproved. The following ballot, however, found the Antifederalists ready for battle. On this occasion, the committee's work was approved. By the time the meeting was coming to a close, a third poll was in prospect. With the two sides evenly matched and tempers getting ragged, a compromise was reached. No instructions were given to the deputies. The third ballot found the vote tied, as predetermined, one in favor, one opposed.[60]

Before long the General Assembly was again presented with a Federalist resolution to convene a ratifying convention. The month was May, 1789. Several new factors now altered the nature of the constitutional struggle. One was the election of George Washington and his inauguration as President of the United States on April 30, symbolizing the determination of the American states to carry on as a nation without Rhode Island. Another was the quickening pace of the liquidation of the public debts of Rhode Island, fast nearing completion in the middle of 1789. Each of these developments influenced the Federalist-Antifederalist division. The country leadership could no longer depend on the paper-money issue to hold the party together. Many country spokesmen wished to rejoin the United States. On the other hand, the problem was a very delicate one. If the country party moved too speedily to adopt the Constitution, it would be repudiated by the freemen; but if it failed to act, its solidarity would be destroyed. In addition, there were outside pressures from the new national government. No one could mistake the truculent tone of those who said Rhode Island would not survive as an independent country.

Facing this difficult situation at the May session of the General Assembly, the country party postponed a motion for a ratifying convention until the people were consulted. The country leaders in the

59. Coventry Town Meeting, Mss., December 20, 1788; Exeter Town Meeting, Mss., December 22, 1788.
60. *Newport Herald*, May 14, 1789.

legislature promised that, if the freemen favored the Constitution, they would not oppose calling a ratifying convention.

When the Assembly reconvened in the middle of June, the prevailing sentiment of the freemen was still antagonistic to the Constitution. The Federalist members were not dissuaded. As a preface to a resolution authorizing a convention, the Federalists recounted their oft-repeated arguments in favor of the new government, taking care to point out that an independent Rhode Island would shortly be laden with duties on international commerce by the United States. The country did not respond. Its Antifederalist deputies announced in the lower house that they were ready to vote without a debate. The silence of the majority members had been prepared in advance. In a caucus the evening before they decided upon this strategy, intending to show by their tactics that they voted No because of the deliberations of the freemen in their town meetings in previous weeks.[61] The people had spoken, and the country party was their tribune.

The imminence of a ballot without a word raised against the Constitution provoked the Federalists. They snapped that the Antifederalists had nothing to say about the Constitution because they were either "ashamed or too ignorant" to make their arguments public. Stung by this outcry, Jonathan J. Hazard spoke briefly about why Rhode Island did not ratify the Constitution, mainly for the edification of the minority. He quickly summed up the reasons why the state was not already a member of the new republic, asserting that no great disadvantage would fall upon Rhode Island for its recalcitrance. It was advisable to be "slow and deliberate" in contemplating the newly instituted government, carefully analyzing every possible ramification. Hazard reassured his listeners that, regardless of how slowly the legislature proceeded, it could rejoin the United States whenever it pleased. He implied without elaboration that it might not be as easy to get out.

The vote of the lower house resulted in another defeat for the Federalists. By a margin of eleven the House of Deputies refused to authorize a ratifying convention. This time, however, there was hope. The reduced margin of the Antifederalist phalanx was an intriguing sign that the country party was receding from its adamant posture.[62] The sky was beginning to brighten on the Federalist horizon.

61. *Ibid.*, June 15, 1789; William Ellery to Benjamin Huntington, Newport, June 18, 1789, Ellery Letters, Mss., R.I.S.A.

62. *Providence Gazette,* June 20, 1789; *Salem Mercury* (Mass.), June 30, 1789; *Pennsylvania Packet* (Philadelphia), July 1, 1789; *Gazette of the United States*

Better evidence of the changing character of Rhode Island's Antifederalism is the testimony of the busy federal officeholder, William Ellery. He was diligent in sounding out the country leaders about their continuing intransigence. "I asked them whether they meant ever to adopt the Constitution," Ellery wrote in a record of his conversations. "Yes," was their reply. "When?" he shot back. "Some time hence." [63]

The country leaders explained that they wanted the paper bills to remain a legal tender for a few more months. After that, they were inclined to join the United States. The country spokesmen also stated that they wanted to wait until Congress amended the Constitution before attempting to reason with their Antifederalist constituents. These frank talks tried Ellery's patience; he had little sympathy for what he felt was the cynicism of the country hierarchy. "You might as well reason with the wind," he wrote, "as with this sort of people." Ellery saw one solution for the problem of Rhode Island's Antifederalism: the blunt and unabashed threat of force. He recommended a policy of economic and military reprisals as the only way to bring Rhode Island into the Union. Shortly afterward, in the middle of September, 1789, Ellery provided another clue to the growing moderation of the country party. He observed in a letter to his frequent correspondent, Congressman Benjamin Huntington, that some of the country politicians, including Jonathan J. Hazard, were convinced that the state had to ratify the Constitution in the near future. They were now angling for federal jobs, he suggested, and would announce their conversion to Federalism when important national offices were dangled as bait.[64]

Liquidation of the public debts induced Governor Collins to call a special session of the General Assembly in September, 1789. Another issue was the Constitution of 1787. Although Congress had temporarily exempted Rhode Island from duties on foreign trade, Collins thought it best to have the legislators consider the situation. The most important act of the Assembly in this meeting was to suspend the legal-tender provisions of the paper-money system, thereby breaking the lingering connection between paper money and the ratification of the

---

(New York), June 27, 1789. The *Federal Gazette* (Philadelphia), August 6, September 10, October 6, 1789, repeatedly intimated that Rhode Island would soon ratify the Constitution.

63. Ellery to Benjamin Huntington, Newport, June 18, 1789, Ellery Letters, Mss., R.I.S.A.

64. Ellery to Benjamin Huntington, Newport, September 13, 1789, Ellery Letters, Mss., R.I.S.A.

Constitution. Now the problem for those who wanted Rhode Island in the Union was to convince the freemen that a convention should be authorized and the Constitution ratified.[65]

The special session, though sympathetic to the pleas of the Federalists that the state must ratify the Constitution, was limited in what it might do. The country party was bound by the Antifederalist ideology with which it had waged the struggle against the federal system before 1789; this philosophy asserted that the issue should be decided by the people directly, through a referendum. As a result, the question was once more submitted to the town meetings, accompanied by the familiar declaration that the freemen "retain in their own hands the entire power of adopting or rejecting the said Constitution. . . ."[66] Inevitably, as everyone suspected, the people of Rhode Island were unwilling to live under the Constitution of 1787. A substantial majority of the town meetings instructed their representatives to vote against calling a ratifying convention. When the legislature reconvened, the expected Federalist motion to authorize a ratifying convention was beaten 39 to 17.[67] Superficially, the movement for the Constitution suffered a humiliating defeat. Below the surface of public commitment, however, the Antifederalists admitted they wished to be reunited with the United States. Unfortunately, they said, they "were restrained from expressing their sentiments, by their instructions."[68] In 1790 there would be greater consistency of thought and action.

65. *Providence Gazette,* September 26, 1789.
66. Rhode Island Records, Mss., R.I.S.A., Vol. 13, pp. 635–36; Bartlett, *Records,* X, 338.
67. *Providence Gazette,* October 31, 1789.
68. *Newport Herald,* November 5, 1789.

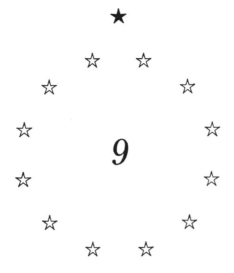

The Nation Again Complete

THERE COULD BE no mistaking that the autumn of 1789 was a season of change in Rhode Island politics. Everywhere below the level of outright public disclosure there were hints and whispers that most of the country party's leaders were certain that Antifederalism was a lost cause. With paper money no longer an obstacle to ratification, the successful operation of the new federal government seemed an invitation, not a threat, to growing numbers of people. The men who governed the state had little doubt that Rhode Island would have to rejoin the United States, but the majority of freemen were still unconvinced.

North Carolina's ratification of the Constitution on November 1, 1789, sharpened the urgency with which the freemen pondered their lingering doubts about the United States.[1] Rhode Island was now left behind in solitude as the only state that spurned the new federal sys-

---

1. The news of North Carolina's ratification was printed in the *Providence Gazette,* December 12, 1789, and the *Newport Mercury,* December 16, 1789.

tem. It was not a comfortable feeling. If the United States government had in any way been restrained from taking overt action against Rhode Island because of North Carolina, the fourth-largest American state, this restraint was now gone. Greater credibility would have to be given to continuing threats of hostilities by the United States against the tiny and defenseless state. The accession of North Carolina also affected Rhode Island's Antifederalism because it accentuated the state's newly acquired sovereignty and contrasted ominously with the pattern of harmony that characterized the United States. The effect was electric. Only Rhode Island stood outside the nation, observed two Connecticut newspapers, casting "the shadow of a schism on the Bond that unites the great Federal Republic"; there could be "no doubt" it would soon see the light of reason and self-interest.[2] Similarly, Henry Barber, publisher of the *Newport Mercury*, reassured his out-of-state readers that a rapid change of sentiment was taking place among a growing number of Antifederalists; they were coming to understand that "nature, reason, and every circumstance" dictated Rhode Island's re-entrance into the Union. Time would tell, Barber declared, provided that moderation prevailed in federal and state councils.[3]

The ratification by North Carolina hardened the attitude of the United States government in New York City. In a letter to former Deputy Governor Jabez Bowen, President Washington warned that the General Assembly should "consider well" the possible consequences before it again refused to call a ratifying convention.[4] There can be little doubt that Washington's word of caution was judiciously circulated among the state's leaders. Rhode Island's status as a leper was further revealed when President Washington took a circuitous route on his tour of New England in 1789, carefully avoiding Rhode Island. This snub dashed the hopes of the freemen of Providence who were eager to honor the Revolutionary leader, "a Character so justly revered by the world." [5] Rhode Island's novel sovereignty precluded the proposed celebration.

Signs of change, however, did not mean that all Rhode Islanders were converted to the Federalist cause. There were still Antifederalists

2. *Connecticut Journal* (New Haven), December 9, 1789; *Connecticut Gazette* (New London), December 11, 1789.

3. *Newport Mercury*, December 23, 1789.

4. Washington to Bowen, New York, December 27, 1789, Emmet Collection, Mss., N.Y.P.L., Em. 9585.

5. Providence Town Meeting, Mss., October 24, 1789.

exalting the state's independence as the year 1790 neared. Some delighted in Rhode Island's solitude, noting that its history and tradition had been that of self-rule and freedom from external control. Consistency with the past was recommended as the highest virtue.[6] Other Antifederalist commentators rejoiced as they contemplated the material blessings which an independent future would bring to Rhode Island. Prosperity and progress were twin gifts of complete sovereignty. Should Rhode Island open its ports to the entire world in defiance of the United States, wrote an Antifederalist, it would become "the wealthiest, the happiest, and the most envied State in all the world." Nor was there need to fear attack, for no one could doubt that Rhode Island would be protected by foreign powers. Summing up the Antifederalist case, the conclusion was inescapable: "Let the constitution be immediately rejected, we have dallied with it too long."[7]

This Antifederalist reasoning was greeted with expressions of ridicule and with undisguised threats of dismemberment. A partition of Rhode Island, suggested reports in the American press, would return the state to the Union most quickly.[8] Other informed observers insisted that economic sanctions should be instituted if Rhode Island tried to remain an independent country.[9] Congress, in fact, had already taken steps to impose duties on Rhode Island shippers and exclude the state's products from United States ports;[10] some Federalists were ready to proceed with a total embargo on commerce with the state and the use of force to ensure that Rhode Island paid its share of

6. Letter from "Solon, Jr.," *Providence Gazette*, February 27, 1790.

7. For these statements and one of the most authoritative patterns of Antifederalism, see the anonymous letters of "Greenwichiensis," *Newport Herald*, February 25, March 18, April 8, May 13, 1790. "Greenwichiensis" was answered in a cogent series of anonymous letters from "Agricola," *Newport Herald*, March 11, April 20, and May 20, 1790.

8. One of these news dispatches boasted that if Rhode Island continued to be "obnoxious," Worcester County in Massachusetts would invade and capture the state with its own forces in three weeks (*Federal Gazette* [Philadelphia], January 2, 1790). See also "Extract of a letter from a very distinguished Member of Congress," *Providence Gazette*, October 3, 1789; letter from "Manlius," *Daily Gazette* (New York), October 15, 1789; and items in *Gazette of the United States* (New York), June 27, 1789; *Salem Mercury* (Mass.), June 30, 1789.

9. Roger Sherman to David Howell, New York, May 16, 1789, Archives, Mss., B.U.L.

10. *Debates and Proceedings in the Congress of the United States, 1789–1824*, 42 vols. (Washington, D.C., 1834–56), II, 2214, 2236. (Hereafter cited as *Annals of Congress*.) This first economic reprisal against Rhode Island and North Carolina was enacted on July 31, 1789; its operation was suspended until January 15, 1790 by an act of Congress passed on September 16.

the Revolutionary debts.[11] In Rhode Island, William Ellery, in particular, was unflinching in calling for severe measures as the only way to convince the freemen that they must adopt the federal Constitution.[12] He believed that firmness alone would work the wonder of ratification in Rhode Island.

The danger of dismemberment was threatened not only by forces outside Rhode Island but also by a secessionist movement among the commercial towns. Providence and Newport were preparing to secede from Rhode Island and rejoin the United States if the General Assembly did not authorize a ratifying convention.[13] In laying the groundwork for this eventuality, the Federalists were careful to sound out the United States government in the hope of gaining its protection should the commercial towns apply for admission to the Union or annexation to their neighboring states. Rhode Island's Federalists were coming to see the new government as their last chance of escape "from the nest of freebooters" who controlled the state.[14] Just prior to the scheduled January, 1790, meeting of the General Assembly, Benjamin Bourne of Providence, a prominent attorney and influential Federalist, asserted that, if the legislature failed to convene a ratifying convention, the minority was determined to call its own convention and approve the Constitution. Bourne acknowledged that this might be a dangerous maneuver, but, in a letter to Silas Talbot, a friend then living in New York, he defended this policy as the only means by which the Federalists could rejoin the United States. He hoped that Congress itself would favor the strategy; congressional protection might be necessary.[15]

11. Letter from "A Federalist," *Newport Mercury*, January 6, 1790; letter from "A Federalist," *Daily Advertiser* (New York) , May 18, 1790. See also *The Journal of William Maclay: United States Senator from Pennsylvania, 1789–1791,* ed. Edgar Maclay (New York, 1927) , p. 183.

12. Ellery to Benjamin Huntington, Newport, September 8, 1789, Ellery Letters, Mss., R.I.S.A.

13. Ellery to Benjamin Huntington, Newport, March 10, May 14, 1789, April 17, May 3, 1790, *ibid.; Gazette of the United States* (New York) , April 15, 1789; *Federal Gazette* (Philadelphia) , April 20, 1789; *State Gazette of North Carolina* (Edenton) , May 28, 1789; *Daily Gazette* (New York) , January 1, 1790. A dispatch printed in the *Federal Gazette* (Philadelphia) , January 1, 1790, flatly predicted a "revolt" of the seaport towns in the event the General Assembly failed to authorize a convention at its January session.

14. *Daily Advertiser* (New York) , January 27, 1789; *Connecticut Journal* (New Haven) , February 4, 1789; *Maryland Journal and Baltimore Advertiser,* February 6, 1789; *Virginia Herald* (Fredericksburg) , February 19, 1789.

15. Bourne to Talbot, Providence, January 9, 1790, Peck Collection, Mss., R.I.H.S.

A Ratifying Convention

Leaders of the Antifederalist forces were not blind to the grave crisis confronting Rhode Island in the waning days of 1789. They were well aware of the difficult course the state would have to tread if it attempted to remain independent. Even among the irreconcilables, few saw much chance of success. A number began thinking about jobs under the new system, seeking to make the best of all possible worlds for both Rhode Island and themselves through a belated ratification of the Constitution.[16] Indeed, it is ironic that the most critical period of Rhode Island's Confederation history came after the summer of 1789, when the administration of President Washington was already in office and the Federal period had begun. During these uncertain months outside the United States the dangers of internal dissolution and external attack were most real.

It was thus with a strong feeling of emergency that the General Assembly convened on January 11, 1790. The main issue of the session was that of a constitutional convention. Peter Edes, writing in his *Newport Herald,* noted that "without friend or ally" the problem of reunion was a question of profound magnitude.[17] The Federalists needed no reminder. They spared no effort to be present and seized every opportunity to win country party members over to the apparent inevitability of their viewpoint.[18] Everything depended on this meeting of the legislature.

On Friday morning, January 14, Benjamin Bourne, representing Providence in the lower house of the Assembly, offered the expected resolution calling for a ratifying convention. After a lengthy debate of several hours, the resolution carried by a vote of 34 to 29; the Federalists were surprised at their easy victory and majority in the House of Deputies.[19] The next day, however, their pleasure was dampened. The

16. William Ellery to Benjamin Huntington, Newport, February 19, 1789; June 12, 1790, Ellery Letters, Mss., R.I.S.A.; *Newport Herald,* January 21, 1790.

17. January 21, 1790.

18. Colonel [Jeremiah] Olney to General Henry Knox, Providence, January 17, 1790, Knox Papers, Mss., M.H.S., Vol. XXV, p. 99; Jabez Bowen, John I. Clarke, Benjamin Bourne, John Brown, and Z. Brown to Christopher Champlin and George Gibbs, Providence, January 12, 1790, Wetmore Collection, Mss., M.H.S.

19. Colonel [Henry] Shelburne to General [Henry] Knox, Newport, January 18, 1790, Knox Papers, Mss., M.H.S., Vol. XXV, p. 102.

upper house defeated the first bill authorizing a constitutional convention by a division of 5 to 4.[20]

Mindful of the possible consequences of this veto, the Antifederalists in the upper house asked for a conference of party leaders in the hope of superseding the convention call with an alternative plan of action. The conference broke up in complete failure. Undaunted, the Assistants recommended to the House of Deputies that the constitutional problem be delivered once more to the freemen for their deliberation and decision.[21] This bill was rejected by a margin of fourteen deputies. In order to keep the issue alive, the lower house approved a second convention resolution, varying only the time for the convocation of a convention so that the motion would be in order as a new bill. The upper house again refused its concurrence; but instead of bringing the session to a close, the Assistants adjourned to the following day, Sunday, January 16.

The Lord's Day proved an auspicious occasion for Rhode Island Federalism. Its strength was increasing in the House of Deputies, while the upper house, pressed by the logic of events, seemed to be unreasonable. When the legislators reassembled, the Federalists were ready with a third bill authorizing a constitutional convention. The resolution carried by a substantial margin, 32 to 11. The great throng of spectators that witnessed the debate turned its eager attention to the Assistants. Supposedly, the clergy were without listeners on that Sabbath morning.[22] In the upper house, where two previous bills had been lost by a single vote, the absence of an Antifederalist assistant, the Elder John Williams, now resulted in a deadlocked ballot, 4 against 4.[23] The decision rested with Governor John Collins.

20. The best accounts of this meeting of the General Assembly may be found in the *Newport Herald* and *U.S. Chronicle* (Providence), both published on January 21, 1790. Useful information is also printed in the *Providence Gazette*, January 16, 1790, and the *Daily Gazette* (New York), January 15, 25, 1790.

21. This proposal was introduced by Deputy Governor Daniel Owen. For the text and an explanatory note see the Acts and Resolves of the General Assembly, Mss., R.I.S.A., Vol. 25, p. 98.

22. *Federal Gazette* (Philadelphia), January 30, 1790.

23. Several weeks after the session had ended a curious explanation circulated that the absence of John Williams, reputedly a descendant of Roger Williams, came about because Williams was "obliged to attend to the cure of Souls, [and] was under a Necessity of banishing *Worldly Cares* on that Day" (*Providence Gazette*, February 6, 1790). Later Tristam Burges offered a radically different interpretation of the Reverend Williams' devotion. "The Elder was doubtless greatly grieved and distressed that the wicked political men should take such advantage of his pious call to preach on that day," Burges observed; "and Mr. John Brown was so much gratified

Long before January 16, 1790, John Collins had become a resolute Federalist. How he would decide could not have been in doubt.[24] In the speech that preceded his vote, Collins expounded on the many dangers threatening Rhode Island and the certainty of greater ill fortune if the state continued to disdain reunion with the United States. For these reasons, Collins affirmed, he favored calling a ratifying convention.

Rhode Island's constitutional convention was scheduled to convene on March 1, 1790. The place of the meeting was South Kingstown, an Antifederalist agricultural town. Delegates to the convention were chosen by the freemen on February 9 on the same basis as the lower house of the legislature. The opposing forces waged a spirited campaign to secure a dominant representation. When the General Assembly had agreed to call a convention, the Federalists were sanguine that a speedy re-entrance into the Union would be accomplished by the delegates at South Kingstown. In this expectation, the General Assembly petitioned Congress to extend Rhode Island's exemption from the burden of commercial legislation until the convention completed the task of ratification. On February 8, in response to Rhode Island's request, Congress agreed to extend this relief until April 1, but "no longer." [25] The country party, however, instead of surrendering wholesale to the rising star of Federalism, was indefatigable in securing the election of its delegates to the convention. At the conclusion of the balloting, the country members held a majority of approximately ten, a reduction by half of its majority in the lower house of the legislature.[26]

The Federalist minority was also active during this last phase of the

---

by the pious Elder's attention to the spiritual concerns of his flock that he soon after sent him a clear deed of a very considerable farm in the vicinity as a reward for his religious zeal and attention to the spiritual wants of his church and congregation" (Memoir of Welcome Arnold, unpublished biography, R.I.H.S., p. 5).

24. Collins gives an account of his Federalist views and an apologia for remaining as nominal head of the country party after 1787 in Collins to George Washington, Newport, May 24, 1790, in Gaillard Hunt, "Office Seeking in Washington's Administration," *American Historical Review*, I (1896), 279–80.

25. Rhode Island Records, Mss., R.I.S.A., Vol. 13, p. 724; John R. Bartlett, ed., *Records of the Colony of Rhode Island and Providence Plantations in New England,* 10 vols. (Providence, 1856–65), X, 373–74; *Annals of Congress,* II, 2260.

26. Brown and Benson to Hewes and Anthony, Providence, February 4, 1790, Brown Papers, Mss., J.C.B.L.; Henry Marchant to William Marchant, Newport, February 15, 1790, quoted in Robert C. Cotner, ed., *Theodore Foster's Minutes of the Convention held at South Kingstown, Rhode Island, in March, 1790, which failed to Adopt the Constitution of the United States* (Providence, 1929), p. 20 n. 75; letter from "Alpha," *U.S. Chronicle* (Providence), February 11, 1790.

constitutional struggle in Rhode Island. It met with some success, but not enough to control political events in the state. The Federalists conducted a forceful campaign, stinting neither cost nor effort.[27] Defeat throughout the Confederation era had not dimmed their ardor. The struggle to elect delegates and the meeting of the convention itself were preceded by a brief flurry of Federalist exhortation. Nothing new was said, but the Federalists carried on as though repetition might win out where their logic had failed before. The Articles of Confederation was again faulted as a frame of government, needing radical reform before it collapsed. To continue under the Articles, the Federalists asserted, involved the risk of bankruptcy and disorder. This sorry picture contrasted sharply with the expanding economic and political prospects of the United States under the Constitution of 1787. The new government's success was hailed, while Rhode Island was said to be rapidly "driving towards inevitable ruin and disgrace." [28] Another Federalist writer reminded the freemen of the possibility that the United States would use its economic and military power to force Rhode Island to enter the Union. "Why not make a virtue of necessity," he chided, "and take a part in the first organization of the new Government?" [29] Corroborating the menace of an involuntary reattachment to the United States, Congressman Caleb Strong of Massachusetts advised his Rhode Island friends that anything short of ratification would bring reprisals from the national government.[30]

A troubling paradox of the campaign to elect delegates to the convention was the position of the country leaders. Since they had consented to call a convention, they were prepared to rejoin the United States; but their strenuous efforts to elect country delegates seemed almost certain to result in an Antifederalist majority. In other words, even though the country leadership was ready to accept the Constitution of 1787, its struggle to dominate the convention was calculated to forestall ratification. During the deliberations of the convention this paradox was resolved.

27. Letter of John Brown and John Francis, Providence, June 11, 1790, in Hunt, "Office Seeking in Washington's Administration," pp. 279–80; George Champlin to Welcome Arnold, Newport, February 23, 1790, Welcome Arnold Papers, Mss., J.C.B.L. See also the letters of "Centinel" and "A.B.C.D. etc." in the *U.S. Chronicle* (Providence), April 15, 1790.
28. Anonymous letter, *U.S. Chronicle* (Providence), February 5, 1790.
29. Letter from "An Independent Elector," *ibid.*, March 5, 1790.
30. Strong to Theodore Foster, New York, February 29, 1790 Correspondence, Foster Collection, Mss., R.I.H.S.

The controlling factor governing the country party's actions was Rhode Island politics. The country leaders were determined to stay in power after the ratification of the Constitution; they were also anxious to hold the paper money–Antifederalist coalition together. In order to secure these objectives, they could hardly carry the dead weight of acknowledged Federalism around their necks in the spring elections of 1790. In consequence the country leadership worked out an intricate political strategy. Instead of rejoining the Union when the convention assembled, the country members intended to adjourn the meeting after adopting a bill of rights and a series of amendments to the Constitution. Having accomplished this, the country leaders planned to present their bill of rights and proposed amendments to the freemen and seek re-election to state offices. The country party would thus take a noncommittal approach to the Constitution of 1787. After the elections were completed and the country party was ensconced in power for another six months to a year, a reconvened session of the ratifying convention would accept the Constitution. The scheme, moreover, offered another highlight among its already attractive prospects. If everything went according to plan and the country party retained control of the General Assembly, it would be able to select Rhode Island's first two United States senators.[31]

The Rhode Island ratifying convention met on March 1, 1790. It proceeded to business much as other conventions before it, reading and debating the Constitution clause by clause and appointing a special committee to prepare a list of amendments.[32] The first divisions in the convention showed the strength of the country party. Deputy Governor Daniel Owen, an Antifederalist, was chosen president without opposition; Daniel Updike, country-affiliated clerk of the House of Deputies, was elected secretary of the convention over Theodore Foster

31. Henry J. Shelburne to Henry Knox, Newport, March 7, 1790; Jeremiah Olney to Henry Knox, Providence, May 31, 1790, both in Knox Papers, Mss., M.H.S., Vol. XXV, p. 60; Vol. XXVI, p. 67; William Ellery to Benjamin Huntington, Newport, March 8, 28, 1790, Ellery Letters, Mss., R.I.S.A.; letter from "S.K.," *Providence Gazette*, March 6, 1790; Welcome Arnold to Samuel A. Otis, Providence, February 23, 1790, Welcome Arnold Papers, Mss., J.C.B.L.

32. There was no official journal of the convention's debates. The best source is the record of the debates at South Kingstown kept by Theodore Foster, who was not a delegate, in Cotner, *Foster's Minutes*. Daniel Updike, secretary of the convention, kept a skimpy minute book of the convention sessions that met in South Kingstown and Newport. Updike's notes may be consulted in William R. Staples, ed., *Rhode Island in the Continental Congress: With the Journal of the Convention that Adopted the Constitution 1765–1790* (Providence, 1870), pp. 640–57. Valuable information also appears in the *Providence Gazette*, March 13, May 29, June 5, 1790.

by a margin of 12 votes.[33] For the most part, there was remarkable agreement among the delegates with regard to the major provisions of the Constitution of 1787. This harmony was surprising and very different from the climactic battles in the Virginia and New York conventions. The most important conflicts came over the proposed amendments.

Provision for national taxation under the federal system, particularly the possibility that direct taxes might be laid by Congress, was a subject of concern throughout the constitutional struggle in Rhode Island. In West Greenwich, a town unflagging in its opposition to the proposed frame of government, Antifederalists charged that within three years of the adoption of the Constitution, their property would "all be taken away" by federal levies.[34] Not everyone shared this dread. But William Barton of Providence, a Federalist member of the convention, spoke out against the wisdom of giving Congress power to lay direct taxes upon the states, demonstrating that fear of national taxation was a nonpartisan issue in Rhode Island. Joseph Stanton complained that the tax provisions of the Constitution were "obscure" and would result in loathsome poll taxes. Responding to criticism, Henry Marchant and Nathan Miller, formerly a member of Congress, predicted that the national government would rarely, if ever, levy direct taxes or take advantage of the American people. Marchant was especially careful to recall the problem of federal taxation under the Articles of Confederation, asserting that it would be best to leave the constitutional framework unchanged with respect to national taxes.[35]

Several delegates were also critical of the powers of the President under the new federal system. Joseph Stanton attacked the executive authority as too extensive and dangerous in scope. Henry Marchant again defended the Constitution. He counterclaimed that the President's power was necessary to offset the strengthening of other federal agencies, believing that it was wise to entrust the powers of government to equal branches.[36] Other Federalists celebrated the range of presidential authority as an admirable focus for national unity and an effective check on sectional strife.

33. *Newport Herald,* March 4, 1790; *Connecticut Journal* (New Haven), March 10, 1790; *New-York Packet* (New York), March 13, 1790.

34. Letter from "A Friend to Justice and Good Government," *Newport Mercury,* February 15, 1790; "Journal of William Loughton Smith, 1790–1791," ed. Albert Mathews, *Massachusetts Historical Society Proceedings,* LI (1918), 39.

35. Cotner, *Foster's Minutes,* pp. 39–43, 54–55.

36. Staples, *R.I. in the Continental Congress,* pp. 645–46.

The principal controversy in the Rhode Island ratifying convention was over the problem of slavery. The state's association with slavery had a long history. Rhode Island merchants were among the leaders in profiting from the slave trade, and during the colonial period the Narragansett country had sustained the largest slave population in New England. The plight of the Negro in America had agitated Rhode Islanders before the Revolution, and the struggle for the natural rights of man, announced in 1776, gave another perspective to the problem. Subsequently, Rhode Island had provided for the gradual abolition of slavery during the War for Independence and finally prohibited the slave trade in 1786.[37] The Constitution of 1787 reopened the question. Throughout the ratification controversy there had been powerful Antifederalists among the Quakers in Rhode Island. They were repelled by the constitutional tolerance of slavery among the states and appalled that the traffic in Africans would be legal until 1808. Moses Brown and other Quaker leaders, who might otherwise have befriended the new government, were consequently unenthusiastic or hostile to the proposed federal system. Brown reported that "there is not a sensible friend I have conversed [with] on this subject but had not been disagreeably affected." [38] The issue was more prominent in the convention because of an unusually long and acrid dispute that had raged in Rhode Island's newspapers throughout 1789. This controversy arose out of a futile campaign waged by several merchants, including Moses' brother John, to legalize the slave trade for Rhode Island citizens.

Joseph Stanton led the Antifederalists in attacking the Constitution because it tried "to encourage the African trade." [39] Stanton and his supporters wanted the convention to bear witness against the iniquitous trade by rejecting the Constitution. Benjamin Bourne responded to Stanton's strictures, barely hiding his scorn for what he considered

---

37. The subject of Negro slavery and the slave trade in Rhode Island has a relatively large literature. Among the better studies one might consult Elizabeth Donnan, "Agitation Against the Slave Trade in Rhode Island, 1784–1790," in *Persecution and Liberty: Essays in Honor of George Lincoln Burr* (New York, 1931); Irving H. Bartlett, *From Slave to Citizen: The Story of the Negro in Rhode Island* (Providence, 1954); or James F. Reilly, "The Providence Abolition Society," *Rhode Island History,* X (1961), 33–48. A noteworthy examination of the period between 1774 and 1790 is presented by Mack Thompson, *Moses Brown: Reluctant Reformer* (Chapel Hill, 1962), pp. 92–106, 175–202, and 293–342.
38. Thompson, *Moses Brown,* p. 193; Robert M. Hazelton, *Let Freedom Ring! A Biography of Moses Brown* (New York, 1957), pp. 104–5.
39. Cotner, *Foster's Minutes,* p. 47.

a naïve idealism: "We are not a Society of Friends to publish our Tes-
timonials to this." [40] Bourne, however, was in a minority at the convention. Joe Comstock, an irreconcilable member from Portsmouth, spoke
for the majority when he expressed his suspicion that Congress would
not prohibit the slave trade in 1808. Such a possibility should be beyond the discretion of Congress. Only justice and morality would exalt
the nation, Comstock declared; iniquity was a reproach to humanity.[41]

The moderation of the country leadership and its desire to embrace
the new government were clearly represented by the fact that Jonathan J. Hazard chose to reassure his colleagues on the issue of slavery.
He could not permit an overheating of the Negro problem to wreck
both the delicate plans of the country leaders and Rhode Island itself.
Hazard said there was little the convention could do to alter this un-
pleasant compromise of the Constitution of 1787; he wanted the convention to propose only those amendments that stood a chance of
general acceptance. Besides, Hazard complained, the South—as the
greatest offender against the Negro—must answer for itself and ar-
range its own affairs.[42] Continuing along a more practical vein, Hazard
found himself in agreement with his Newport namesake, George Hazard, who explained that, if slavery were destroyed in the South, it
would bring drastic poverty to the region, thereby further burdening
the northern states with the costs of the federal government and the
national debt.[43] In the end, the problem of the Negro was relegated to
the committee on amendments, and the sentiment against slavery was
embodied in one of the amendments to the Constitution approved by
the convention.

Amendments and a Bill of Rights

After four days of desultory debate, during which the cause of Antifederalism came to focus on only a few issues, the convention took up
the report of the committee assigned to suggest changes and additions
to the Constitution of 1787. The committee presented a bill of rights
and a list of amendments. The bill of rights was accepted without a
dissenting voice, and the amendments did not occasion prolonged

40. *Ibid.*, pp. 73–75.
41. *Ibid.*, p. 48; Staples, *R.I. in the Continental Congress*, p. 645.
42. Cotner, *Foster's Minutes*, p. 48.
43. *Ibid.*, pp. 49–52; Staples, *R.I. in the Continental Congress*, pp. 647–48.

dispute.[44] Only two of the proposed twenty-three amendments were rejected by the delegates. One would have prohibited the federal government from appointing to national office men who held any state position. This amendment, greatly restricting the federal government in the selection of its officers, was thought an unnecessary inhibition of national power. The second unsuccessful amendment proposed that direct federal taxation be based on wealth instead of population. The delegates were apparently satisfied with Henry Marchant's assurance that Rhode Island and other small states would fare better in the future if direct taxes were levied on the states in proportion to population. An amendment prohibiting the slave trade was accepted by a single vote over the objection of delegates who asserted that "a Traffic in the human species was so wicked in its Nature, and so inconsistent with the spirit of a free government" that Congress would not be negligent in interdicting the trade after 1808. The majority wanted to be sure.

In writing a bill of rights and presenting amendments, Rhode Island's ratifying convention kept in step with its sister states. The bill of rights was, in large measure, a duplication of the influential Virginia document,[45] reaffirming the heritage of freedom inherited from England; it did, however, give evidence of the state's fear of outside control. Suspicion of national power led the delegates to assert the right of Rhode Island's freemen to "nominate and elect all state officers." The convention also declared that the Constitution of 1787 established a federal system that granted only limited powers to the nation. It stated emphatically that the presence of clauses in the Constitution prohibiting Congress from the exercise of certain powers did not imply that, where these limitations were absent, Congress was authorized to act.

The Rhode Island convention had already been preceded by other states in proposing amendments to the Constitution.[46] These amendments were mostly repetitive of those suggested by New York, North

44. The bill of rights and Rhode Island's amendments may be consulted in Staples, *R.I. in the Continental Congress*, pp. 650–55, 674–83. Most of this information was printed in the *Newport Mercury*, May 31, 1790; *U.S. Chronicle* (Providence), June 3, 1790; and *Providence Gazette*, March 13, 1790.

45. It was commonly reported that Rhode Island's bill of rights was "a copy" of the Virginia document. See, for instance, *Gazette of the United States* (New York), March 20, 1790; *State Gazette of North Carolina* (Edenton), April 10, 1790; *Maryland Gazette* (Annapolis), April 1, 1790.

46. The other states that proposed amendments were Massachusetts, New Hampshire, Virginia, New York, and North Carolina.

Carolina, and Virginia, but here again the convention included items characteristic of the state and its people. Of Rhode Island's twenty-one amendments, only five had not been urged by previous ratifying conventions.[47] All the amendments are of special interest as a concrete record of the precise nature of Antifederalism in Rhode Island; presumably they are indicative of the reasons why so many freemen found the Constitution of 1787 objectionable and unacceptable, and the amendments written solely by Rhode Island have added significance as a guide to those points where Antifederalism in the state took on its own unique dimension.

Among the amendments which only Rhode Island proposed was a suggestion that after 1793 changes in the Constitution receive the consent of eleven of the original thirteen states before becoming operative, regardless of the number of additions to the Union that might come later. Another amendment, again designed to increase the power of the state and make the Constitution more palatable to the freemen, was a plan to prohibit the imposition of direct taxes by Congress without the concurrence of three-fourths of the states.[48] The convention also recommended a change in the Constitution that would have barred compulsory service in the military forces of the United States except in cases of general invasion. A surprising suggestion, both in terms of granting greater responsibility to Congress and its subject matter, was an amendment authorizing the national government to establish a uniform system for the settlement of the poor throughout the country. Perhaps the convention feared that tiny Rhode Island would be unable to provide a livelihood for a growing population and hoped that this proposition would make federal assistance possible. The last amendment offered solely by Rhode Island concerned the slave trade. "As a traffic tending to establish or continue the slavery of any part of the human species, is disgraceful to the cause of liberty and humanity," the convention declared, Congress should be given power to prevent the importation of slaves immediately.

Other amendments were less novel. They limited the range of national power and perpetuated the influence of the states. These amendments represented positive evidence of the strength of states' rights sentiment among the people of Rhode Island and the desire of

47. Frank Green Bates, *Rhode Island and the Formation of the Union,* Columbia University Studies in History, Economics, and Public Law, Vol. X, No. 2 (New York, 1898) , 201–12.

48. Cotner, *Foster's Minutes,* p. 57; Staples, *R.I. in the Continental Congress,* p. 649.

the state to carve out as wide a circle of power in the Union as feasible.

Along with five other state conventions, the Rhode Island delegates offered as their first amendment a sweeping declaration reserving "to each state its sovereignty, freedom and independence, and every power, jurisdiction and right which is not by this Constitution expressly delegated to the United States." This statement was a stark reminder of the Articles of Confederation. The convention also recommended that every state legislature be given the authority to withdraw or change its senatorial delegation at will. Two other amendments in the Confederation tradition sought to prohibit Congress from imposing direct taxes of any kind, thus forcing the national government to rely on requisitions upon the states. In each instance the convention wanted to increase the power of the states.

Limitations on national power characterized the rest of the convention's twenty-one amendments. One amendment sought to ensure that Rhode Island would have full control over every aspect of the election of its representatives to the United States Congress. Two recommendations of special interest asked for a two-thirds congressional majority before Congress could declare war (an item that would be revived during the War of 1812) and a two-thirds margin for Congress to borrow money. Restraints on national power were also sought by amendments outlawing monopolies and standing armies in time of peace. Finally, a number of the Rhode Island amendments were concerned with the paper-money experiment; they attempted to preclude any congressional interference with Rhode Island's redemption of its public debt in paper currency. A key amendment would have banned suits by private citizens in the federal courts against the states of the Union. A clause in the amendment explained: "to remove all doubts . . . Congress shall not, either by themselves, or through the judiciary, interfere with any one of the states, in the redemption of paper money already emitted . . . or in liquidating or discharging the public securities of any one state." A separate amendment limited the judicial authority of the United States to cases that arose after the ratification of the Constitution. Rhode Island hoped to close its books forever on the paper-money system.

Adjournment and Politics

After the twenty-one amendments were approved by the convention, the Federalists tried to include them in an over-all resolution with the bill of rights and a motion to ratify the Constitution. At this point the country party took control. Led by Job Comstock and other country leaders, the convention voted to send its work to the freemen for their consideration before deciding on the momentous question of ratification. Jonathan J. Hazard asserted that every citizen of Rhode Island should be given an opportunity to discuss the convention's actions and add further amendments to the list drawn up in South Kingstown.[49] Then there would be time enough to vote on the Constitution.

The motion for an adjournment brought frustrated outcries from the Federalist minority. The Federalists were sure that the Constitution would be ratified if a vote were taken; their problem was to avoid delay. William Barton spoke first for the Federalists. He objected to the proposed adjournment, noting that after April the United States government would certainly levy tariffs and tonnage duties and would apply its system of mercantile legislation against Rhode Island. Such an eventuality, Barton remonstrated, would disrupt the economy of the seaport towns. Henry Marchant also rose to denounce the proposed adjournment. He protested that two and a half years had already passed since the summer of 1787, when the Constitution was written. This was time enough for everyone in Rhode Island to have made up his mind, Marchant insisted, and too much time to expect Congress to tolerate further delay. Other Federalists forecast that, if the state failed to enter the Union immediately, Congress would probably levy special duties on Rhode Island farm products imported into the United States. The Federalists complained that, having been called into session to ratify or reject the Constitution, the delegates were not authorized to adjourn without coming to a decision.[50]

The country leadership reserved its greatest effort for this extended debate over adjournment. "We [are] the Servants of the People. We act for them," Job Comstock announced. "The Constitution is the Proper Word of the People. I cannot act against their Consent. When the People have had Time to think of it it will be proper to meet again." Jonathan J. Hazard followed the same line of reasoning. "We derive our Power from the People. They have a Right to be consulted," he declared. "They expect the Amend[men]ts will be made and sent to them." [51] As for economic reprisals from the United States, Hazard ex-

49. *Providence Gazette,* March 13, 1790; Cotner, *Foster's Minutes,* pp. 62–63, 76–77.

50. Cotner, *Foster's Minutes,* pp. 78–79, 82–86; *Providence Gazette,* March 13, 1790.

51. Cotner, *Foster's Minutes,* pp. 81–82, 87–89.

pressed a hope that Congress would continue to exempt the state from its trade laws. He countered the Federalist plea for prompt action by saying: "The Most Haste The Worse Speed is a Maxim."

On March 6, by a majority of thirteen, the convention agreed to adjourn and refer its proceedings to the freemen. A dispute followed over the length of adjournment. The Federalists proposed that the delegates reassemble as quickly as possible, seeking to shorten the adjournment to a few weeks and reconvene at the end of March. This move lost by seven votes. Instead the convention agreed, by a thin margin of five delegates, to meet again at the end of May.[52] This would place the concluding session of the convention well after the annual spring elections. The country leaders had no intention of ratifying the Constitution until they were returned to power.

In fact, before the convention brought its deliberations to a close, the forthcoming general elections scheduled for April became a dominant topic of interest among the delegates. Both the Federalist and Antifederalist parties devoted considerable thought to their prospective candidates and the nature of their campaigns. The Federalists were in a nearly hopeless situation. If they made ratification of the Constitution a major issue in the election, they might force the country party to assume an inflexibly Antifederalist position. On the other hand, if the Federalists failed to contest the elections, the country party was bound to remain in control of the state. Neither alternative was comforting. Fearful of defeat, therefore, and unwilling to provoke the country leaders into a continuing Antifederalist stand, the Federalists recommended a combined slate of candidates in the oncoming campaign, a ticket of state unity. They offered to divide all state offices on an equal basis between the parties and run a single "coalition" list of nominees.[53] This suggestion was instantly spurned by the country leadership. It was supremely confident of victory without any help from the merchants.

The country party strategy for the campaign of 1790 was to appear before the voters as the spokesman of the freemen, ready to do their will. The leadership's Federalism was unavowed. In order to protect this posture, the convention's bill of rights and amendments were sent directly to the people for consideration at the annual spring town

52. Staples, *R.I. in the Continental Congress,* pp. 656–57; *Providence Gazette,* March 13, 1790.
53. *Providence Gazette,* March 27, 1790; *U.S. Chronicle* (Providence), April 1, 1790.

meetings. At these same meetings the townsmen would cast their ballots for state offices. Obviously, although the country leaders were prepared to accept the Constitution, they did not want to be identified with Federalism. In the hope of making this policy appear consistent, John Collins, the incumbent governor whose tie-breaking vote had made the ratifying convention possible, was dropped as a candidate. In his place, Arthur Fenner, Jr., a Providence merchant, was presented to the voters. Fenner, though a moderately prosperous merchant from an old Rhode Island family, had favored the paper-money system in past years and was sympathetic to Rhode Island's Antifederalism. The Providence merchant offered other qualifications for the state's highest office. He was popular in Providence, despite his country connections, and had served in various town offices. His natural skills as a politician were commonly noted by contemporaries, skills so necessary in this period of transition in Rhode Island politics.[54] As its candidate for deputy governor, the country party offered Samuel J. Potter of North Kingstown, hoping to counter its Antifederalist image by deleting Daniel Owen from the 1790 ticket.

The Federalists had little inclination to oppose the country party. They knew well the growing moderation among the country leaders and the likelihood that the Constitution would be ratified at the next session of the convention. Rather than have the Constitution divide the parties, the Federalists sought, like the country party, to obscure the issue. Therefore, the Federalists revived the coalition proposal and accepted Arthur Fenner, Jr., as their candidate for governor, seeking in return to get the country leaders to admit some opposition nominees to their party list. These tactics, the Federalists believed, would give the country party no reason to exploit the constitutional question as a party issue, while adding minority candidates to the country slate.[55]

The Federalists put their plan into effect at a Providence town meeting on March 22, 1790. Providence formally voted to support a coalition of parties. A special committee consisting of John Brown, Welcome Arnold, David Howell, Jabez Bowen, and Zephaniah Andrews, all prominent inhabitants and Federalists, was appointed to win the

54. William Ellery to Benjamin Huntington, Newport, April 15, 1790, Ellery Letters, Mss., R.I.S.A. For comments on Fenner's political abilities see the *Gazette of the United States* (New York), April 28, 1790; Burges, Memoir of Welcome Arnold, unpublished biography, R.I.H.S., pp. 12–13.

55. William Ellery to Benjamin Huntington, Newport, March 28, April 5, 1790, Ellery Letters, Mss., R.I.S.A.

concurrence of Newport in this undertaking. This was quickly accomplished. On March 24, two days after the Providence town meeting, a Newport committee composed of George Champlin, Henry Marchant, George Gibbs, James Robinson, and Isaac Senter joined with the Providence group in addressing a public letter to Arthur Fenner, Jr., soliciting his aid in achieving a combination of parties. The letter lamented the divisions that characterized Rhode Island political life and "threatened destruction to all." For the future well-being of the state, Fenner was urged to accept nomination on a unity ticket and agree to a division of political offices. The coalition sponsors suggested Fenner for governor, a Federalist for deputy governor, and an equal division of candidates in the upper house of the General Assembly.[56]

Arthur Fenner rejected the coalition plan in a public letter.[57] He began by reproaching the merchants and Federalists for their obstructionism during the paper-money era, taking special care to associate the coalitionists with this unpopular political interest. In a free republican society, Fenner stated, the reasonable wishes of the people must always guide government or its "voice will reach and influence the seat of legislation." This was the situation in 1786, and the paper-money revolution was its result. If parties developed in Rhode Island by reason of this legislative overturn, Fenner observed, the most prudent way to have allayed corrosive political turmoil was to accept the will of the majority. The merchants adopted a different policy. Their bitterness and invective displaced democratic persuasion in the years following May, 1786. This was the root of Rhode Island's troubles in the recent past. "The public opinion may be wrong for a time, but it will generally settle on what is right, especially if the proper means are used for the public information," wrote Fenner. "The great principle of republics is, that the majority shall govern. . . ." Fenner refused the coalition suggestion as wholly improper. He complained that only the people could nominate a candidate for political office, and to address a public letter to any individual inviting him to become a candidate was inappropriate. After this sharply worded deference to the political traditions of his native state, however, the crafty Fenner failed to forswear the support of the Federalists if it was offered.

56. *Providence Gazette,* March 27, 1790; *U.S. Chronicle* (Providence) , April 1, 1790.
57. The original of Fenner's response may be found among the Rhode Island Historical Society Manuscripts, Vol. 14, p. 143. The letter was printed in the *U.S. Chronicle* (Providence) , April 1, 1790, and the *Providence Gazette,* April 3, 1790.

Notwithstanding this stinging rebuff, the Providence and Newport committees went ahead with their plan and presented a coalition ticket for the consideration of the freemen. Arthur Fenner, Jr., and Samuel J. Potter, the country party candidates for governor and deputy governor, were supported for office, making their elections a certainty. But six of the coalition nominees for the upper house were Federalists.[58] Their platform in the election offered an understated advocacy of "re-union" with the United States. The coalitionists admitted that the agricultural towns had prevailed in Rhode Island since 1786. In direct answer to Fenner, they acknowledged that the majority should govern, but here they drew the line. "A majority most clearly have no right to associate, nullify, or to impair their obligations to the lesser numbers," a coalition letter declared. The same communication called attention to the mutual interests of commerce and agriculture in Rhode Island, noting that injury to one would be likely to retard the prosperity of the other. "If therefore, a majority under the pretence of upholding the country interest, should seat themselves exclusively in power—to monopolize the offices of government, and to prostrate the other orders in society, ought they to receive countenance and support in a pursuit so unwarranted?" [59] An answer was self-evident: support a coalition of parties for the best future of Rhode Island.

The coalitionist appeal for conciliation found few aherents among the freemen. There was only one issue in the campaign, a country publicist intoned, and that was whether to continue the present leaders in power or surrender the management of public affairs to the merchants.[60] This message was understood and accepted by the majority of Rhode Island voters. The issue of reunion with the United States was deliberately obscured. In the elections the country party was continued in power. It won every contest.

Ratification

With the elections concluded, interest mounted regarding the soon-to-be reconvened session of the ratifying convention. That it was

58. For a complete list of the candidates offered by the two major parties see the *Providence Gazette,* April 3, 10, 1790; relevant also is the letter of David Howell in the same newspaper on April 17, 1790.

59. Letter from "The Friends to a Coalition of Parties," *ibid.,* April 17, 1790.

60. Letter from "A Countryman," *U.S. Chronicle* (Providence) , April 17, 1790.

scheduled to meet again in Newport, a Federalist town, perhaps offered some slight reason for hope. The fate of the convention depended entirely on what the country leadership was prepared to do. The Federalists had their fingers crossed that the country party, headed by Governor Arthur Fenner, Jr., would bow to the necessity of reunion with the United States.[61] Their aspiration for a speedy and peaceful re-entrance into the Union, however, did not preclude a determination to secure this event by any means at their disposal. Led by the Federalists, the commercial towns threatened to secede from Rhode Island. Providence, for example, on May 24, announced that if the convention rejected the Constitution or adjourned without rejoining the United States, it would apply to President Washington "for the same privileges and protection" as other members of the nation.[62] Other seaport communities were similarly resolved to follow the lead of Providence. By the time the convention reassembled, the Federalists had obtained an unofficial pledge of protection for any Rhode Island town that desired admission into the United States.[63] The matter of the Union had reached a climax at the end of May, 1790, and the Federalist minority prepared for desperate measures if they proved necessary—even, whispered William Channing in a somber letter to Theodore Foster, "a deposition of government." [64]

Among the United States the reaction to the convention's adjournment was one of exasperation. Patience and restraint were sorely strained by what seemed to be Rhode Island's dalliance with the Constitution. "Affairs are brought to the point of maturity and time, and if you are not with us you are against us," wrote an anonymous "Citizen of America" in a Pennsylvania newspaper. "Though you may cautiously avoid to draw the sword, you will by your conduct, declare yourself hostile to our tranquility. . . ." [65] Another writer, in a petulant mood, recalled the state's long association with paper money in the colonial and Confederation periods, exclaiming that "public indig-

61. Brown and Benson to Thayer, Bartlett, and Co., of Charlestown, Providence, May 12, 1790, Brown Papers, Mss., J.C.B.L.

62. Providence Town Meeting, May 24, 1790, Staples, *R.I. in the Continental Congress*, p. 666; *U.S. Chronicle* (Providence) , May 27, 1790.

63. Benjamin Huntington to William Ellery, New York, May 8, 1790, Ellery Letters, Mss., R.I.S.A. See also items in the *Virginia Herald* (Fredericksburg) , May 20, 1790; and the *Virginia Independent Chronicle* (Richmond) , May 20, 1790.

64. Channing to Foster, Newport, May 18, 1790, Correspondence, Foster Collection, Mss., R.I.H.S.

65. Letter published in the *Federal Gazette* (Philadelphia) , reprinted in the *Providence Gazette,* May 22, 1790.

nation is so highly raised, and the possibility of inconveniences and injuries from you has so quickened the feeling of our people, that an immediate reduction of your State is the wish of many." [66] These threats coincided with increased activity in Congress to bar commercial intercourse with Rhode Island.[67] A senator from Pennsylvania, the suspicious and antiaristocratic William Maclay, remembered that the nation's legislators were determined to put Rhode Island into "a kind of commercial coventry." Maclay was alone in the Senate when he denounced attempts to intimidate Rhode Island. "I was twice up," he wrote of debates on May 11, 1790, "said a good deal, but it answered no purpose whatever." The members of Congress attributed overt measures against Rhode Island to motives of "self-defence, self-preservation, [and] self-interest," suggesting something of the rationale that impelled the United States to seek Rhode Island's ratification. As Maclay observed, "terror" and "fear" were employed to secure the adoption of the Constitution, "a thing despaired of from their own free-will or judgment." [68] This atmosphere, charged with critical danger, was cultivated by Federalists in the state who felt that Rhode Island would be reconciled to the Union only by a conviction that ratification was a matter of extreme urgency.[69] Near the end of this era, as at its start, Rhode Island accepted the Union of necessity.

When the convention reassembled on May 25 the country leadership was prepared to ratify the Constitution. Despite this willingness, binding instructions from the towns made it difficult to muster the necessary votes to re-enter the United States. John Howland, a contemporary and later president of the Rhode Island Historical Society, recollected that many of the country party "were glad of the adoption, though they were so pledged to the opposition that they dared not vote for it." [70] It was certain that the balloting on ratification would be very

66. Letter "To Rhode Island Citizens," *Federal Gazette* (Philadelphia), reprinted in the *Providence Gazette*, May 15, 1790.

67. *Providence Gazette*, May 22, 29, 1790.

68. Maclay, *Journal of William Maclay*, pp. 249–50, 253, 257, 260.

69. William Ellery to Benjamin Huntington, Newport, May 11, 1790, William Ellery Letters, Mss., R.I.H.S. For the role of a key Connecticut Federalist in Congress see Elizabeth C. Barney Buel, "Oliver Ellsworth," *New England Magazine*, XXX (1904), 611–26.

70. Edward M. Stone, *The Life and Recollections of John Howland* (Providence, 1857), p. 166. After the convention disbanded, the *Providence Gazette* reported on June 5, 1790: "Many members of the Convention were convinced of the propriety of an adoption of the Constitution, and the majority would, it appears, have been much larger [than two] had not a number of the members been restricted by instructions."

close. "Many of the Antifederalists wish the Business done," observed Theodore Foster, "but do not love to do it themselves." [71]

The first order of business before the convention was to read the instructions of the towns. For more than two and a half years the freemen considered the Constitution of 1787. In some towns, such as Middletown and Portsmouth, there had been a change of sentiment from an early attitude of opposition and defiance to a more pliant awareness of the need for reunion with the United States. [72] Middletown voted its approval of the new government with the addition of Rhode Island's bill of rights and twenty-one amendments on April 21; on May 29, the very day the convention adopted the Constitution, it instructed its delegates once again to favor ratification. Other Antifederalist towns, however, were true to their initial convictions that the Constitution was a bad scheme. Nothing that happened since September of 1787 had made them waver in this belief. West Greenwich, North Kingstown, Richmond, and Coventry found the Constitution unacceptable even with amendments, and in West Greenwich the freemen expressed their dislike of the convention's attempt to amend the federal system. Some Antifederalist towns were dissatisfied, but they were not completely irreconcilable. Two of them, Charlestown and Gloucester, refused to tell their delegates to ratify the Constitution until the convention's amendments were actually added to the new frame of government. [73]

Reading the instructions of the delegates authenticated what everyone already knew: the decision on ratification would be made by a razor-thin margin. Nearly all the delegates were bound by instructions. Before the balloting began, eleven towns and 30 votes were pledged to favor the ratification of the Constitution, while sixteen towns with 34 delegates were prepared to block ratification. [74] This meant that nei-

71. Foster to William Channing, Providence, May 24, 1790, Channing-Ellery Papers, Mss., R.I.H.S., Vol. 4.
72. According to the manuscript records of Portsmouth and Middletown, both towns, as late as October 19, 1789, were opposed to the Constitution and the convocation of a ratifying convention. Each favored ratification in the period after the adjournment of the ratifying convention in March, 1790.
73. West Greenwich Town Meeting, Mss., April 21, 1790, Charlestown Town Meeting, Mss., April 21, 1790, Gloucester Town Meeting, Mss., April 21, 1790, and Coventry Town Meeting, Mss., April 21, 1790; North Kingstown Town Meeting, April 21, 1790, and Richmond Town Meeting, April 15, 1790, in Staples, *R.I. in the Continental Congress*, p. 655.
74. Newport, Providence, Portsmouth, Bristol, Middletown, Jamestown, Tiverton, Warren, Cumberland, Barrington, and Little Compton were in favor of ratification; North Kingstown, Gloucester, Charlestown, Coventry, West Greenwich, Richmond,

ther of the parties had an absolute majority of the 70 delegates in the convention, although the sixteen Antifederalist towns constituted a majority of the thirty in Rhode Island.[75]

On May 28, after three days of discussion, Job Comstock, an implacable Antifederalist, moved that the convention adjourn. Henry Marchant proposed instead that the delegates ratify the Constitution. Marchant declared that the Antifederalists had undertaken no real criticism of the Constitution, and he warned the delegates that Congress was readying vigorous sanctions against Rhode Island. The president of the convention, Daniel Owen, in what might have been a critical procedural ruling, held that Comstock's motion to adjourn took precedence over any other business. The adjournment resolution was defeated by a majority of nine, a positive indication that the country party was prepared to accept the Constitution.[76]

The next day, May 29, 1790, after a brief overnight recess to permit the delegates some last-minute consultations, Marchant's ratification resolution was put to a vote and passed by a margin of two delegates, 34 to 32.[77] Rhode Island had accepted a reformed Union, and the nation was again complete.

Foster, Warwick, South Kingstown, East Greenwich, Exeter, Cranston, Johnston, North Providence, Smithfield, and Scituate were opposed to the Constitution.

75. Three towns for which the evidence is unclear are Hopkinton, Westerly, and New Shoreham. It is possible that these delegates were uninstructed.

76. Staples, *R.I. in the Continental Congress,* pp. 669–72; *Providence Gazette,* May 29, 1790.

77. *U.S. Chronicle* (Providence) , June 3, 1790; *Providence Gazette,* June 5, 1790. The count of the towns given previously was eleven towns and 30 delegates instructed to favor ratification, with sixteen towns and 34 delegates opposed. In the final balloting, 3 Antifederalist votes were lost when 2 delegates broke their instructions and supported ratification, while Daniel Owen, representing Antifederalist Gloucester, could not vote because he served as president of the convention. The Federalists lost 2 ballots when a member from Portsmouth broke his instructions and voted against the Constitution and another Federalist was absent. The net loss for the Antifederalists, therefore, was 2 votes and one town. The final count thus stood at eleven towns and 30 delegates for ratification, fifteen towns and 32 delegates opposed; one town was evenly divided. Of the three remaining towns, New Shoreham's delegates were not present, while Hopkinton and Westerly voted in favor of accepting the Constitution.

10

Aftermath

REUNION with the United States came easily for Rhode Island after the ratification of the Constitution. Considering the bitter words and deeds of the years since 1786, this gentle accommodation may have been surprising. But everywhere there was a desire to forgive and forget past quarrels now that the sister states were finally reunited.[1]

Notice of Rhode Island's ratification was immediately dispatched to President George Washington in an official letter from Daniel Owen, president of the convention.[2] Governor Fenner was equally prompt. Within a week of ratification the General Assembly was called into ses-

1. For a sampling of opinion inside and outside Rhode Island, see Robert Rogers to Welcome Arnold, Newport, June 1, 1790, Welcome Arnold Papers, Mss., J.C.B.L.; letters from "Peter" and "A Gentleman at New York," both in the *Providence Gazette,* June 1, 12, 1790; and the *Independent Chronicle* (Boston) , June 3, 1790.

2. Owen to Washington, Newport, May 29, 1790, William R. Staples, ed., *Rhode Island in the Continental Congress: With the Journal of the Convention that Adopted the Constitution 1765–1790* (Providence, 1870) , p. 681.

sion, and all officers of the state were asked to swear or affirm their support for the Constitution of 1787; there were no reports of nonjurors. Urged by the governor, the legislature added its consent to the first ten amendments to the federal Constitution and passed a lengthy statute prescribing the mode of electing two United States senators and a representative. Rhode Island would not be unrepresented in federal councils a moment longer than was necessary. The Assembly closed its momentous session with the invocation, "God save the United States of America," which had been in disuse for more than a year.[3]

Congress and President Washington also acted speedily to welcome Rhode Island back into the Union. On June 1, 1790, the very day he received news of Rhode Island's adoption of the Constitution, Washington informed the members of Congress. Doubtless, the First Congress was relieved that peaceful measures had sufficed in the case of Rhode Island. In the House of Representatives, William L. Smith of South Carolina asked that the House cease further consideration of a bill to ban commercial intercourse with Rhode Island. Smith's motion was instantly approved. Completing the smooth process of reunion, Congress passed statutes extending to Rhode Island the operation of various laws enacted earlier, including the Judiciary Act of 1789, several bills respecting tariffs and customs collections, and the enumeration initiated by the federal Census Act of 1790.[4] President Washington was especially anxious that Rhode Island's re-entrance into the United States be as gracious and complete as possible. Accordingly, hoping to vindicate his rebuff of 1789, when he had ignored Rhode Island on a tour of New England, Washington decided to make a special visit to the state at the close of the summer of 1790, during an adjournment of Congress.

George Washington was unrivaled among the heroes of Rhode Island. He was revered as the citizen-soldier of the War for Independence, the savior of American liberty. Now he was to be venerated as the father of his country. Washington was aware of the esteem in which he was held in the state. He wanted to turn this reverence to the useful purpose of a perfect reconciliation between Rhode Island and

3. John R. Bartlett, ed., *Records of the Colony of Rhode Island and Providence Plantations in New England,* 10 vols. (Providence, 1856–65), X, 380–81, 385–86, 379; *Providence Gazette,* June 19, 1790.

4. *Debates and Proceedings in the Congress of the United States, 1789–1824,* [*Annals of Congress*] 24 vols. (Washington, D.C., 1834–56), II, pp. 1628–33, 2229–33; "The Adjustment of Rhode Island in the Union in 1790," *Proceedings of the Rhode Island Historical Society,* VIII (1900), 104–36.

the Union. His trip was a great success. The President arrived in Providence on August 19 accompanied by a small but politically balanced entourage, including the Secretary of State, Thomas Jefferson, Governor George Clinton of New York, formerly an Antifederalist, Senator Theodore Foster, and other members of Congress. On the President's disembarking, a stirring blast of cannon joined with a prolonged ringing of bells throughout the town. According to all accounts, the crowds that greeted Washington were tremendous. The entire affair was perfection itself. It was not, however, without its peculiarities. Washington was flooded with fulsome expressions of adoration as well as tactless messages of congratulation at his election as President of the United States two years before. These latter felicitations must have ruffled the Virginian, reminding him of the days of hostility before ratification.[5] His visit, however, and the adulation with which he was received, helped to cement relations between Rhode Island and the Union.

Indicative of the accommodation in state and federal relations were the signs of harmony that now began to crop up in local politics. The old split between town and country in Rhode Island politics was coming to an end.

The elections for a United States representative and two senators provided an occasion to test the nature of party divisions now that Rhode Island had entered a new era of history. Would the old issues of paper money and the Union continue to divide the freemen when they cast their ballots for national officers? The struggle for a seat in the House of Representatives promised to be the most revealing, since this election was conducted on a popular basis. Several candidates entered their names in hope of victory. Significantly, the Antifederalist-country coalition was not united on a single man for this influential national office. Three prominent country party leaders—Job Comstock, James Sheldon, and Simon Potter—tried and failed to win the favor of the electorate. The winning candidate was Benjamin Bourne, a key Providence Federalist and important figure in the ratifying convention. His Federalist and anti-paper-money viewpoints were well known, but he was still elected by a majority of 239 in the balloting.[6] The principal

5. Bartlett, *Records*, X, 390, 410; *Providence Gazette*, July 17, August 21, 1790; *Newport Mercury*, August 23, 1790; "Journal of William Loughton Smith, 1790–1791," ed. Albert Mathews, *Massachusetts Historical Society Proceedings*, LI (1918), 20–90.

6. *Providence Gazette*, August 28, September 4, 11, November 6, 1790; *Newport Mercury*, September 13, 1790.

issue against Bourne was his stand opposing the convention's slavery amendment. However, none of these issues stood in the way of his election.

The contest for the Senate was more intense. An equal division between the former parties resulted. Theodore Foster, an enterprising Providence Federalist, was appointed to one seat by the legislature. The other place went to Joseph Stanton. Considering that the country party controlled the General Assembly, Stanton's election was not surprising. The country strategy in the spring elections of 1790 had been designed to secure just such an eventuality. Foster's election was unexpected. The most likely possibility for the seat which Foster won had been Jonathan J. Hazard; he had helped prepare the country plan to control the Assembly and had given out undisguised hints throughout the spring that he wanted an important national office after Rhode Island adopted the Constitution. Unfortunately, Hazard's ambitions conflicted with the preferences of Governor Arthur Fenner, Jr., the new power in Rhode Island politics. Fenner recognized clearly that a time of transition was in progress in his native state, and he was determined to control events. The governor decided to support his brother-in-law, Theodore Foster, for election to the second Senate seat.[7] Fenner's influence as the state's chief executive and his power within the country coalition, added to Foster's Federalist connections, were too much for Hazard to overcome. Though he campaigned vigorously, Hazard was beaten. Obviously, Fenner's intervention in the senatorial struggle demonstrated again that the country party was disintegrating. Moreover, his support for Foster not only served to win over an important ally in state politics, but it also revealed that the governor wished to walk a middle road between the old parties. If possible, Fenner wanted to make over Rhode Island politics in his own image, and so successful was he in this endeavor that he served sixteen consecutive terms as governor until his death in 1805, when he was succeeded by his son James. The senatorial election introduced a new balance into Rhode Island political life, a balance that led to harmony. "In politics we have nothing," James Burrill, Jr., informed his friend Theodore

7. Governor Arthur Fenner, Jr., to Theodore Foster, Providence, July 27, 1790, Correspondence, Foster Collection, Mss., R.I.H.S., Vol. I; Henry Marchant to Elbridge Gerry, Newport, June 12, 1790, Elbridge Gerry Papers, 1772–1782, Mss., M.H.S.; William Ellery to Benjamin Huntington, Newport, June 12, 1790, Ellery Letters, Mss., R.I.H.S.

Foster, already in attendance at Congress. "State politics is now of little Consequence & you are at the Fountain head of the Continental."[8] A new era had begun.

If an unwonted harmony characterized Rhode Island history during the early years of the Federal period, it was not without a serious challenge. The most dangerous threat came from an expected source, the paper-money tangle. On all sides there had been continuing doubts that the paper-money controversy could be left behind so easily in 1789; the reason was the state debt.

The country leadership had turned Antifederalist largely because it feared that the Constitution of 1787 would impede the operation of the paper-money system before the state debts were liquidated. When this was accomplished in 1789, the country party prepared to rejoin the United States. Ironically, now that Rhode Island was ready to enter the new federal system the administration of President Washington placed a stumbling block in its way. In obedience to a resolution of Congress passed on September 21, 1789, the Secretary of the Treasury, Alexander Hamilton, prepared a report on the public credit in which he proposed that the national government assume the remaining debts of the states.[9] The paper-money controversy was in this way reborn, for the question arose as to whether Rhode Island still had a state debt. Nominally, the process of the paper-money system had redeemed the entire sum of Rhode Island's indebtedness. Those who accepted paper currency had received their compensation; those who refused forfeited all their securities. In the event the United States Treasury was willing to accept the forfeited securities as an unpaid Rhode Island state debt—since its owners had received no compensation—a dangerous political and economic conflict might ensue.

Fortunately for the cause of Rhode Island's Federalism, the assumption of the state debts played an unimportant role in the ratification struggle. The reason was simple. Aside from the fact that the assumption issue paled in significance when compared with the fundamental problem of Rhode Island's survival as an independent country, no one could be certain that an assumption would ever take place. Prior to May 29, 1790, the day Rhode Island adopted the Constitution, it seemed unlikely that Hamilton's plans would prove acceptable to an

8. Burrill to Foster, Providence, July 24, 1790, Correspondence, Foster Collection, Mss., R.I.H.S., Vol. I.
9. *Annals of Congress,* II, 1992–2021.

unmanageable Congress. On the eve of the last session of the Rhode Island ratifying convention, Royal Hunt, a knowledgeable New York City merchant, commented on the uncertain prospects of the assumption proposal in a letter to the Reverend Enos Hitchcock of Providence. "The assumption is again under discussion [in Congress], and its fate is not less doubtful than it has been for many weeks past," remarked Hunt in a mood of exasperation. "The parties on the question are nearly equal in strength, and there are some among them, wavering characters, who change their opinion often, or rather have not any opinion at all." [10]

Although the assumption issue was insignificant to the outcome of the ratification controversy, this did not mean that Rhode Islanders were uninterested. Hamilton's suggestions as Secretary of the Treasury attracted attention from all parties in the state. The country party had no sympathy for any assumption of the state debts. As far as it was concerned, Rhode Island was completely free from debt. Country partisans looked askance at Hamiltonian policies, asserting that his assumption scheme was "a trick of the devil, and a devilish trick." [11] When Rhode Island finally re-entered the Union, it joined to this act several proposed amendments intended to bar any federal interference with its Confederation paper-money settlements. By contrast, the mercantile minority was favorable to Hamilton's programs, but it was unsure of the political wisdom of reawakening the dormant paper-money contention. A representative appraisal was that of William Ellery, who waited impatiently for the victory of Federalism in Rhode Island. "I have read the summary of Mr. Hamiltons report, and I like the honest ground he proceeds upon.—The establishment of public credit is certainly right . . . , and to execute this sufficient funds must be established; but whether it would be best that Congress should assume the State debts incurred by the late war or not I am not able to determine." Ellery was inclined to guess that an assumption of the forfeited Rhode Island state debts might calm future discord by paying off those who received nothing for their securities. Until this was done, he wrote, "we shall probably be forever in hot water." [12]

On August 4, 1790, after months of wrangling, Congress agreed on a

10. Hunt to Hitchcock, New York, May 26, 1790, Hitchcock Letters, Mss., R.I.H.S.; see also the earlier letter of William Ellery to Benjamin Huntington, Newport, March 28, 1790, Ellery Letters, Mss., R.I.S.A.

11. Letter from "Z," *Providence Gazette*, May 1, 1790.

12. William Ellery to Benjamin Huntington, Newport, February 2, 1790, Ellery Letters, Mss., R.I.S.A.

plan to assume the debts of the states.[13] Rhode Island was seriously affected. The total amount assumed from Rhode Island came to $200,000, far short of the actual state debt, regardless of how it was calculated. The full amount for which the state had been liable stood at $587,312.75, more than three and a half times the sum set aside by Congress. Furthermore, if the Rhode Island state debt was understood to include only the forfeited securities, totaling $344,259.49, the congressional fund was still inadequate. Even more unsettling was an edict of the newly appointed commissioner of the Loan Office for Rhode Island, Jabez Bowen, who ruled that no securities which had already been reclaimed in paper currency would be acceptable in exchange for federal stock. As a result, only those individuals who had attacked the paper-money system and refused to surrender their securities in accordance with the law were to be compensated. This was a hard blow to harmony in state politics and a threat to reconciliation between Rhode Island and the Union.

The good will and cooperation that prevailed among Rhode Island's political leaders in this difficult crisis was a manifest indication that the Confederation era had come to an end. There were no blasts against Congress for upsetting the paper-money settlements, nor did anyone disclose a thought of secession from the recent federal compact. Likewise, the mercantile minority proved itself the soul of reason in a quest for justice for every Revolutionary creditor of the state, supporting each effort at compromise. The merchants let pass a golden opportunity for revenge; they sought peace instead. A solution lay in two directions. The General Assembly intervened in the situation in an attempt to give all creditors an equitable share of the assumption fund. The other remedy was an endeavor to gain a second assumption of the unpaid state balance.

13. The only authoritative account of the assumption controversy in print is that of E. James Ferguson, *The Power of the Purse: A History of American Public Finance, 1776–1790* (Chapel Hill, 1961), pp. 201–19, 306–33. The material in Ferguson focuses on Virginia and Massachusetts, and skillfully traces the connection between the assumption issue and the settlement of state accounts. Another examination of the assumption conflict is that of Whitney K. Bates, "The Assumption of the State Debts 1783–1793." (Ph.D. diss., University of Wisconsin, 1951), pp. 40–45, 193–231. Among other studies, the most familiar are Rayfael A. Bayley, *The National Loans of the United States, From July 4, 1776, to June 30, 1880*, 2d ed. (Washington, D.C., 1882), pp. 30–34, 109–11; Albert S. Bolles, *The Financial History of the United States, From 1774 to 1789: Embracing the Period of the American Revolution* (New York, 1879), pp. 24–28; and Benjamin Ratchford, *American State Debts* (Durham, N.C., 1941), pp. 46–49, 70–72.

The principal obstructions to a settlement of the issue were the United States Treasury Department and its agent in Rhode Island, Jabez Bowen. They would not receive any previously paid claim, irrespective of whether it had been redeemed at a depreciated rate that fell short of the nominal value of the securities. After almost a year of persuasion failed, Governor Fenner asked the legislature to take a hand in circumventing the adamant position of the federal government; he was fully supported by the merchants.[14] The General Assembly passed a comprehensive statute in June, 1791, resurrecting the Revolutionary debts of Rhode Island. All previous acts relating to the paper currency and liquidation of the state debts were repealed. In every case where securities had been surrendered for paper money, they were reissued to creditors with an endorsement on the back of each document deducting the specie value of the bills, calculated at a rate of fifteen to one. Creditors who had refused paper-money payments and were subjected to the forfeiture of their securities were released from the burden of this penalty, at least in terms of state law.[15] Rhode Island was once more deeply in debt. It was anticipated that all creditors would now be entitled to a proportional share of the federal stock.

Unfortunately, this plan was rejected by the Treasury Department. Confronted by this defeat, Governor Fenner recalled the General Assembly and addressed it in person on November 1, 1790, on the subject of the assumption entanglement. Despite the emotional and inflammable nature of the problem, Fenner adjured the legislators to deal with the crisis "on cool and deliberate reflection, most likely to promote common and equal justice, and the peace, tranquility and happiness of the state, and of the nation at large." [16] Evidently, the Confederation years were still remembered. The governor cogently summarized the economic and moral implications of the assumption question in his speech to the Assembly. He left no doubt that injustice to a large class of state creditors, those who complied with the requisitions to receive paper money, had to be corrected. The governor also asserted that the original sum of $200,000 assigned Rhode Island did not even cover the entire amount of the confiscated securities. Rhode Island did not in

14. Tristam Burges, Memoir of Welcome Arnold, unpublished biography, R.I.H.S., p. 23.

15. Bartlett, *Records*, X, 447–50.

16. Petitions to the General Assembly, Mss., R.I.S.A., Vol. 26, p. 72; Bartlett, *Records*, X, 452–54.

fact get enough money. Fenner calculated that, insofar as Rhode Island was generally prorated as having one-fiftieth of the wealth of the nation, its share of the total assumption fund of $21,500,000 should have been $430,000.

The General Assembly gave patient and sympathetic consideration to the governor's examination of the assumption problem. There was no disagreement. A special committee appointed to evaluate Fenner's presentation recommended the preparation of a strongly worded address to the United States Congress, pleading the justice of Rhode Island's cause and calling for a further assumption of its state debts.[17] The state had not been backward in approaching the federal government before. Just as soon as it became certain that an assumption of the state debts was going to take place, Rhode Island's Senators, Theodore Foster and Joseph Stanton, tried to secure as large a sum as possible for their constituents. But they had little success. The members of Congress, however, did guarantee Foster that "justice would hereafter be done to the State, either by a further assumption of the remainder of the debts that accrued on account of the war . . . or in the settlement of the accounts of the United States with the individual states." [18] No second assumption ever took place, and the settlement of accounts between the states and the Union was not completed until 1793. In the interval, Rhode Islanders had to wait.

The settlement of accounts between the states and the nation was one of the most arduous legacies of the War for Independence. Its resolution was a long time in coming. Every state was expected to pay no more than its prorated share of the wealth of the United States to the costs of the American Revolution. Excessive contributions were supposed to be returned from the common treasury, with the delinquent states making up the capital in this fund. After endless bickering, Rhode Island was declared a creditor state of the Union; it was offered a sum of $299,000 as its surplus investment in winning the Revolution.[19] As many states found the original assumption operation inadequate to compensate their creditors to the full value of their se-

17. Reports to the General Assembly, Mss., R.I.S.A., Vol. 5, p. 30; Bartlett, *Records*, X, 454, 465–66.
18. Letter of Theodore Foster, *Providence Gazette*, October 22, 1790; unknown writer to Benjamin Bourne, November 3, 1791, Miscellaneous Manuscripts, N.H.S., Box 25, Folder 9.
19. Ferguson, *Power of the Purse*, p. 333; Report on the Registered State Debt, Ms., R.I.S.A., p. 28.

curities, Congress authorized recipients of the new federal stock to transfer these funds to those who still held unpaid claims against the respective states.[20] Acting upon this congressional authorization, the General Assembly ordered the state's General Treasurer to pay out the federal stock to every remaining Rhode Island creditor.[21] Regrettably, this sum fell short of the total amount of the existing Rhode Island state debts. In consequence the legislature continued periodically to redeem abiding debts for several generations. The state of Rhode Island was thereby placed in the unexpected role of assuming the obligations of the nation. Not until the third decade of the nineteenth century did Rhode Island close its financial books on the American Revolution.

During the years between the assumption of the state debts and the settlement of accounts, 1791 to 1795, another era of speculation occurred in Rhode Island's financial affairs. This came about despite repeated assurances that the federal government would surely make some provision for the payment of all categories of Rhode Island securities.[22] Many Rhode Islanders lost faith, however, and many others were doubtless forced by circumstances to sell their holdings to speculators at less than par value. The issue of speculation was a potentially divisive one, with occasional rumblings against "a certain class of men among us" who would do anything to turn a profit.[23] But Governor Fenner and a nonpartisan political coalition kept a firm hand on the issue, seeking an equitable return to the parties concerned. When the remaining Rhode Island securities were exchanged for federal stock in 1795, evidence of considerable speculation was readily apparent. Approximately 445 state creditors presented claims against Rhode Island in 1795. Of this number, 65 owned amounts in excess of $1,200, and 24 persons offered securities valued at more than $3,485. These 24 creditors owned more than half the state debt in 1795, slightly under $264,000. Moreover, out-of-state residents had accumulated a substantial sum of the Rhode Island state debt since 1790. The best instance was the case of John Peck, a Boston merchant and financier, who was the largest creditor of Rhode Island in 1795, presenting securities amounting to $50,098.46.[24] He had owned no securities in 1790.

20. *Providence Gazette,* January 17, 1795.
21. Rhode Island Records, Mss., R.I.S.A., Vol. 13, pp. 612–16, 664, *Providence Gazette,* February 7, 14, 1795; *Newport Mercury,* February 17, 1795.
22. *Newport Mercury,* September 3, 1791; *Providence Gazette,* September 10, 1791.
23. Letter from "Y.S.," *Newport Mercury,* August 27, 1791.
24. These details on the financial operations of 1795 are based on tabulations in Certificates Issued by Henry Shelburne, General Treasurer, to the several creditors

The last resurgence of the problems of the Confederation period came in 1795. Thereafter, new issues would shape the mold of Rhode Island's future. Already in 1794 signs of political and ideological divisions along the lines of foreign policy were evident, centering on the challenges to the young republic growing out of the wars of the French Revolution. This represented the future. Rhode Islanders prided themselves in the turbulent winter of 1794–95 that their state was the very model of peace and comfort in comparison with other members of the United States. It "must afford infinite Pleasure to the patriotic Mind, to reflect that our own Citizens and Yeomanry are so generally united in supporting the great Interests of their Country," cheered a publicist in the press.[25] The antagonisms of the Confederation past had finally subsided.

A Look Back

Looking back, this study ends as it began, with Rhode Island again united on the question of a national government. The course of this history, however, took several contradictory turns. The state's first response to the need for intercolonial unity had been unpredictable. One of the most despised and fiercely autonomous of the colonial outposts of Great Britain, its experience of isolation was hardly a preparation for the interdependence and cooperation required by the American Revolution. It seems that Rhode Island favored unity from instinct. If the colony was going to be free and separated from the

---

of said state for their proportions of the funded stock belonging to this state now in the office of Jabez Bowen, Commissioner of the Loans. Also certificates for balances, over and above their proportions of said stock, agreeable to the two acts of the General Assembly passed at January Session and the other at June A.D. 1795, Mss., R.I.S.A. As noted earlier, the funded stock no longer was enough to extinguish all claims against Rhode Island. The balance of slightly over $80,000 was credited to each claimant, obtaining the generic title of the "Registered State Debt." Over the years until 1830 the legislature liquidated these claims; thereafter, it refused to honor any further accounts. In the 1840's, John Wilkes Richmond, a Rhode Island citizen, began to gather up remnants of these Revolutionary debts, which in every instance had already been paid at least twice, hoping to redeem them with compound interest since the War for Independence. For details about Richmond's activities consult the Report on the Registered State Debt, Ms., R.I.S.A., or any of the items Richmond published charging that Rhode Island had "repudiated" its Revolutionary debts.

25. *Providence Gazette,* October 11, 1794.

mother country, a firm Union of all the former colonies was an undertaking of the most urgent priority. The only alternatives were suicide or surrender.

Although Rhode Island's support for an inter-American Union had not been a by-product of the colonial past, its later rejection of the nation in 1789–90 was far from inevitable. The radical change in policy which became apparent during the struggle over the Impost of 1781 depended both on factors growing out of the War for Independence and on a calculation by Rhode Islanders—merchants and farmers alike—that further steps toward a strengthened federal government were not in their interest or in that of the state as a whole. This approach to the problem of organizing the nation was even more clearly defined during the prolonged battles over paper money and the liquidation of the state debt. Despite the vigor and emotion of these conflicts, each side took careful measure of how a stronger central government would affect its interests. The merchants—disregarding their states' rights position of 1781 to 1784—were now fully persuaded of the useful part which a powerful central government might play in controlling the excesses of the state legislatures, especially their own General Assembly. The country party leaders, in turn, needed little time to recognize the dangers which the Philadelphia Convention and the Constitution of 1787 might hold out for their paper-money program. Only after the country party had paid off the state debt did Rhode Island rejoin the United States, but even then most Rhode Islanders were still suspicious that the ratification of the Constitution was a mistake. What made the difference in May, 1790, were the variety of threats by the United States government and the danger of secession by the largest towns, all of which indicated that Rhode Island would not be permitted to survive as an independent country. The alternative to reunion may well have been dismemberment.

To say that Rhode Island accepted a stronger central government under duress in 1790 is not meant to argue that the state contributed nothing to the constitutional reformation of 1787. Ironically, Rhode Island's experience with paper money during this era was itself an important factor in the quest for a stronger national government. The state's paper-money system had been everywhere condemned as an adventure in fraud and confiscation. After unrelenting vilification in the country's newspapers, there were few who doubted the allegation that state sovereignty, exemplified by Rhode Island, would result in despotism and the confiscation of private property. Rhode Island's image had been projected as evidence of the futility of the Articles of Confederation and the pitfalls inherent in its dominant principle of state sovereignty.

The state of Rhode Island, therefore, followed an inconsistent policy toward the central government from 1774 to 1795, sometimes favoring and sometimes opposing the movement toward national unity. No one pattern of class division, political philosophy, or patriotism offers an embracing framework within which to understand the history of Rhode Island and the Union. Changing local needs and interests, together with the paper-money question and a swing in the balance of political power from the mercantile seaports to the country towns, all help explain the contradictory responses to the organization of a national government. This approach, moreover, can be extended beyond the history of Rhode Island alone. Maryland's tortuous process in ratifying the Articles of Confederation, as well as New York's about-face on the Impost amendments of 1781 and 1783, give further indications of how changing local situations resulted in a complex federal-state interaction on questions of national importance. The same perspective can be applied to other members of the Union and will help to clarify the varied ways in which the American states reacted to the organization of a central government. It demonstrates that the form of the federal system which emerged from the Revolutionary era was not the product of an inevitable flow of history. The future of the American Republic was never assured until it had, in fact, arrived.

Bibliography

I. *Manuscript Sources*

1. Archives, Historical Societies, and Libraries
BROWN UNIVERSITY LIBRARY
  Archives.
  Solomon Drowne Collection (manuscripts and transcripts).
HOUGHTON LIBRARY, HARVARD UNIVERSITY
  Papers of Nicholas Cooke.
  The Sparks Manuscripts, Rhode-Island and Georgia.
HISTORICAL SOCIETY OF PENNSYLVANIA
  Charles Francis Jenkins Collection, Members of the Old Congress.
  Dreer Collection, Letters of the Members of the Old Congress.
  Gratz Collection.
  Pemberton Papers.
JOHN CARTER BROWN LIBRARY, BROWN UNIVERSITY
  Brown Papers.
  Welcome Arnold Papers.
LIBRARY OF CONGRESS
  Jefferson Papers
MASSACHUSETTS HISTORICAL SOCIETY
  Knox Papers.
  Miscellaneous Bound Documents.
  Warren Papers.
  Wetmore Collection on Rhode Island Commerce.
NATIONAL ARCHIVES
  Papers of the Continental Congress.
    History of the Confederation, 1774–1789.
    Letter Books of the President of Congress, December 11, 1778–August 9, 1787.
    Letters and Reports from Robert Morris, Superintendent of Finance and Agent of Marine, 1781–1785. 2 vols.
    Letters of the Board of Treasury, 1785–1788. 2 vols.
    Letters from Bache and Hazard, Postmasters General, 1777–1788, and Committee Reports on the Post Office, 1776–1788.
    State Papers of New Hampshire and of Rhode Island and Providence Plantations, 1775–1788.
  Rhode Island Records, Accounts for the Loan of 1790, 1790–1835. 32 vol⁰
  "Old Loans" Records of the Bureau of Public Debt. Record Group 53.

NEWPORT HISTORICAL SOCIETY
  Miscellaneous Manuscripts (Currently Collected in Folders).
  William Ellery, Loan Office and Custom House Letter Book, 1786–1794.
NEW YORK PUBLIC LIBRARY
  Abraham Yates Papers.
  Chalmers Collection, Papers Relating to Rhode Island, 1637–1785.
  Emmet Collection.
RHODE ISLAND HISTORICAL SOCIETY
  Broadsides, 1774–1795 (Printed Materials).
  Carter-Danforth Papers, 1770–1799.
  Champlin Papers, 1781–1794.
  Channing-Ellery Papers, 1694–1814.
  Eighteenth Century Rhode Island Election Proxies (Printed Materials).
  Enos Hitchcock Papers.
  Frederick S. Peck Collection, 1761–1845.
  Memoir of Welcome Arnold, by Tristam Burges, 1850.
  Moses Brown Papers.
  Olney Papers, 1775–1820.
  Rhode Island Historical Society Manuscripts.
  Theodore Foster Collection.
  Updike Papers, 1673–1898.
  Ward Manuscripts.
  Warner Papers.
RHODE ISLAND STATE ARCHIVES
  Abstract of State Debt (1795).
  Accounts with the United States, Ledger A, 1776–1782.
  Acts and Resolves of the Rhode Island General Assembly.
  An Account of the Persons who have Received the First Quarter Part of the
    Principal & Interest of the 4 p c Notes.
  Books of Manifests 1785–1789 (Providence).
  Certificates Issued by Henry Shelburne, General Treasurer to the several
    creditors of said state for their proportions of the funded stock belong-
    ing to this state now in the office of Jabez Bowen, Commissioner
    of Loans. Also certificates for balances, over and above their proportions
    of said stock, agreeably to the two acts of the General Assembly passed
    at January Session and the other at June A.D. 1795.
  Council of War Records, 1776–1782.
  Description of Notes (on which the State have paid a part) agreeable to
    an Act of Assembly passed at June Session A.D. 1791.
  General Treasurer's Accounts 1712–1731 [and] Auditor's Reports 1732–
    1812.
  General Treasurer's Papers: Lodged Money, One Folder (Paper Money
    Materials).
  Grand Committee Office [Paper Money], Account Books A & B, 1786–1803.

Impost Accounts.

Journals of the Conventions of the New England States.

Journals of the House of Deputies.

Journals of the Senate.

Letters from the Governor, 1731–1800.

Letters to the Governor, 1731–1800.

Lists of Notes issued for Consolidating the Securities issued from General Treasurer's Office Sept. 1782–June 1784.

Maritime Papers, Manifests; Import Cargoes, 1775–1789 (Newport).

Papers Relating to the Adoption of the Constitution of the United States.

Petitions to the Rhode Island General Assembly, 1725–1867.

Report on the Registered State Debt With Certificates, 1849.

Reports to the General Assembly, 1728–1860.

Reports—Secretary of State 1761–1798: Henry Ward, One Folder.

Rhode Island Records, 1646–1851.

William Ellery Letters, 1783–1790.

2. Town Meeting records

Barrington [Town Meeting] Records, 1770–1793. Vol. I. Barrington Town Hall.

Bristol Town Meeting Records, 1781–1811. Vol. 3. Town Clerk's Office, Bristol Town Hall.

[Charlestown] Town Council and Probate Records, Nos. 3 and 4 [Town Meeting Records, 1779–1793]. Town Clerk's Office, Charlestown Town Hall (Carolina, R.I.).

Coventry Council Records, 1772–1789 [includes Town Meeting Records, 1767–1789] and Coventry Town Meeting Records, 1741–1806. Town Clerk's Office, Coventry Town Hall.

[Cranston] Town Meeting Records, 1754–1802. Nos. 1 and 2. City Clerk's Office, Cranston City Hall.

Cumberland Council Records [Town Meeting Records, 1746–1816]. No. 1. Town Clerk's Office, Cumberland Town Hall (Valley Falls, R.I.).

[East Greenwich] Town Meeting Records 1752–1793. Town Clerk's Office, East Greenwich Town Hall.

Exeter Annual April Town Meeting, 1766–1801. Rhode Island Historical Society.

Exeter Town Meeting Records, 1779 [to 1805]. Town Clerk's Office, Exeter.

Foster Town Meeting Records, 1781–1865. Town Clerk's Office, Foster Centre Town Hall.

Gloucester Town Meting Records, 1731–1864. 2 vols. Town Clerk's Office, Chepachet Town Hall.

Hopkinton Town [Meeting] Records, 1757–1825. Nos. 1 and 2. Town Clerk's Office, Hopkinton Town Hall.

Jamestown Book of Records [includes Town Meeting Records], 1744–1796. No. 3. Town Clerk's Office, Jamestown Town Hall.

Johnston Town Meeting Records [Transcripts], 1754–1791. Rhode Island Historical Society.

Little Compton Town Records, 1759–1855 [includes Town Meeting Records, 1774–1795]. Town Clerk's Office, Little Compton Town Hall.

Middletown Town Meeting Records, 1743–1808. Town Clerk's Office, Middletown Town Hall.

New Shoreham Land Evidences, Vital Records, Town Meetings, 1761–1803. Vols. 3 and 4. Town Clerk's Office, New Shoreham Town Hall (Block Island, R.I.).

Newport Town Proceedings [Town Meeting Records], 1779 1816. Vol. 1. Newport Historical Society.

[North Kingstown] Town Council Records [Town Meeting Records], 1696–1803. Vol. 1. Town Clerk's Office, Wickford Town Hall.

[North Providence] Town Meeting Records, 1765–1808. Recording Office, Pawtucket City Hall.

Portsmouth Town Meeting Records, 1697–1835. 2 vols. Town Clerk's Office, Portsmouth Town Hall.

[Providence] Town Meetings, 1772–1804. Nos. 6 and 7. City Clerk's Office, Providence City Hall.

Richmond Land Evidence, 1771–1786 [includes Town Meeting Records, 1780–1795]. No. 3. Town Clerk's Office, Richmond Town Hall.

Scituate Town Meeting Records, 1731–1825. Nos. 1 and 2. Town Clerk's Office, North Scituate Town Hall.

Smithfield Town Meeting Records, 1771–1816. City Clerk's Office, Central Falls City Hall.

South Kingstown Town Meeting Records, 1776–1836. Town Clerk's Office, South Kingstown Town Hall (Wakefield, R.I.).

Tiverton Town Meeting Records, 1774–1798. Town Clerk's Office, Tiverton Town Hall.

[Warren] Town [Meeting] Records, 1746–1811. No. 1. Town Clerk's Office, Warren Town Hall.

Warwick Town Meeting Records, 1776–1795. Rhode Island Historical Society.

West Greenwich Town Meeting Book. No. 2, 1773–1811. Rhode Island State Archives.

Westerly Town Meetings, Births, Marriages and Ear Marks, 1719–1819. No. 4. Town Clerk's Office, Westerly Town Hall.

II. *Newspapers*

For details on the dates of publication and the continuity of the journals listed see Clarence S. Brigham, *History and Bibliography of American News-*

papers 1690–1820, 2 vols., Worcester, 1947. Brigham's admirable work may sometimes be supplemented by new listings found in the major newspaper collections.

The American Journal and General Advertiser. Providence.
Gazette Françoise. Newport.
The Newport Gazette.
Newport Herald.
Newport Mercury.
The Providence Gazette; and Country Journal.
The United States Chronicle: Political, Commercial, and Historical. Providence.
American Herald. Boston.
The Boston Gazette and Country Journal.
The Continental Journal and the Weekly Advertiser. Boston.
The Essex Journal and the Massachusetts and New-Hampshire General Advertiser. Newburyport, Mass.
Exchange Advertiser. Boston.
The Herald of Freedom and the Federal Advertiser. Boston.
The Independent Chronicle, and the Universal Advertiser. Boston.
Massachusetts Centinel: And the Republican Journal. Boston.
Massachusetts Gazette. Boston.
The Salem Mercury: Political, Commercial, and Moral. Salem, Mass.
Thomas's The Massachusetts Spy; Or, Worcester Gazette.
Worcester Magazine.
The American Mercury. Hartford.
The Connecticut Courant and Weekly Intelligence. Hartford.
The Connecticut Gazette and the Universal Intelligencer. New London.
The Connecticut Journal. New Haven.
The Middlesex Gazette. Middletown, Conn.
The Norwich Packet: and the Connecticut, Massachusetts, and Rhode Island Weekly Advertiser. Norwich, Conn.
The Country Journal and Poughkeepsie Advertiser. Poughkeepsie, N.Y.
The Gazette of the United States. New York City.
The Independent Journal: Or the General Advertiser. New York City.
New York Daily Advertiser. New York City.
New York Daily Gazette. New York City.
New-York Packet. New York City.
The New-Jersey Gazette. Trenton.
The New-Jersey Journal. Elizabeth Town.
The Federal Gazette, and Philadelphia Evening Post.
The Freeman's Journal: Or, North American Intelligencer. Philadelphia.
The Independent Gazeteer. Philadelphia.
The Pennsylvania Gazette. Philadelphia.

The Pennsylvania Herald. Philadelphia.
The Pennsylvania Journal, and The Weekly Advertiser. Philadelphia.
The Pennsylvania Packet or the General Advertiser. Philadelphia.
The Delaware Gazette. Wilmington.
Maryland Gazette. Annapolis.
The Maryland Journal and Baltimore Advertiser.
The Virginia Herald and Fredericksburg Advertiser.
The Virginia Independent Chronicle. Richmond.
The Virginia Journal and the Alexandria Advertiser.
Martin's North-Carolina Gazette. Newbern.
The North-Carolina Chronicle; or, Fayetteville Gazette.
State Gazette of North Carolina. Edenton.
The State Gazette of North Carolina. Newbern.
Columbian Herald. Charleston.
State Gazette of South-Carolina. Charleston.
The Gazette of the State of Georgia. Savannah.
The Georgia State Gazette or Independent Register. Augusta.

III. *Printed Source Collections, Official Documents, and Contemporary Books*

"Abstracts from the Records of Newport Relative to the Adoption of the Constitution of the United States, 1788–1789." *The Newport Historical Magazine,* IV (1883), 92–99.

Adams, Charles Francis, *et al.,* eds. "Commerce of Rhode Island 1726–1800." *Collections of the Massachusetts Historical Society,* 7th ser., IX and X (1914–1915).

[Annals of Congress] *Debates and Proceedings in the Congress of the United States, 1789–1824.* 42 vols. Washington, D.C., 1834–1856.

Bartlett, John Russell, ed. *Records of the Colony of Rhode Island and Providence Plantations in New England.* 10 vols. Providence, 1856–1865.

Burnett, Edmund C., ed. *Letters of the Members of the Continental Congress.* 8 vols. Washington, D.C., 1921–1936.

Clinton, George. *Public Papers of George Clinton, First Governor of New York, 1775–1795, 1801–1804.* Edited by Hugh Hastings *et al.* New York, 1899–1914.

Cooke, Nicholas. "Revolutionary Correspondence of Governor Nicholas Cooke, 1775–1781." Edited by Matt B. Jones. *Proceedings of the American Antiquarian Society* n.s., XXXVI (1926), 231–53.

Cotner, Robert C., ed. *Theodore Foster's Minutes of the Convention held at South Kingstown, Rhode Island, in March, 1790, Which Failed to Adopt the Constitution of the United States.* Providence, 1929.

DeChastellux, Marquis. *Travels in the Years 1780, 1781, and 1782 by the Marquis DeChastellux.* Translated and edited by Howard Rice. 2 vols. Chapel Hill, 1963.

DeWarville, J. P. Brissot. *New Travels in the United States of America: Performed in 1788.* New York, 1792.

Elliot, Jonathan, ed. *Debates on the Adoption of the Federal Constitution in the Convention Held at Philadelphia in 1787; With a Diary of the Debates of the Congress of the Confederation; As Reported by James Madison, A Member, and Deputy from Virginia, Supplemental to Elliot's Debates.* 5 vols. Washington, D.C., 1845.

———, ed. *The Funding System of the United States and of Great Britain, With Some Tabular Facts of Other Nations Touching the Same Subject.* Washington, D.C., 1845.

Ford, Worthington C., *et al.*, eds. *Journals of the Continental Congress, 1774–1789.* 34 vols. Washington, D.C., 1904–37.

Franklin, Benjamin, and Greene, Catherine Ray. *Benjamin Franklin and Catherine Ray Greene: Their Correspondence, 1775–1790.* Edited by William G. Roelker. Philadelphia, 1949.

Hadfield, Joseph. *An Englishman in America: Being the Diary of Joseph Hadfield.* Edited by Douglas S. Robertson. Toronto, 1933.

Hamilton, Alexander. *The Papers of Alexander Hamilton.* Edited by Harold C. Syrett and Jacob E. Cooke. 11 vols. In Progress. New York, 1961—.

Hoadly, Charles J., and Labaree, Leonard W., eds. *The Public Records of the State of Connecticut, 1776–1796.* 8 vols. Hartford, 1894–1951.

Howell, David. "Charge Delivered to the Graduates of Providence College on Commencement Day (Sept. 17, 1791)." *The Baptist Annual Register,* I (1791), 216–19.

[David Howell.] "Tombstone Inscription." *Narragansett Historical Register,* V (1886), 70.

Hunter, Robert, Jr. *Quebec to Carolina 1785–1786: Being the Travel Diary of Robert Hunter, Jr., a Young Merchant of London.* Edited by Louis Wright and Marion Tinling. San Marino, Calif., 1943.

Jefferson, Thomas. *The Papers of Thomas Jefferson.* Edited by Julian P. Boyd *et al.* 17 vols. In progress. Princeton, 1950—.

Jones, Joseph. *Letters of Joseph Jones.* Edited by Worthington C. Ford. Washington, D.C., 1889.

Kimball, Gertrude S., ed. *Pictures of Rhode Island in the Past 1642–1833: By Travelers and Observers.* Providence, 1900.

Maclay, William. *The Journal of William Maclay: United States Senator from Pennsylvania, 1789–1791.* Edited by Edgar S. Maclay. New York, 1927.

Madison, James. *The Writings of James Madison: Comprising his Public Papers and his Private Correspondence, including Numerous Letters and*

Documents Now for the First Time Printed. Edited by Gaillard Hunt. 9 vols. New York, 1900–1910.

———. *The Papers of James Madison*. Edited by William T. Hutchinson *et al.* 4 vols. In progress. Chicago, 1962—.

Merritt, Richard L. *Symbols of American Community 1735–1775*. New Haven, 1966.

Minot, George Richards. *The History of the Insurrections in Massachusetts in the Year MDCCLXXXVI, and the Rebellion Consequent Thereon*. Worcester, 1788.

Paine, Thomas. *Six New Letters of Thomas Paine: Being Pieces on the Five Per Cent Duty Addressed to the Citizens of Rhode Island*. Edited by Harry H. Clark. Madison, 1939.

———. *The Complete Writings of Thomas Paine*. Edited by Philip Foner. 2 vols. New York, 1945.

"Revolutionary Correspondence from 1775–1782." *Collections of the Rhode Island Historical Society*, VI (1867).

Sanders, Jennings B. *Evolution of the Executive Departments of the Continental Congress, 1774–1789*. Chapel Hill, 1935.

Secret Journals of the Congress of the Confederation. 4 vols. Boston, 1824.

Smith, William Loughton. "Journal of William Loughton Smith, 1790–1791." Edited by Albert Mathews. *Massachusetts Historical Society Proceedings*, LI (1918), 20–90.

Staples, William R., ed. *Annals of the Town of Providence*. Providence, 1843.

———, ed. *Rhode Island in the Continental Congress: With the Journal of the Convention that Adopted the Constitution 1765–1790*. Providence, 1870.

Updike, Wilkins. *History of the Episcopal Church in Narragansett, Rhode Island and, including a history of other Episcopal Churches in the State, with an Appendix containing a reprint of a work now extremely rare, entitled "America Dissected," by the Rev. J. MacSparran, D.D.* Newport, 1847.

Varnum, James M. *The Case, Trevett against Weeden: On Information and Complaint, for refusing Paper Bills in Payment for Butcher's Meat, in Market, at Par with Specie. Tried before the Honourable Superior Court, in the County of Newport, September Term, 1786. Also, The Case of the Judges of said Court, Before the Honourable General Assembly, at Providence, October Session, 1786, on Citation for dismissing said Complaint. Wherein the Rights of the People to Trial by Jury, etc., are stated and maintained, and the Legislative, Judiciary and Executive Powers of Government examined and defined*. Providence, 1787.

Ward, Samuel. "Diary of Governor Samuel Ward: Delegate from Rhode Island in the Continental Congress 1774–1776." Edited by John Ward. *Magazine of American History*, I (1871), 438–42, 503–6, and 549–61.

———. *Correspondence of Governor Samuel Ward, May 1775–March 1776*. Edited by Bernhard Knollenberg. Providence, 1952.

Wharton, Francis, ed. *Revolutionary Diplomatic Correspondence.* 6 vols. Washington, D.C., 1899.

IV. *Secondary Materials*
Printed Books, Articles, Biographical
and Bibliographical Works

"The Adjustment of Rhode Island into the Union in 1790." *Proceedings of the Rhode Island Historical Society,* VIII (1900), 104–36.

Alden, John Eliot. *Rhode Island Imprints, 1727–1800.* New York, 1949.

Alden, John R. *The American Revolution 1775–1783.* New York, 1954.

Andrews, Charles M. *The Colonial Period of American History.* 4 vols. New Haven, 1934–1938.

Andrews, Neil. "The Development of the Nominating Convention in Rhode Island." *Papers from the Historical Seminary of Brown University,* No. I. Edited by J. Franklin Jameson. Providence, 1894.

Arnold, James N. "The Causes of the Popularity of the Revolutionary Movement in Rhode Island." *Narragansett Historical Register,* IV (1885), 81–85.

Arnold, Samuel Greene. *History of the State of Rhode Island and Providence Plantations: From the Settlement of the State, 1636, to the Adoption of the Federal Constitution, 1790.* 2 vols. New York, 1859–1860.

Bartlett, Irving. *From Slave to Citizen: The Story of the Negro in Rhode Island.* Providence, 1954.

Bartlett, John Russell. *Bibliography of Rhode Island: A Catalogue of Books and Other Publications Relating to the State of Rhode Island, With Notes, Historical, Biographical and Critical.* Providence, 1864.

Bates, Frank G. "Rhode Island and the Impost of 1781." *American Historical Association Reports,* I (1894), 351–61.

———. *Rhode Island and the Formation of the Union.* Columbia University Studies in History, Economics, and Public Law, X, No. 2. New York, 1898.

Bayley, Rayfael A. *The National Loans of the United States From July 4, 1776 to June 30, 1880.* 2nd ed. Washington, D.C., 1882.

Beard, Charles A. *An Economic Interpretation of the Constitution of the United States.* New York, 1913.

Bezanson, Anne. *Prices and Inflation During the American Revolution: Pennsylvania, 1770–1790.* Philadelphia, 1951.

Bicknell, Thomas W. *The History of the State of Rhode Island and Providence Plantations.* 3 vols. New York, 1920.

Biographical Cyclopedia of Representative Men of Rhode Island. Providence, 1881.

Bishop, Hillman M. "Why Rhode Island Opposed the Federal Constitution: The Continental Impost; The Paper Money Era; Paper Money and the Constitution; Political Reasons." *Rhode Island History,* VIII (1949), 1–10, 33–44, 85–95, 115–26.

Bjork, Gordon C. "The Weaning of the American Economy: Independence, Market Changes, and Economic Development." *The Journal of Economic History,* XXIV (1964), 541–60.

Black, Robert C, III. *The Younger John Winthrop.* New York, 1966.

Bolles, Albert S. *The Financial History of the United States, From 1774 to 1789: Embracing the Period of the American Revolution.* New York, 1879.

Bongartz, J. Harry. *Check List of Rhode Island Laws. Containing a Complete List of the Public Laws and Acts and Resolves of the State of Rhode Island to Date. With Notes and Pagings.* Providence, 1893.

Brant, Irving. *James Madison, the Nationalist.* Indianapolis, 1950.

———. *James Madison and American Nationalism.* Princeton, 1968.

Bridenbaugh, Carl. *Cities in Revolt: Urban Life in America, 1743–1776.* New York, 1955.

Brigham, Clarence S. "Report on the Archives of Rhode Island." *Annual Report of the American Historical Association,* I (1903), 543–644.

———. *History and Bibliography of American Newspapers 1690–1820.* 2 vols. Worcester, 1947.

Brockunier, Samuel H. *The Irrepressible Democrat: Roger Williams.* New York, 1940.

Bronson, Walter. *The History of Brown University.* Providence, 1914.

Buel, Elizabeth C. B. "Oliver Ellsworth." *New England Magazine,* XXX (1904), 611–26.

Bullock, Charles J. *The Finances of the United States from 1775 to 1789, With Especial Reference to the Budget.* Bulletin of the University of Wisconsin, Economics, Political Science, and History Series, I, No. 2. Madison, 1895.

Burnett, Edmund C. *The Continental Congress.* New York, 1941.

Cady, John Hutchins. *Rhode Island State Boundaries 1636–1936.* State of Rhode Island and Providence Plantations, State Planning Board, Special Report, No. 7. Providence, 1936.

Channing, Edward. *The Narragansett Planters: A Study in Causes.* Johns Hopkins University Studies in Historical and Political Science, 4th ser., III. Baltimore, 1886.

Channing, Edward T. *Life of William Ellery.* Boston, 1836.

Chapin, Howard M. *Bibliography of Rhode Island Bibliography.* Providence, 1914.

———. "Eighteenth Century Rhode Island Printed Proxies." *The American Collector,* I (1925), 54–59.

Coleman, Peter J. *The Transformation of Rhode Island 1790–1860.* Providence, 1963.

Conley, Patrick T. "Rhode Island Constitutional Development 1636–1775: A Survey." *Rhode Island History,* XXVII (1968), 49–63, 74–94.

Cowell, Benjamin. *Spirit of Rhode Island, Sketches of the efforts of the Government and the People in the War of the Revolution.* Boston, 1850.

DePauw, Linda Grant. *The Eleventh Pillar: New York State and the Federal Constitution.* Ithaca, 1966.

"The Destruction of Property in the Town of Middletown, R.I., During the Revolution." *Newport Historical Magazine,* II (1881), 241–43.

Dewey, Davis R. *Financial History of the United States.* 11th ed. New York, 1931.

Donnan, Elizabeth. "Agitation Against the Slave Trade in Rhode Island, 1784–1790." *Persecution and Liberty: Essays in Honor of George Lincoln Burr.* New York, 1931.

Dorfman, Joseph. *The Economic Mind in American Civilization.* 3 vols. New York, 1946–1949.

Dunn, Richard S. "John Winthrop, Jr., and the Narrangansett Country." *William and Mary Quarterly,* 3rd ser., XIII (1956), 68–86.

Durfee, Thomas. "Gleanings from the Judicial History of Rhode Island." *Rhode Island Historical Society Tracts,* 1st ser., No. 18 (1883).

East, Robert A. *Business Enterprise in the American Revolutionary Era.* Columbia University Studies in History, Economics and Public Law, No. 439. New York, 1939.

Eaton, Amasa M. "The Right to Local Self-Government." *Harvard Law Review,* XIII (1899), 441–54, 570–88, 638–58; XIV (1900), 20–38, 116–38.

Ferguson, E. James. "State Assumption of the Federal Debt During the Confederation." *Mississippi Valley Historical Review,* XXXVIII (1951), 403–24.

————. "Currency Finance: An Interpretation of Colonial Monetary Practices." *William and Mary Quarterly,* 3rd ser., X (1953), 153–80.

————. *The Power of the Purse: A History of American Public Finance, 1776–1790.* Chapel Hill, 1961.

Field, Edward, ed. *State of Rhode Island and Providence Plantations at the End of the Century: A History.* 3 vols. Boston, 1902.

Fiske, John. *The Critical Period of American History.* Boston, 1896.

Foster, William E. "Stephen Hopkins: A Rhode Island Statesman." *Rhode Island Historical Society Tracts,* No. 19 (1884).

————. "Sketch of the Life and Services of Theodore Foster." *Collections of the Rhode Island Historical Society,* VII (1885), 111–34.

————. *Town Government in Rhode Island.* Johns Hopkins Studies in Historical and Political Science, 4th ser., No. II. Baltimore, 1886.

Goodwin, Daniel. "The Counties of Rhode Island." *Magazine of History,* XVI (1913), 66–73.

Greene, George Washington. *The Life of Nathanael Greene.* 3 vols. New York, 1871.

Greene, Evarts B., and Harrington, Virginia D. *American Population Before the Federal Census of 1790*. New York, 1932.

Guild, R. A. *Life, Times and Correspondence of James Manning*. Boston, 1864.

Hammond, Bray. *Banks and Politics in America: From the Revolution to the Civil War*. Princeton, 1957.

Harlow, Ralph W. "Aspects of Revolutionary Finance." *American Historical Review*, XXXV (1929), 46–68.

Hazeltine, Harold D. "Appeals from Colonial Courts to the King in Council, With Especial Reference to Rhode Island." *Papers from the Historical Seminary of Brown University*. No. VII. Edited by J. Franklin Jameson. Providence, 1896.

Hazelton, Robert M. *Let Freedom Ring! A Biography of Moses Brown*. New York, 1957.

Hedges, James B. *The Browns of Providence Plantations: Colonial Years*. Cambridge, Mass., 1952.

Hunt, Gaillard. "Office Seeking in Washington's Administration." *American Historical Review*, I (1896), 270–83.

Jameson, J. Franklin, ed. *Essays in the Constitutional History of the United States in the Formative Period 1775–1789*. Boston, 1889.

Jenkins, William S. *A Guide to the Microfilm Collection of Early State Records*. Washington, D.C., 1950.

———. *Supplement*. Washington, D.C., 1951.

Jensen, Merrill. *The Articles of Confederation: An Interpretation of the Social-Constitutional History of the American Revolution 1774–1781*. Madison, 1940; 4th ptg., 1962.

———. *The New Nation: A History of the United States During the Confederation 1781–1789*. New York, 1950.

Johnson, Allen, and Malone, Dumas, eds. *Dictionary of American Biography*. 22 vols. New York, 1928–1949.

Johnson, Herbert A. "Toward a Reappraisal of the 'Federal Government': 1783–1789." *The American Journal of Legal History*, 8 (1964), 314–25.

"Jonathan Easton's Ratable Estate." *Newport Historical Magazine*, II (1881), 60–61.

Kenyon, Cecilia M. "Men of Little Faith: The Anti-Federalists on the Nature of Representative Government." *William and Mary Quarterly*, 3d ser., XII (1955), 3–43.

Leach, Douglas E. *Flintlock and Tomahawk: New England in King Philip's War*. New York, 1958.

Lester, Richard A. *Monetary Experiments: Early American and Recent Scandinavian*. Princeton, 1939.

Libby, Orin G. *The Geographical Distribution of the Vote of the Thirteen States on the Federal Constitution*. Bulletin of the University of Wisconsin, Economics, Political Science and History, I, No. I. Madison, 1894.

Lovejoy, David S. *Rhode Island Politics and the American Revolution 1760–1776*. Providence, 1958.

Lynd, Staughton. "Abraham Yates's History of the Movement for the United States Constitution." *William and Mary Quarterly*, 3d ser., XX (1963), 223–45.

McDonald, Forrest. *We the People: The Economic Origins of the Constitution*. Chicago, 1958.

———. *E Pluribus Unum: The Formation of the American Republic 1776–1790*. Boston, 1965.

McLaughlin, Andrew C. *The Confederation and the Constitution*. New York, 1905.

McRee, Griffith I. *Life and Correspondence of James Iredell*. 2 vols. New York, 1857–1858.

Main, Jackson Turner. *The Antifederalists: Critics of the Constitution 1781–1788*. Chapel Hill, 1961.

———. *The Upper House in Revolutionary America 1763–1788*. Madison, 1967.

Mason, George C. "Nicholas Easton vs. the City of Newport." *Proceedings of the Rhode Island Historical Society*, V (1875–1876), 15–18.

Miller, John C. *Alexander Hamilton: Portrait in Paradox*. New York, 1959.

Miller, William Davis. "The Narragansett Planters." *Proceedings of the American Antiquarian Society*, n.s., XLIII (1913), 49–115.

Montross, Lynn. *The Reluctant Rebels: The Story of the Continental Congress 1774–1789*. New York, 1950.

Mowry, Arthur M. *The Dorr War: Or the Constitutional Struggle in Rhode Island*. Providence, 1901.

Murphy, William P. *The Triumph of Nationalism: State Sovereignty, the Founding Fathers, and the Making of the Constitution*. Chicago, 1967.

Nettels, Curtis P. *Money Supply of the American Colonies before 1720*. New York, 1934.

———. *The Emergence of a National Economy 1775–1815*. New York, 1962.

Nevins, Allan. *The American States During and After the Revolution 1775–1789*. New York, 1924.

Newbold, Robert. *The Albany Congress and Plan of Union of 1754*. New York, 1955.

Newcomer, Lee N. *The Embattled Farmers: A Massachusetts Countryside in the American Revolution*. New York, 1953.

Noyes, Isaac P. *Reminiscenses of Rhode Island and Ye Providence Plantations*. Washington, D.C., 1905.

Oberholtzer, Ellis P. *Robert Morris: Patriot and Financier*. New York, 1903.

Palmer, Robert R. *The Age of Democratic Revolutions: A Political History of Europe and America; The Challenge*. Princeton, 1959.

Peckham, Howard W. *The War for Independence: A Military History*. Chicago, 1958.

Perry, Amos. "The Town Records of Rhode Island: A Report." *Proceedings of the Rhode Island Historical Society,* I (1892–1893), 99–182.

———. "Rhode Island Revolutionary Debts." *Publications of the Rhode Island Historical Society,* n.s., IV (1896).

Polishook, Irwin H. "The Collins-Richardson Fracas of 1787: A Problem in State and Federal Relations During the Confederation Era." *Rhode Island History,* XXII (1963), 117–21.

———. "Trevett vs. Weeden and the Case of the Judges." *Newport History,* XXXVIII (1965), 45–69.

———. "Peter Edes's Report of the Proceedings of the Rhode Island General Assembly, 1787–1790." *Rhode Island History* XXV–XXVI (1966–1967), 33–42, 87–97, 117–28; 15–31.

Potter, Elisha R., and Rider, Sidney S. "Some Account of the Credit or Paper Money of Rhode Island: From the First Issue in 1710, to the Final Issue, 1786." *Rhode Island Historical Society Tracts,* 1st ser., No. 8 (1880).

Preston, Howard W. "The Varnum House." *Rhode Island Historical Society Collections,* XX (1927), 115–20.

Ratchford, Benjamin. *American State Debts.* Durham, 1941.

Ravits, Abe C. "Anarch in Rhode Island." *Rhode Island History,* XI (1952), 117–24.

Reilly, James F. "The Providence Abolition Society." *Rhode Island History,* X (1961), 33–48.

Rider, Sidney S. "Omnipotence of the General Assembly." *Book Notes,* I, No. 6 (1883).

———. "Legislative History in Rhode Island." *Book Notes,* IV, No. 27 (1887).

Ross, Arthur R. *A Discourse Embracing the Civil and Religious History of Rhode Island.* Providence, 1838.

Rossiter, Clinton. *Alexander Hamilton and the Constitution.* New York, 1964.

Rutland, Robert A. *The Ordeal of the Constitution: The Antifederalists and the Ratification Struggle of 1787–1788.* Norman, 1966.

Schlesinger, Arthur M. *The Colonial Merchants and the American Revolution, 1763–1776.* New York, 1939.

———. *Prelude to Independence: The Newspaper War on Britain 1764–1776.* New York, 1958.

Smith, Joseph J. *Civil and Military List of Rhode Island.* Providence, 1900.

Stone, Edward M. *The Life and Recollections of John Howland.* Providence, 1857.

Sumner, William Graham. *The Financier and the Finances of the American Revolution.* 2 vols. New York, 1891.

Taylor, Robert J. *Western Massachusetts in the Revolution.* Providence, 1954.

Thayer, Theodore. *Nathanael Greene: Strategist of the American Revolution.* New York, 1960.

Thompson, Mack E. "The Ward-Hopkins Controversy and the American Revolution in Rhode Island: An Interpretation." *William and Mary Quarterly*, 3d ser., XVI (1959), 363–75.

————. *Moses Brown: Reluctant Reformer.* Chapel Hill, 1962.

Turner, Henry E. *Greenes of Warwick in Colonial History.* Newport, 1877.

Updike, Wilkins. *Memoirs of the Rhode Island Bar.* Boston, 1842.

Van Tyne, Claude H. "Sovereignty in the American Revolution: An Historical Study." *American Historical Review*, XII (1905), 529–45.

Varnum, James M. *A Sketch of the Life and Public Services of James Mitchell Varnum of Rhode Island.* Boston, 1906.

Ver Steeg, Clarence L. *Robert Morris: Revolutionary Financier.* Philadelphia, 1954.

Ward, Harry M. *The United Colonies of New England 1643–1690.* New York, 1961.

————. *The Department of War 1781–1795.* Pittsburgh, 1962.

Warren, G. F., and Pearson, F. A., "Wholesale Prices for 213 Years, 1720–1932." *Cornell University Experimental Station*, Memoir 142 (1932).

Weeden, William B. *Economic and Social History of New England 1620–1789.* 2 vols. Boston, 1894.

Willcox, William B. "Rhode Island in British Strategy, 1780–1781." *Journal of Modern History*, XVII (1945), 304–31.

Williamson, Chilton. *American Suffrage from Property to Democracy 1760–1860.* Princeton, 1960.

Winslow, John. *The Trial of the Rhode Island Judges: An Episode Touching Currency and Constitutional History.* Brooklyn, 1887.

V. *Unpublished Materials*

Bates, Whitney K. "The Assumption of the State Debts 1783–1793." Ph.D. dissertation, University of Wisconsin, 1951.

Brock, Leslie Van Horn. "The Currency of the American Colonies 1700–1764: A Study in Colonial Finance and Imperial Relations." Ph.D. dissertation, University of Michigan, 1941.

Coyle, Franklin S. "The Survival of Business Enterprise in the American Revolutionary Era (1770–1785)." M.A. thesis, Brown University, 1960.

MacInnes, John B. "Rhode Island Bills of Public Credit 1710–1755." Ph.D. dissertation, Brown University, 1952.

Index

Adams, John, 89
Agriculture, 104–7, 123
Allen, Samuel, 125
American Revolution: aftermath, 103–7; financing, 48; financing, problems of, 55–56; French assistance, 54; military security, 13; military planning in Rhode Island, 9; need for common defense, 9–10, 11; unequal distribution of costs, 10, 12, 15–16, 48
Anarchiad, 168
Andrews, Zephaniah, 224
Annapolis convention of 1786, 111, 182
Antifederalism: anticipated by Howell, 71; in country party, 206; in Rhode Island, 190, 197
Arnold, Benjamin, 41
Arnold, Jonathan, 85, 91, 92, 99
Arnold, Peleg, 167
Arnold, Welcome, 41–42, 118, 224
Articles of Confederation: inadequacies, 53, 174; lack of taxing power, 48, 59; provisions, 16, 71; ratification, 16, 59
Assemblymen, 34
Assistants, 22–23

Barber, Henry, 208
Barker, Abraham, 125
Barrington: opposed legal-tender laws, 128 n; opposed Impost, 79; supported Constitution, 229; supported second constitutional convention, 202
Barton, William, 216, 222
Bill of rights, 192, 218–19
Boston Tea Party, 10
Boundary controversies, 5–6
Bourne, Benjamin: accepted paper-money loan, 160; called minority ratifying convention, 210; elected to Congress, 234–35; supported slavery provisions, 217–18
Bowdoin, James, 177. *See also* Collins-Richardson fracas
Bowen, Jabez, 124–25, 224; delegate to

Annapolis convention, 111; supported federal assumption of debt, 237–38
Bradford, William, 32, 153
Bristol: opposed country, 127 n; opposed Impost, 79; opposed legal-tender laws, 128 n; opposed paper money, 163; supported Constitution, 199, 229
Brown and Benson, 118
Brown, John, 41, 224; compromise paper-money proposals, 151; refused paper-money payments, 156; speculator, 115, 117, 118
Brown, Joseph, 75–76
Brown, Moses, 169–70, 217
Brown, Nicholas, 117, 156
Burges, Tristam, 41
Burrill, James, Jr., 234–35

Carrington, Edward, 190
Carter, John, 68, 89
Census Act of 1790, 232
Champlin, Christopher, 111 n, 225
Channing, William, 141, 153
Charles II, 4
Charlestown: changed position on paper money, 120 n, 122; dissatisfaction with charter, 45; opposed Constitution until amended, 229; opposed legal-tender laws, 128 n; supported legal-tender laws, 162
Charter of 1663: attempts to reform, 147; autonomy under, 7; basis of government, 24, 137; dissatisfaction with, 45; lacked bill of rights, 135; satisfaction with, 24; separation of church and state, 5; unequal representation of towns, 147
Childs, Francis, 166–67
"Citizen" (James Mitchell Varnum) letters, 67
Clark & Nightingale: accepted paper-money loans, 160, 164; creditor of state, 117; refused paper-money payments, 156
Clarke, Joseph, 173